FAITH OF OUR FATHERS

JOSEPH PEARCE

Faith of Our Fathers

A History of True England

IGNATIUS PRESS   SAN FRANCISCO

Cover art:
A stained glass window depicting
Joseph of Arimathea planting his staff on
Wearyall Hill near Glastonbury,
Church of St. Peter & St. Paul,
Longbridge Deverill, Wiltshire, England
Photograph © ASP Religion/Alamy Stock Photo

Cover design by John Herreid

© 2022 by Ignatius Press, San Francisco
All rights reserved
ISBN 978-1-62164-435-4 (PB)
ISBN 978-1-64229-203-9 (eBook)
Library of Congress Catalogue Number 2021940710
Printed in the United States of America ⊗

For Benedict Nicholson
May your future be filled with the presence of the past

Faith of our Fathers,
Mary's prayers
Shall win our country back to Thee;
And through the truth that comes from God,
England shall then indeed be free.

—Frederick W. Faber

CONTENTS

PROLOGUE

True and Timeless England

If England was what England seems
An' not the England of our dreams,
But only putty, brass, an' paint,
'Ow quick we'd chuck 'er! But she ain't!

—Rudyard Kipling,
from "The Return"

England, like all things, is subject not merely to the truth but to the Truth Himself.

It is this true England, an England "charged with the grandeur of God" and in communion with Christ and His Church, which is celebrated in these pages. It is an England which is as alive as the saints because, like all the saints, and like all of time and all of eternity, it exists in God's omnipresence.

In order to understand this true and timeless England more fully, we need to understand the relationship of time to eternity. With our finite perception, we can perceive only the past. Even the present, by the time that we perceive it, has become the immediate past. In psychological terms, the present is as empty of time as the geometrical point is empty of space. It exists only in metaphysics, even if our physical existence depends on it. And

wherever we find ourselves in the present, it is always a
direct consequence of where we have been in the past.
The past has put us where we are, and we cannot now be
present anywhere else. Our perceptions of the future, on
the other hand, can be a figment only of our imagination.
It is what might happen. The nearer the future is to us,
the more predictable it is. The further the future is from
us, the less predictable it becomes. We can be fairly sure
of what we'll be doing tomorrow but can have no idea of
what we'll be doing five years from now. This rootedness
of reality in the concrete presence of the past is one of
the things which makes history so important. We need to
know where we've been in order to know where we are
and where we're going.

For God, however, there is no past and there is no
future. For God everything is present. This is the deeper
meaning of divine omnipresence—not that God is present
everywhere, though He is, but that everything is present
to God. For God, therefore, we cannot say that history *was*
but only that history *is*. It is always present to Him. It is
this ever-present history which is celebrated in the pages
that follow.

God's omnipresence relates to the history of True
England because it means that all of England, past, present,
and future, is present to God in the eternal now. Those
who happen to be wandering around today on the geo-
graphical stage on which the drama of England is being
performed are sharing that stage simultaneously with all
Englishmen in all ages. Most people walking around on
that stage today might have no idea of what England is, or
of who they are, but England is not dependent on them.
Insofar as contemporary Englishmen have lost sight of the
truth to which True England owes its allegiance, they have
lost their place in the cosmological passion play in which

True England plays its part. They have answered Hamlet's conundrum of "to be or not to be" by choosing not to be. Like the souls in C. S. Lewis' *Great Divorce*, they are pathetic and relatively insubstantial shadows. They are certainly less real as Englishmen than Alfred the Great, Bede the Venerable, St. Edward the Confessor, Chaucer, St. Thomas More, the hundreds of English Martyrs, Shakespeare, Newman, Chesterton, or Tolkien. All these people *are* England, now and always.

Seeing True England through the omnipresent perspective of the Triune splendor of the Good, the True, and the Beautiful, we know that such an England can never die, not because it lingers like a fading coal in the memory of mortal men, but because it exists as a beautiful flower in the gardens of eternity. This is the England which is celebrated in these pages.

Chapter One

A Christ-Haunted Country

And did those feet in ancient time
Walk upon England's mountains green:
And was the holy Lamb of God,
On England's pleasant pastures seen!

—William Blake,
from "Jerusalem"

William Blake's romantic poem, later set to music by Sir Hubert Parry, has become so popular in contemporary England that it could almost be said to be an unofficial *English* national anthem, as distinct from the *British* national anthem, *God Save the Queen*. Yet most of those singing it will know nothing of the legend which inspired Blake's vision. "Those feet in ancient time," to which Blake refers, were those of the Christ Child, who, according to legend, had been brought to England by St. Joseph of Arimathea, a close and wealthy friend of the Holy Family who would later provide the tomb for Christ's burial. Whereas the latter fact is of course scriptural, there's no evidence that "those feet" ever actually walked "upon England's mountains green", or that "the holy Lamb of God" was ever seen on England's pastures or anywhere else "in England's green and pleasant land" (to quote the poem's final line). It is a pious legend, indicative of the deep faith of the English people and expressive of the fervent *desire* for Christ's physical presence on their native soil, thereby sanctifying it and making it His own. It is the hope that something *would* be true because it *should* be true.

A similar legend tells of St. Joseph of Arimathea's arrival as a Christian missionary to England in A.D. 63. It is said that he planted his staff on Wearyall Hill in Glastonbury and that, like Aaron's rod, it budded and blossomed. The Glastonbury Thorn, as it became known, bloomed every Christmas for centuries until the Puritans cut it down. Cuttings were saved and planted and these have also continued to bloom every Christmas. Even to this day, blossoms from the Glastonbury Thorn are sent to the queen every Christmas and they can sometimes be seen adorning the backdrop during Her Majesty's Christmas broadcast to the nation.

It is also said that St. Joseph of Arimathea brought two sacred vessels with him, one containing the blood and the other the water that had flowed from Christ's side at the Crucifixion. These sacred vessels, or at least one of them, became the Holy Grail of Arthurian legend. It is little wonder, therefore, that G. K. Chesterton in *A Short History of England* devotes a chapter to "The Age of Legends", in which he waxes lyrical on the sudden transformation of English history from the stolid facts of Roman occupation to the mythopoeic fancy of an Arthurian Elfland:

> All of a sudden we are reading of wandering bells and wizard lances, of wars against men as tall as trees or as short as toadstools. The soldier of civilization is no longer fighting with Goths but with goblins; the land becomes a labyrinth of faërie towns unknown to history; and scholars can suggest but cannot explain how a Roman ruler or a

Welsh chieftain towers up in the twilight as the awful and unbegotten Arthur.[1]

Fr. Roger Huddleston, O.S.B., says something similar in his entry on Glastonbury Abbey in the *Catholic Encyclopedia*, though he says it somewhat more prosaically. There was now such an accretion of stories surrounding the history and name of Glastonbury, "a mass of tradition, legend, and fiction, so inextricably mingled with real and important facts, that no power can now sift the truth from the falsehood with any certainty".[2]

Although there can be no reliable sifting of the true from the false, as Fr. Huddleston reminds us, we can at least distinguish between the implausible and the impossible. It is possible that St. Joseph of Arimathea set out as an early missionary, to France and then to England, as pious legend suggests, and it is therefore possible that he arrived at Glastonbury in A.D. 63 as legend also suggests. It might be considered implausible but it is not impossible. What is certain is that there was a chapel at Glastonbury from the early years of the Roman occupation, dedicated to the Blessed Virgin, which means that missionaries had arrived in the area at around the time that St. Joseph of Arimathea is said to have been there. The story of the miraculous staff and the Holy Grail might be little more than wishful thinking or, as H. M. Gillett thinks (perhaps wishfully!), they "may indeed be based on old and half-remembered traditions".[3]

---

[1] G. K. Chesterton, *A Short History of England*, Phoenix Library ed. (London: Chatto and Windus, 1929), 19–20.

[2] Fr. Roger Huddleston, O.S.B., *The Catholic Encyclopedia*, s.v. "Glastonbury Abbey"; quoted in H. M. Gillett, *Shrines of Our Lady in England and Wales* (London: Samuel Walker, 1957), 144.

[3] Gillett, *Shrines of Our Lady in England and Wales*, 145.

Shrouded as they are in mist, mysticism, and mystery, the holy legends surrounding Glastonbury have shaped England's history, and indeed the history of the whole of Christendom, as Chesterton explains:

> St. Joseph carried the cup which held the wine of the last Supper and the blood of the Crucifixion to that shrine in Avalon which we now call Glastonbury; and it became the heart of a whole universe of legends and romances, not only for Britain but for Europe. Throughout this tremendous and branching tradition it is called the Holy Grail. The vision of it was especially the reward of that ring of powerful paladins whom King Arthur feasted at a Round Table, a symbol of heroic comradeship such as was afterwards imitated or invented by mediaeval knighthood.[4]

The mythical or legendary presence of the Holy Grail somewhere on English soil, and the figure of King Arthur, the once and future king, have transformed England's "green and pleasant land" into a Christ-haunted country. This spirit was present in the final lines of Robert Stephen Hawker's *The Quest of the Sangraal*:

> Ah! native England! wake thine ancient cry:
> Ho! for the Sangraal! vanished vase of heaven,
> That held, like Christ's own heart, one hin of blood.

We will end with the final lines of the poem with which we began our Arthurian quest. This is William Blake's impassioned battle cry, a Christ-haunted plea for the resurrection of True England:

---

[4] Chesterton, *Short History of England*, 26–27.

Bring me my Bow of burning gold:
Bring me my arrows of desire:
Bring me my Spear: O clouds unfold!
Bring me my Chariot of fire!

I will not cease from Mental Fight,
Nor shall my sword sleep in my hand:
Till we have built Jerusalem,
In England's green & pleasant Land.

Chapter Two

The England Before England

Before the Roman came to Rye or out to Severn strode,
The rolling English drunkard made the rolling English road.

—G. K. Chesterton, from "The Rolling English Road"

Even allowing for poetic licence, Chesterton was taking a few liberties with the strict letter of historical accuracy in claiming that there were any Englishmen in what is now known as England before the Roman occupation. England gets its name from *Englaland*, Angle-Land, the land of the Angles, one of the several Germanic tribes which settled the country during and especially after the Roman occupation. This "England before England" was called Albion by the Romans, from the Latin *albeo*, which means *white*, a reference, presumably, to the white cliffs of chalk along the coastline of southeast England, which is the first feature of the landscape which anyone sees when sailing to England from the continent. This name of Albion referred to the whole British Isles and not merely to that part of it which is now known as England. Another name used by the Romans for the British Isles was Britannia, a reference to the name of the tribes inhabiting the "English" part of the island.

Julius Caesar had invaded the country in 55 B.C., during the Gallic Wars, in order to curtail the support given by the

Celtic tribes of Britain to the enemies of Rome. Having succeeded in subjugating the Britons, the Roman legions departed and would not return for almost a century, finally occupying the country and making it part of the empire in A.D. 43. At first, the imperial legions encountered relatively little resistance. Most of the south and east of what is now England was under Roman control by A.D. 47. The first serious resistance was that led by the warrior queen Boadicea (or Boudicca) in A.D. 60, the queen of the Iceni tribe in what is now Norfolk, in the east of the country. Boadicea formed an alliance with another tribe, the Trinobantes, from what is now Essex, just to the east of London; she rose against Roman rule with an estimated 120,000 men at her command. They sacked Colchester, one of the largest of the newly established Roman towns, and also London (Londinium), which was a thriving and prosperous city, full of merchants.

Boadicea's uprising was brutal and merciless, killing around seventy thousand people—men, women, and children. It was almost successful in routing the Romans because the regular Roman troops were relatively few in number and many of them were deployed to the west, in what is now Wales, leaving London largely undefended as Boadicea's army descended upon it. Eventually, however, the Roman army, under the command of Gaius Suetonius Paulinus, defeated Boadicea's insurgents in a bloody battle somewhere north of London. The warrior queen was killed either in this ultimately decisive battle or in a subsequent smaller battle shortly afterwards. Her rebellion had been crushed and peace was restored.

As we have seen already, legend tells that early missionaries, allegedly led by St. Joseph of Arimathea, had established a Christian presence at Glastonbury in A.D. 63, only three years after Boadicea's uprising. Whether this is historically accurate, it is known that a church and later an abbey were established here from the earliest times. "It is ... accepted that long before the Saxons came to England, the little chapel of St. Mary of Glastonbury was considered ancient," thus writes the historian H. M. Gillett.[1] It was on this account that Glastonbury was considered the oldest abbey in Christendom and its abbot given due precedence on this account at Councils of the Church.

By the middle of the second century, the work of Christian missionaries had borne fruit across the country, converting much of the Celtic population to the Gospel of Jesus Christ. The Venerable Bede records in his history of England, written in A.D. 731, that Lucius, a British king, wrote to the pope, Eleutherius, asking to be received into the Church. "The pious request was quickly granted," writes St. Bede, "and the Britons received the Faith and held it peacefully in all its purity and fullness until the time of the Emperor Diocletian."[2] Thus, by around A.D. 180, it can be reasonably presumed that the people of what is now England were mostly believing Catholics and that the region of Albion, ruled by King Lucius, was now officially a Catholic kingdom. England was therefore Catholic before England became "England", illustrating that the faith goes back to the very dawn of English history and indeed beyond it.

And yet, even if the Celtic people of Albion were embracing the faith, the same could not be said of the Roman Empire. Bede does not mention the anti-Christian laws enacted by the emperor Severus in A.D. 209, nor the persecution a few decades later during the reign of

---

[1] H. M. Gillett, *Shrines of Our Lady in England and Wales* (London: Samuel Walker, 1957), 146.

[2] Bede, *Ecclesiastical History of the English People*, ed. D. H. Farmer and Ronald Latham (London: Penguin Classics, 1991), 49.

the emperor Valerian, the latter of which claimed the lives in Rome of St. Lawrence and Pope Sixtus II. According to Bede, the first martyr in England, St. Alban, was killed during the Diocletian persecutions of the early years of the fourth century. It's possible that Albion, a far-flung corner of the empire, escaped the earlier persecutions in Rome, which would explain Bede's omission of any mention of them; but it's also possible, as argued by the historian John Morris, that St. Alban was actually martyred during the persecutions under the emperor Severus a century earlier.[3]

Irrespective of its actual date, Bede's telling of the story of St. Alban's martyrdom merits our attention. We are told that Alban was a pagan who, out of charity and pity, sheltered a priest fleeing his persecutors. When Alban observed the priest's "unbroken activity of prayer and vigil", he was "touched by the grace of God and began to follow the priest's example of faith and devotion".[4] When it became clear that Alban's house was to be searched by the priest hunters, Alban dressed in the priest's robe, enabling the priest to escape and allowing himself to be taken in the priest's place. Following his being scourged on the orders of the judge, in the hope that such treatment might induce Alban to renounce his newfound faith, he was sentenced to death by decapitation. Bede's account tells of a large crowd of mostly Christian observers, keen to witness the first martyrdom on Albion's shore, and of the refusal of the executioner to carry out the sentence, moved by awe at Alban's evident sanctity in the face of impending death. This executioner was beheaded at the same time as Alban, in punishment for his insubordination. "The soldier who

[3] John Morris, "The Date of Saint Alban", in *Hertfordshire Archaeology*, vol. 1 (East Herts Archaeological Society, 1968).
[4] Bede, *Ecclesiastical History*, 51.

had been moved by divine intuition to refuse to slay God's confessor was beheaded at the same time as Alban," Bede writes. "And although he had not received the purification of Baptism, there was no doubt that he was cleansed by the shedding of his own blood, and rendered fit to enter the kingdom of heaven." Bede also tells us that the judge was himself so moved by witnessing these events that he called an end to the persecution, "and whereas he had formerly fought to crush devotion to Christ, he now began to honour the death of the saints".[5]

The spilling of the blood of these first English martyrs happened in the Roman city of Verulanium, about twenty-five miles north of London. The city, which is in Hertfordshire, is now known as St. Albans.

Following the ending of the persecution, Bede speaks of the spread of the faith in the times of peace that followed. Those faithful Christians, "who during the time of danger had taken refuge in woods, deserted places, and hidden caves, came into the open, and rebuilt the ruined churches".[6] Shrines were erected in honour of the recent martyrs, their blood truly serving as the seed of the resurrected Church.

A snapshot of London at this time reveals a city in which the faith was already firmly established. Simon Jenkins, in *A Short History of London*, records a church in the vicinity of what is now the Tower of London, being built in around A.D. 300, and the Church Council held at Arles in 314 was attended by a bishop called Restitutus "from Londinium".[7]

The next major blight to hit the Christians of Albion was not a renewal of persecution but the spreading of heresy by

---

[5] Ibid., 54.
[6] Ibid.
[7] Simon Jenkins, *A Short History of London* (London: Viking, 2019), 12.

Pelagius, a British monk, in allegiance with Julian of Campania, a deposed and renegade bishop. Essentially, Pelagius denied the existence of Original Sin and taught that men could go to heaven through the triumph of their own will, merely choosing to do what Christ commands. This belief denied that any supernatural assistance was necessary from God, which was effectively a negation of the doctrine of grace. If men did not need grace, they did not need the sacraments or indeed the Church. They could get to heaven without any such help. This "self-help", do-it-yourself religion proved very popular in the fifth century, especially in Pelagius' native Britain. "Pelagius spread far and wide his noxious and abominable teaching that man had no need of God's grace," writes Bede, adding that, even though St. Augustine and other orthodox theologians quoted numerous authorities in refutation of Pelagius' error, his followers "refused to abandon their folly".[8] He then quotes Prosper of Aquitaine's poetic riposte to Pelagius:

> Against the great Augustine see him crawl,
> This wretched scribbler with his pen of gall!
> In what black caverns was this snakeling bred
> That from the dirt presumes to rear its head?
> Its food is grain that wave-washed Britain yields,
> Or the rank pasture of Campanian fields.[9]

Admirers of the twentieth-century writer and Catholic apologist Hilaire Belloc will be familiar with Belloc's "Song of the Pelagian Heresy":

> Pelagius lived in Kardanoel,
> And taught his doctrine there:
> How whether you went to heaven or hell,

[8] Bede, *Ecclesiastical History*, 56.
[9] Ibid.

It was your own affair;
How whether you rose to eternal joy,
Or sank forever to burn,
It had nothing to do with the church, my boy,
But was your own concern.

Oh, he didn't believe in Adam or Eve—
He put no faith therein;
His doubts began with the fall of man,
And he laughed at original sin.

Even as Pelagius was sowing seeds of dissent and division throughout Britain, further upheaval was caused by the sudden withdrawal of Roman troops from the British Isles as Rome itself fell to the invading Goths. This calamitous turn of events would prove catastrophic for Europe as a whole, precipitating the fall of the Roman Empire and causing chaos throughout the length and breadth of Christendom. Nor would Albion be spared.

In Bede's description, "the part of Britain inhabited by the Britons", that is, what is now England, as distinct from what is now Scotland, "had been hurriedly stripped of all troops and military equipment and robbed of the flower of its young men, who had been led away by ambitious despots and were never to return".[10] Bereft of its young men of military age who had gone to defend Rome from the barbarian onslaught from the north, the people of Albion were left defenceless from the pagan hordes to their own north. They sent desperate messages to Rome, "promising perpetual submission if only the Romans would drive out their enemies".[11] At first, the Romans sent military help but, increasingly besieged themselves, they were no longer

[10] Ibid., 58.
[11] Ibid.

able to maintain a garrison in the far-flung reaches of the fast disintegrating empire.

With no hope of help, the Britons fled from the wave of terror sweeping across the northern part of their land, abandoning their homes and their cities to the Picts and other Scottish tribes. "The slaughter was more ghastly than ever before," Bede tells us, "and the wretched citizens were torn in pieces by their enemies, as lambs are torn by wild beasts."[12] The Britons who had been driven from their homesteads and farms turned in starvation-driven desperation on their own people living farther south, plundering and pillaging. In this way, the entire agricultural infrastructure was ruined in a debauch of anarchy, resulting in a great famine.

As the physical lives of the Britons were being wracked by war and famine, their spiritual lives were being threatened by the continued presence of Pelagianism. Intent on defending the faith from error, the beleaguered faithful requested help from the bishops of Gaul who responded in 429 by sending two bishops to Britain, Germanus of Auxerre and Lupus of Troyes. Apart from using the power of reason to refute the errors of Pelagius, as St. Augustine and others had done already, Germanus refuted the Pelagian denial of the existence or power of grace by the employment of the supernatural power of grace itself in the form of miracles performed by invoking the intercession of the saints. He took a reliquary from around his neck and placed it on the eyes of a blind girl who was healed instantly, "to the joy of her parents and the amazement of the crowd".[13] The power of miraculous grace speaking louder than the thousands of words that Augustine and others had used to

---

[12] Ibid., 60.
[13] Ibid., 67.

counter Pelagianism, the people who had been bewitched by error returned to the true fold. Practising what they preached, the two bishops made a pilgrimage to the tomb of the martyred St. Alban in thanksgiving for the success of their mission.

In 433, only four years after Germanus and Lupus were strengthening the faith of the people of Britain, another great bishop and saint of the Church, St. Patrick, was said to be visiting the monks at Glastonbury, which, being far from the ravages and savages in the north, had escaped the turmoil and terror afflicting much of the rest of the country. Although St. Patrick's visit to Glastonbury is disputed by many modern historians, it was evidently accepted by the mediaeval historian William of Malmesbury. Writing in the twelfth century, he accepted the account he had been given that St. Patrick had not only visited Glaston-bury, reforming the community of hermits into a more formal monastic mode of life, but that he had died there and was buried in the original first-century chapel known as the *Vetusta Ecclesia* (Old Church). According to William of Malmesbury, St. Patrick was succeeded as abbot of Glastonbury by his disciple Benignus. The same account also attests to the fact that St. Brigid settled on a marsh-enclosed islet, near to Glastonbury, and that St. David, the patron saint of Wales, visited Glastonbury in the sixth century, as did St. Gildas the Wise.[14]

All of these events at Glastonbury are disputed by historians, and there's no denying that we are entering a period of history which is truly shrouded in mystery. What happened when the sun finally set on the England before England? It's a twilight zone of myths and legends, from which the Christ-haunted story of King Arthur and the

---

[14] Gillett, *Shrines of Our Lady in England and Wales*, 146–47.

quest for the Holy Grail emerge as shadows barely visible amidst the mist settling on the marshes surrounding Avalon. Charles Coulombe in *A Catholic Quest for the Holy Grail* does his best to find the facts obscured by the fogs of legend that surround them. Here's what he says about King Arthur himself:

> Some claim he never existed—and certainly he did not exist as the quasi-medieval king familiar to us from the tales of the Grail and later film! But in all likelihood he was a leader of the Briton resistance to the Saxons—perhaps the last *Dux Bellorum*, "Duke of Battles". One can imagine him leading his cavalry from one end of Britain to the other, striking at the Saxons wherever they advanced. And Camelot? Well, instead of the walled and turreted city the name has come to conjure up in our imaginations, it was more probably a hill fort, like Cadbury Castle in Somerset—which local legend has always claimed to have been his headquarters. At least this is the first picture that we have of him in Nennius' *Historia Brittonum*, written around 830—which would have been around three and one-half centuries after the time when he is said to have flourished.[15]

Although Nennius offers the "first picture" of King Arthur, as Charles Coulombe states, there are tantalizing and suggestive glimpses of the legendary king in earlier sources. The aforementioned St. Gildas the Wise, in his *De Excidio et Conquestu Britanniae*, written some time in the early sixth century (at least three hundred years before Nennian), speaks of the warrior king Ambrosius Aurelianus, who led the British resistance to the Saxons and

---

[15] Charles A. Coulombe, *A Catholic Quest for the Holy Grail* (Charlotte, N.C.: TAN Books, 2017), 28.

whom some have suggested was a relative of King Arthur, if not perhaps another name for Arthur himself. Bede, using Gildas as his source and writing a century before Nennius, also writes of Ambrosius Aurelianus' victory over the Saxons.

Nennius describes the legendary Arthur as fighting no fewer than twelve victorious battles against the Saxons, giving the location for each but with place names that continue to baffle historians. In the eighth of these battles, Nennius tells us that "Arthur carried the image of the holy Mary, the everlasting Virgin, on his [shield], and the heathen were put to flight on that day, and there was a great slaughter upon them, through the power of Our Lord Jesus Christ and the power of the holy Virgin Mary, his mother."[16]

Charles Coulombe records that the fourteenth-century monastic chronicler John of Glastonbury claimed that King Arthur had placed the image of the Blessed Virgin on his shield after an apparition of the Virgin and the Infant Jesus which was miraculously gifted to him while he was staying near Glastonbury.[17] Mr. Coulombe also cites a Breton legend which derives the unique coat of arms of Brittany to an ermine cloak that the Blessed Virgin was said to have placed on King Arthur's shield while he was in mortal combat with a pagan of giant stature. The legend states that Arthur was so grateful for the Virgin's supernatural assistance that he ordered his nephew, Hoel, the first Duke of Brittany, to place the ermine pattern on his arms.[18]

It is difficult to give credence to these pious legends, which should be attributed to the Christ-haunted

---

[16] Quoted in ibid., 136–37, from Nennius, in *Arthurian Period Sources*, vol. 8 (Chichester: Phillimore, 1980), 35.

[17] Coulombe, *Catholic Quest for Holy Grail*, 137.

[18] Ibid.

imagination of bards and storytellers, and to the chroni-
clers who were happy to weave such legends into the fabric of their histories. It does illustrate, however, the deeply
religious faith of those who told the stories and of those of
whom the stories were told.

As the Catholic sun was setting on the England before
England, the Christians of the time must have wondered
if Christ Himself was about to be eclipsed by a new pagan
darkness. It was, however, Christ Himself, working
through the Church, His Mystical Body, who would rise
from the ruins of Roman Britain.

Chapter Three

A Land of Saints

Fonts of Saxon rock stood full of God,
Altars rose, each like a kingly throne,
Where the royal chalice with its lineal blood,
The glory of the presence, ruled and reigned.

—Robert S. Hawker, from
"The Quest of the Sangraal"

Having watched the sun set in an Arthurian mist on Roman Britain, we'll now look at the birth of England, *Englaland*, the land of the Angles, Saxons, and Jutes. It was long presumed and taught that the Germanic pagan tribes moved into England after the withdrawal of the Romans in the early fifth century. In fact, however, there was already a considerable Germanic presence during the Roman occupation and possibly even before it. By the middle of the third century, much of the Roman army was German, and at the end of that century, the war lord Carausius took control of England, albeit briefly, bringing large numbers of German-speaking soldiers with him. By the middle of the fourth century, explains Hilaire Belloc, "the eastern and southern shores of England were probably already fortified and garrisoned with Saxons taken into the pay of the

Empire."[1] So prominent was this Germanic presence that the whole of the east and south coast from the Wash to the Isle of Wight was known as "the Saxon shore". This Germanic presence was overlooked by Bede, who states that the Angles were invited to Britain by King Vortigern in the middle of the fifth century to help him repel the raids by the Picts in the north:

> It was not long before such hordes of these alien peoples vied together to crowd into the island that the natives who had invited them began to live in terror. Then all of a sudden the Angles made an alliance with the Picts ... and began to turn their arms against their allies. They began by demanding a greater supply of provisions; then, seeking to provoke a quarrel, threatened that unless larger supplies were forthcoming, they would terminate their treaty and ravage the whole island. Nor were they slow to carry out their threats.[2]

Bede speaks of a "conflagration from the eastern to western shores" and the subsequent "stranglehold" that the Angles now had "over nearly all the doomed island". A widespread persecution of the Christian population followed. Churches were burned, "priests were slain at the altar," and the people were put to death by "fire and sword". Bede then describes the grim aftermath of the slaughter, which would sound the death knell of Romano-British power in England:

> A few wretched survivors captured in the hills were butch-ered wholesale, and others, desperate with hunger, came

---

[1] Hilaire Belloc, *A Shorter History of England* (London: George G. Harrap, 1934), 47.

[2] Bede, *Ecclesiastical History of the English People*, ed. D. H. Farmer and Ronald Latham (London: Penguin Classics, 1991), 63.

out and surrendered to the enemy for food, although they were doomed to lifelong slavery even if they escaped instant massacre. Some fled overseas in their misery; others, clinging to their homeland, eked out a wretched and fearful existence among the mountains, forests, and crags, ever on the alert for danger.[3]

As for King Vortigern, the British king who had made the fateful and fatal decision to invite the Angles to his realm, he seems to have fled for his life to the inaccessible mountains of Wales. And yet, as we have already discussed, the sixth-century chronicler St. Gildas the Wise records in his history of the period that the Romano-British remnant mounted a spirited resistance, winning several battles culminating in their victory over the Angles at the Battle of Badon Hill, sometime between 493 and 500. There seems no reason to doubt the veracity of Gildas' account, considering that he was writing only forty or so years after the battle itself and is therefore a near contemporary source. Gildas moved to Brittany, in what is now France, in the later years of his life, founding a monastery; it might well be that he and other British exiles were the source of the Arthurian legends which would emerge, embellished greatly, in the poetry of Chrétien de Troyes in the twelfth century.

Were we to try to disentangle Bede's account of the Angles being invited into the country from overseas with the apparent fact that there was already a considerable Germanic presence along the coast of England, we might be tempted to conjecture that King Vortigern sought an alliance with his Saxon neighbours, rather than inviting Saxons from overseas to defend his realm, or perhaps he did both. Irrespective of such details, the inescapable reality is that Romano-British Albion met its doom and

[3] Ibid., 64.

that Anglo-Saxon England emerged in its place. We can assume that only some of the Romano-British population remained in England, subsumed within, and subjugated by, the triumphant English ascendancy, whereas others went into exile in the west to Wales and Cornwall, or to Brittany across the sea, all these places retaining the Celtic tongue as their linguistic connection to their Romano-British ancestors.

For about a century, pagan darkness returned. It was ended in 596, when Pope St. Gregory the Great sent St. Augustine and a small company of other monks to England. In the following year, Augustine preached before King Ethelbert, who was impressed enough to grant Augustine permission to preach the Gospel to the people of Kent. In 602, with the king's assistance, Augustine repaired and then consecrated a church which had been established centuries earlier by Roman Christians. Two years later, Pope Gregory appointed Mellitus as Bishop of London, thereby reestablishing a see which had existed under the Romans since at least three hundred years earlier. Mellitus' first major act as bishop was to build St. Paul's Cathedral, probably on the site of a previous church.

Even as Augustine and Mellitus were planting seeds of faith and building churches in the south of England, war was raging in the north. Ironically, it was now the army from Scotland and Ireland which was Christian, whereas the invading English army was pagan, under the rule of the ruthless King Ethelfrid of Northumbria. Although the pagan English triumphed at the Battle of Degsastan in 603, they would succumb to Christ a little over two decades later, in 627, when Ethelfrith's brother-in-law, King Edwin, converted to the faith, making Northumbria a Christian kingdom. With all the zeal of a new convert, King Edwin persuaded King Earpwald of East Anglia to accept Christ in baptism, also in 627, so that in one glorious year the east and the north of England embraced the faith. In that same year, a veritable *annus mirabilis*, St. Honorius became Archbishop of Canterbury. During his twenty-five years as Primate, he would oversee the transformation of England into an avowedly Christian country and a land of saints. He sent St. Felix to evangelize East Anglia and lived to see the apostolate of St. Aidan in Northumbria; he replaced St. Birinus of Wessex with another saint, Agilbert, as Bishop of Dorchester, and had the joy of seeing the conversion of King Peada and the kingdom of the Middle Angles. It was also during St. Honorius' time that the first English convent of Benedictine nuns was founded, in 630, by St. Eanswith at Folkestone in Kent, beginning a monastic tradition of religious sisters in England which would span nine hundred years until Henry VIII's dissolution of the monasteries in the sixteenth century.

In 642, St. Oswald, the king of Northumbria, fell in battle against the pagans of Mercia. Bede reports miracles at the site of his death, including the healing of a paralytic girl. Miracles were also reported nine years later after the death of St. Aidan, the Irish monk who was the first bishop and abbot of Lindisfarne (Holy Island), off the coast of Northumbria.

Two of Aidan's students, St. Cedd and St. Chad, who had received their education at Lindisfarne, would become great evangelists for the faith in the struggle to wrest the soul of England from the grip of paganism. St. Cedd preached to the East Saxons, in what is now Essex, and proved so successful that he was appointed bishop and subsequently founded monasteries. St. Chad, his brother, would become the first Bishop of Mercia, in the English midlands.

Perhaps the most important event with respect to the spread of Christianity throughout England was the Synod of Whitby, held in 664, which conformed the practice of the faith in England with that of the universal Church. At this time, those parts of England still under the influence of the remnant of the Romano-British Church, which had been influenced in turn by the teaching of Irish monks, was celebrating Easter at a different time from that celebrated by Rome. This anomaly was resolved at the synod, ensuring a unified practice of the Church's liturgy thereafter.

One of the most colourful characters of the mid-seventh century was St. Etheldreda, a queen who would become the foundress and abbess of Ely, on the fens of what is now Cambridgeshire. A princess by birth, the daughter of the king of East Anglia, she became a nun and founded a monastery in 673 on the site of what is now the magnificent Ely Cathedral. She also restored an old church, which had been reputedly destroyed by Penda, the pagan king of Mercia, and lived an austere and holy life of penance and prayer. She ate only one meal a day and wore clothes of coarse wool instead of linen. Dying in 679, her body was discovered seventeen years later to be incorrupt and the tumour on her neck, the presumed cause of her death, was found to be healed. According to those who witnessed the exhumation of her body, including St. Wilfrid, the linen cloths in which her body had been wrapped were as fresh as they were on the day of her burial. Her shrine at Ely became a popular place of pilgrimage, and devotion to her was flourishing many centuries later. Known by the name of St. Audrey, a contraction of "Etheldreda", St. Audrey's Fairs were held on her feast day of October 17. The silk and lace sold at these fairs was not always of the finest quality; even to this day, something of poor or questionable quality is said to be *tawdry*, a corruption of *St. Audrey*.

Another great abbess of the Church and contemporary of St. Etheldreda was St. Ethelburga, foundress of Barking

Abbey in Essex, to the east of London. It would become one of the most prominent religious houses in England, surviving until its destruction by Henry VIII. The abbey had been founded for St. Ethelburga by her brother, St. Erkenwald, sometime before the latter had become Bishop of the East Saxons in 675. Such was the rise to prominence of Barking Abbey and such was the reputation for holiness of its foundress that St. Bede, writing only a few decades after St. Ethelburga's death, spends several chapters on the events of her life, including accounts of several miracles, such as visions of the afterlife and the healing of a blind woman while praying in the convent burial ground.

A saint of an altogether different sort was Caedwalla, a pagan king of Wessex who had a reputation for ruthlessness and violence until he fell under the benign and holy influence of St. Wilfrid. Experiencing a dramatic conversion, he abdicated in 688 and travelled to Rome on penitential pilgrimage, desiring to be received into the Church. He was baptized on Holy Saturday 689 by Pope Sergius and given the name of Peter. Although he was only thirty years old, he was taken ill suddenly and died. It is said that he was still wearing his white baptismal robes at the moment of death. He was buried in the crypt of St. Peter's, and his epitaph, written by Crispus, Archbishop of Milan, is quoted by Bede. Caedwalla would be the first of four Anglo-Saxon kings to end his days in Rome, two of whom became monks upon their arrival in the Eternal City.

The late seventh century was also a time of great scholarship and culture. St. Adrian of Canterbury established a school, teaching Greek, Latin, Scripture, theology, law, and astronomy, at which many future bishops and abbots were educated. St. Adrian had a reputation for sanctity as well as scholarship; when his body was exhumed in 1091, almost four hundred years after his death, it was found to be incorrupt. Similarly, the body of St. Cuthbert, the Bishop of Lindisfarne, was found to be incorrupt in 698, eleven years after his death, and miraculous healings were reported at his tomb and in association with his relics.

Two years later, St. Egwin, Bishop of Worcester, and several attendants were gifted with an apparition of the Blessed Virgin at Evesham in what is now Worcestershire. In gratitude for such a blessing, St. Egwin, with the financial support of King Ethelred, began building a church over the place of the apparition. The shrine and church were put under the care of Benedictine monks, and a great abbey was then built to honour Our Lady of Evesham. Following St. Egwin's death, he was buried at the foot of the shrine, which became one of the major pilgrimage sites of Anglo-Saxon England. The shrine was pillaged by the Danes and then rebuilt on an even grander scale in the eleventh century, just prior to the Norman Conquest.

The late seventh and early eighth centuries also heralded the birth of English literature. Caedmon, the earliest known of all English poets, was a monk at Whitby Abbey, and it is to this period that *Beowulf*, the great English epic, belongs. A profoundly Catholic work, irrespective of its woeful and willful misreading by modern critics, *Beowulf* was almost certainly written by a monk who was probably a contemporary of Bede. It is little surprise, therefore, that the poet should share Bede's preoccupation with the continued presence of Pelagianism, which had been condemned as recently as 634 by Pope Honorius[4] for the growth of its influence, especially in Ireland. *Beowulf* warns against Pelagianism in the narrative's depiction of its eponymous protagonist as the strongest man alive who

[4] Not to be confused with the aforementioned Honorius of Canterbury.

believes he can defeat all evil through the power of his own strength, reflecting the heretical teaching of Pelagius that men could get to heaven through the power of their own will, without the need of God's grace. Beowulf discovers, in spite of his great strength, that he is unable to defeat the supernatural power of Grendel's Mother without the supernatural assistance of a miraculous sword, signifying grace. The last part of *Beowulf*, which tells of the hero's defeat of the dragon, employs numerical allegory in a manner which would prove very influential to J. R. R. Tolkien, who was a great scholar of the Anglo-Saxon language (Old English) and who translated *Beowulf* and lectured on it. Other great poems written at this time or during the following century are "The Dream of the Rood", "The Ruin", "The Wanderer", and "The Seafarer"—all profoundly Christian works which are so beautiful that they withstand the test of translation, defying Bede's claim, when discussing his own translation of Caedmon's English verse into Latin, that "verses, however masterly, cannot be translated literally from one language into another without losing much of their beauty and dignity."[5] Bede's adage, echoing T. S. Eliot's claim that "between the potency and the existence falls the shadow",[6] is indubitably true; yet it says a great deal about the potency of these wonderful Old English poems that they retain great beauty even after the shadow is cast by translation.

St. Bede, the great chronicler of Anglo-Saxon history, completed the writing of his celebrated and seminal *Ecclesiastical History of the English People* in 731 at a time of turmoil and tribulation for the Church. The armies of the

[5] Bede, *Ecclesiastical History*, 249.
[6] T. S. Eliot, from "The Hollow Men" (1925).

new religion of Islam were conquering many Christian lands and even advanced as far as northern France, before being defeated in 732 at the Battle of Tours. At the same time, an English monk, St. Boniface, was having great success in converting the pagan peoples of Germany, working tirelessly until suffering martyrdom in 754 in the eightieth year of a long and faithful life.

In contrast, St. Bede the Venerable seems hardly to have travelled at all from the monastery in northern England in which he had spent an uneventful and quiet life of prayer and study. Yet his own legacy, though different from that of missionaries such as St. Boniface, is considerable. The knowledge that we now have of Roman Britain and Anglo-Saxon England is largely dependent on Bede's scholarship, and there's no doubt that he deserves the accolade of being "The Father of English History" as well as the accolade of being declared a Doctor of the Church by Pope Leo XIII in 1899.

Bede died in 735, at the halfway mark of the history of Anglo-Saxon England, the first half of which he had chronicled so well. At the time of his death, it had been 325 years since the Romans had left Britain, signalling the dawn of the Anglo-Saxon ascendency, and 331 years before the Norman Conquest would see the sun setting on Anglo-Saxondom. The three centuries which would follow Bede were destined to be at least as eventful and perhaps even more glorious than the three centuries that he had depicted so well.

Chapter Four

Christian Kings and the Queen of Heaven

See you the windy levels spread
About the gates of Rye?
O that was where the Northmen fled,
When Alfred's ships came by.

—Rudyard Kipling,
from "Puck's Song"

In 735, the same year in which Bede died, another great English scholar, Alcuin, was born in the north of England. Destined to become the most influential scholar of the eighth century, he was educated by men whom Bede had taught. This passing of the baton of knowledge from one generation to the next exemplifies the continuum of accumulated wisdom across the ages that rightly bears the name of civilization.

Writing of the flowering of knowledge and scholarship in Anglo-Saxon England, Fr. Aelfric Manson illustrates the connection between the revival of the liberal arts and the Church's insistence on the marriage of faith and reason. "To Alcuin, as to Alfred the Great, study and the pursuit of knowledge was part of the Christian life, and the liberal arts were not practiced as ends in themselves but as sub-serving, in one way or another, the great end of enriching the Christian life and advancing in the understanding of revelation."[1]

Having spent the first forty years of his life building the great library at York, and gaining a reputation for scholarship which was known from one end of Christendom to the other, Alcuin answered the call of Charlemagne to help spread Christian learning to the Franks. Alcuin migrated from England in 782 to Aachen, in what is now Germany, passing out of English history in order to play a major role in the history of Christendom. Charlemagne bestowed three abbeys upon Alcuin for the support of himself and his scholars which became great centers of learning. Alcuin set about raising the standards for the copying of manuscripts, which was such a crucial task in the days before printing, as well as increasing the amount of copying being done. Handpicked scribes would make copies under Alcuin's supervision which were then distributed to monasteries for further copies to be made. In this way, libraries gradually grew up all over the realms that Charlemagne ruled, all of which had Alcuin's own labour as their fount and source.

Charlemagne was himself a student of Alcuin, considering the learned Englishman to be his mentor. In becoming Alcuin's first student, Charlemagne was showing his own people that nobody should consider himself above the pursuit of knowledge. As one whom Charlemagne trusted, Alcuin became what the historian William J. Slattery has described as the empire's unofficial "Minister of Culture". He was, writes Slattery, "a man for whom Charlemagne held deep admiration, whose friendship he cherished, and

---

[1] Maisie Ward, ed., *The English Way: Studies in English Sanctity from Bede to Newman* (Tacoma, Wash.: Cluny Media, 2016), 39.

to whom he gave an important role in formulating policy and in drafting official documents."[2]

Although Alcuin had become one of the most influential figures in the whole of Christendom, he never lost touch with what was happening in his native land. This is evident in letters he sent to three successive kings of Mercia—Offa, Ecgfrith, and Cenwulf—and to Ethelred I, king of Northumbria, beseeching them to rule with virtue and reminding them that corrupt and tyrannical rulers endanger both their kingdoms and themselves. The golden rule for all rulers was that the king who governs himself well will govern his kingdom well.

The situation in England in the years following Bede's death was somewhat complex, the consequence of the gradual coalescence of power into the hands of three dominant kingdoms: Northumbria in the north, Mercia in the midlands, and Wessex in the south and west. The most powerful king in the late eighth century was Offa, king of Mercia, who built the famous Offa's Dyke, a great trench, which served to delineate and defend his kingdom's western border from the Welsh, the remnants of which are still visibly discernible today.

In 802, six years after the death of Offa, Egbert became king of Wessex, a significant landmark in the history of England because he would be the patriarch of all the native kings of England until the time of the Norman Conquest and, through his female descendants, the ancestor of all English monarchs after Henry I until the present day. At the time of his death, in 839, he had consolidated his power to such a degree that he had become the de facto ruler of

[2] William J. Slattery, *Heroism and Genius: How Catholic Priests Helped to Build—and Can Help Rebuild—Western Civilization* (San Francisco: Ignatius Press, 2017), 106–7.

the whole country. "Before him you only have chieftains, many half mythical," wrote Hilaire Belloc. "After him you have true kings who come to rule all England."[3]

During Egbert's reign, a new pagan menace beset the people of England in the form of Viking marauders from what is now Denmark and Norway. Such raids by these Scandinavian pirates had begun as early as 787, including a terrible attack upon the monastery of Lindisfarne in 793, and they would continue, on and off, throughout Egbert's reign. It was, however, not until shortly after his death in 839 that the real onslaught of the Vikings began in earnest. From 840, when an invading force attacked the south coast of England, there were incessant raids over a period of three years during which the invaders made inroads into England from Lincolnshire in the east to Dorset in the southwest. After a brief respite, during which the Vikings turned their attention to mainland Europe, most notably in a great raid on Hamburg, the new Christian town and bishopric in Germany that Charlemagne had founded, the invaders returned in greater numbers than ever before. In 851, they sacked Canterbury, the heart of Christendom in England, and then sailed up the Thames to ravage London. They were finally defeated just outside London, suffering such devastating losses that England was then left in peace for some time.

In 860, the Danes returned. Looting Winchester in the south, they launched a decade-long assault on the people of England. Taking York, they subjugated the whole north of the country. They raped, looted, pillaged, and massacred, wherever they went, burning monasteries to the ground and spreading terror amongst the hapless populace who seemed powerless to stem the tyrannical pagan

[3] Hilaire Belloc, *A Shorter History of England* (London: George G. Harrap, 1934), 82.

tide. Invading East Anglia in 869, the Danes defeated the army of the East Angles, taking their young Christian king prisoner. With great courage, King Edmund refused to deny the faith and was mutilated in terrible fashion as punishment for his Christian witness. The exact nature of his martyrdom is unclear. He might have been scourged, shot with arrows, and then finally beheaded, as tradition maintains, which would have been less gruesome than the traditional Viking "blood-eagling" ritual, which entailed the disemboweling of the still-living victim as an offering to the pagan gods, a practice which, in modified form, would be resurrected by the neo-barbarians of the English Reformation seven hundred years later.

In around 915, about fifty years after his martyrdom, King Edmund's body was exhumed and found to be incorrupt. The body was then reburied at a place which is now called Bury St. Edmunds, becoming a major shrine and place of pilgrimage.

As England appeared defenceless in the presence of the relentless advance of the barbarians, lying prostrate and seemingly doomed to be sacrificed, like St. Edmund, as an offering to the pagan gods, a hero arose who would save both England and the faith she espoused. A grandson of King Egbert, he is known to history as Alfred the Great.

With respect to Alfred's historical importance, Hilaire Belloc insisted that it was crucial not merely to the survival of the faith in England but perhaps to the survival of the whole of Christendom. When Alfred became king of England in 871, Christendom was under siege. Barbarian hordes were pressing Christian Europe from the north and east, and Islam was threatening conquest from the south. By the mid-ninth century, Belloc wrote, "Western Christendom had become a sort of fortress, besieged on all sides." Its territory had contracted to the north and centre of Italy, France, a strip of northern Spain, England, and Ireland, and the valley of the Rhine, with the recently converted and half-civilized German tribes to the east of the valley forming a fragile buffer zone to the pagans beyond. "If, out of this limited territory, the British islands had been swept away the shock would have been severe and might have been final."[4]

If Belloc's assessment of Alfred's importance is to be believed, and it certainly seems credible enough, every Christian, irrespective of his ethnic roots, owes Alfred the Great a great debt of gratitude. Since this is so, let's look a little closer at the man and the legend.

The first seven years of Alfred's reign were perilous in the extreme, the future of Anglo-Saxondom hanging by a thread which the ever-advancing Danes threatened to sever forever. By 877, Alfred and his court had become exiles in their own land, retreating to fortified positions in the marshes of Somerset, on the very southwestern edge of the kingdom. It was from this isolated refuge that Alfred set forth in the spring of 878, gathering an army on the Feast of Pentecost and then advancing to the Danish host stationed at Chippenham. With the future of Christendom balanced on a knife edge, Alfred's army won the day at the Battle of Eddington, or what Chesterton, in *The Ballad of the White Horse*, calls Ethandune, in conformity to the name used in the primary historical sources. As for the battle's significance, it is encapsulated brilliantly in Chesterton's epic poem by the words that the poet places on the lips of the king: "The high tide!" King Alfred cried. "The high tide and the turn!" Alfred's victory turned the tide, ensuring that Anglo-Saxon England would survive, as would the faith which animated it.

[4] Ibid., 87.

Chesterton, perceiving the legendary truth that transcends the historical facts, wrote that "Alfred has come down to us in the best way (that is by national legends) solely for the same reason as Arthur and Roland and the other giants of that darkness, because he fought for the Christian civilization against the heathen nihilism."[5] If this is so, it is indeed a fortunate or providential coincidence that Alfred's victory at Eddington came on the centenary of Roland's heroic death at the Battle of Roncevaux Pass in 778, the legendary battle which inspired the mediaeval French epic *The Song of Roland*, in much the same manner as the legendary Battle of Eddington had inspired Chesterton's epic. As for whether we should consider the coincidence that one battle could be seen as a mystical celebration of the hundredth anniversary of the previous one, we need only hearken to the words of Alfred the Great, in the "Addition" to his translation of Boethius: "I say, as do all Christian men, that it is a divine purpose that rules, and not fate."

There is much more that could and should be said about the achievement and legacy of Alfred the Great: his scholarship, as exhibited in the aforementioned translation of Boethius; his unification of England as a nation, and his elevation of English as an official language, alongside a revival and restoration of Latin; his establishment of a navy, enabling better defence of England's ravaged coast; his reform of the legal system; and his establishment of a court school in emulation of Charlemagne's and Alcuin's example. Such is his enduring reputation that Chesterton could refer to "a chiming unanimity, a chain of polite or popular compliment"[6] which had stretched unbroken

[5] G. K. Chesterton, prefatory note to *The Ballad of the White Horse* (London, Methuen, 1911), viii.

[6] Ward, *English Way*, 53.

from the *Anglo-Saxon Chronicle*, dating from Alfred's own day, until the present day:

> A Scottish rationalist like Hume, a romantic Tory like Scott, a Voltairean sceptic like Gibbon, a prudent Catholic like Lingard, an imprudent pro-Catholic like Cobbett, a practical and (spiritually) rather stupid Protestant like Macaulay, would all at any moment have testified to the solid and unquestioned moral reputation of Alfred.[7]

Let's conclude our discussion of Alfred the Great with the tribute paid to him by the "imprudent pro-Catholic" William Cobbett:

> Where is there one amongst us, who has read anything at all, who has not read of the fame of Alfred? What book can we open, even for our boyish days, that does not sound his praise? Poets, moralists, divines, historians, philosophers, lawyers, legislators, not only of our own country, but of all Europe, have cited him, and still cite him, as a model of virtue, piety, wisdom, valour, and patriotism; as possessing every excellence, without a single fault. He, in spite of difficulties such as no other human being on record ever encountered, cleared his harassed and half-barbarized country of horde after horde of cruel invaders, who, at one time, had wholly subdued it, and compelled him, in order to escape destruction, to resort to the habit and the life of a herdsman. From this state of depression he, during a not long life, raised himself and his people to the highest point of happiness and of fame. He fought, with his armies and fleets, more than fifty battles against the enemies of England. He taught his people by his example as well as by his precepts, to be sober, industrious, brave, and just. He promoted learning in all the sciences; he planted the University of Oxford; to him,

[7] Ibid.

and not to a late Scotch lawyer, belongs "Trial by Jury."
Blackstone calls him the founder of Common Law; the
counties, the hundreds, the tithings, the courts of justice,
were the work of Alfred; he, in fact, was the founder of
all those rights, liberties and laws, which made England
to be what England has been, which gave her a character
above that of all other nations, which made her rich and
great and happy beyond all her neighbours, and which
still give her whatever she possesses of that pre-eminence.
If there be a name under heaven, to which Englishmen
ought to bow with reverence approaching towards adoration, it is the name of Alfred.[8]

King Alfred died at the end of the ninth century, bequeathing to his successors a time of relative peace and political stability, radically different from the perilous and
anarchic England that he had himself inherited less than
thirty years earlier. The slow conversion of the people of
Scandinavia to Christianity removed the threat of pagan
barbarism, and the consolidation of Anglo-Saxon power
meant that the north of the country was being brought
once more under the control of the English monarchy.

As for the Church, she was blessed in the tenth century by the authoritative presence of St. Dunstan, who
became Abbot of Glastonbury in 939 and Archbishop of
Canterbury in 960, serving as the Primate of all England
for twenty-eight years, until his death in 988. His reformation of both monastic and diocesan life was so extensive and so successful that later generations, following the
Norman Conquest, looked upon it as a "golden age".
Belloc attributed the reform of the Church by Pope St.
Gregory VII a century later as having its inspirational roots
in St. Dunstan's reforms in England: "We must always

[8] William Cobbett, *A History of the Protestant Reformation* (Sevenoaks, Kent:
Fisher Press, 1994), 77–78.

remember that the revival of the Catholic Church ... was thus launched in England, and by an Englishman."[9] In addition to Dunstan's influence on the universal Church, he was also a pivotal figure in English history. "It has been well said," wrote the historian David Hugh Farmer, "that the 10th Century gave shape to English history, and Dunstan gave shape to the 10th Century."[10]

Such was Dunstan's reputation and stature, and such was the high regard in which he was held by his contemporaries, that his cult emerged spontaneously after his death and spread rapidly. As early as 999, he was being recognized in a document drawn up by a monk of Canterbury as the "chief of all the saints who rest at Christ Church", and his feast day was being celebrated widely, appearing on several pre-Conquest calendars. As was often the case with the more popular saints, folk tales and legends began to proliferate about his life. One of the most entertaining, if not one of the most believable, is shown in artistic depictions of the saint holding the devil by the nose with a pair of blacksmith's tongs. Hagiographical tradition had made Dunstan a metalworker, a reference to the metalwork he was known to have done while living as a hermit, prior to his becoming Abbot of Glastonbury. It was believed or claimed that some tenth-century blacksmith's tools, still kept as relics at a convent in Mayfield in Sussex, had belonged to Dunstan. These legends are retold and embellished with rambunctious humour by Hilaire Belloc in *The Four Men*, in which St. Dunstan is credited with saving the county of Sussex from being destroyed by the devil.

We have said little of the kings of the tenth century, who are eclipsed in stature by their great forebear Alfred,

[9] Belloc, *Shorter History of England*, 95.

[10] David Hugh Farmer, *The Oxford Dictionary of Saints* (Oxford: Oxford University Press, 1987), 139.

but one incident warrants attention. In 971, King Edgar visited Glastonbury and granted a Charter of Privilege to St. Mary's Chapel, England's oldest shrine to the Mother of God. Significantly, he laid his scepter on the altar as a token of the king's subservience to the Queen of Heaven, as well as an act of investiture granting royal privileges to the shrine. He then broke the scepter, which was described by William of Malmesbury as being "beautifully formed of ivory and adorned with gold", commanding that one half should be kept in the chapel in testimony of his granting of the charter.[11] The charter was then confirmed by the reigning pope, John XIII.

The eleventh century saw a brief period when the Danes at last ruled supreme in England. These Danes were, however, very different from the pagan Vikings who had terrorized the country in preceding centuries. Under the reign of King Canute, a devout Christian, the faith flourished.

Following in the footsteps of King Edgar, Canute made a pilgrimage to the Marian shrine at Glastonbury, bringing "a glistening pall, enriched with peacock feathers" as a donation.[12] He also established the Benedictine order at Gloucester Abbey, and at the height of his power, he went on pilgrimage to Rome. During his reign, new churches were built in London and there were thought to be about twenty-five within the city by the time of his death, including six dedicated to the Norwegian saint Olaf and one to Olaf's son, St. Magnus the Martyr.[13]

King Canute, who reigned from 1016 until 1035, is best known to posterity for the legendary account of his ordering the tide to obey him. Although this is often cited as

[11] H. M. Gillett, *Shrines of Our Lady in England and Wales* (London: Samuel Walker, 1957), 152.
[12] Ibid.
[13] Simon Jenkins, *A Short History of London* (London: Viking, 2019), 21.

evidence of the foolishness of egocentric rulers who "try to stop the tide", the true source of the account, which dates from the twelfth century, demonstrates Canute's piety and humility, not his folly and pride. According to the twelfth-century account by Henry of Huntingdon, Canute ordered his throne to be placed on the beach, and then, sitting on it, he ordered the incoming tide to stop. When the tide lapped against his feet, in defiance of the royal command, he used the incident to teach a priceless lesson to his flattering courtiers. "Let all men know how empty and worthless is the power of kings," he declaimed, "for there is none worthy of the name, but He whom heaven, earth, and sea obey by eternal laws." He then hung his crown on a crucifix and, according to the account, never wore it again "to the honour of God the almighty King".[14] The episode shows King Canute to be a kindred spirit to the chastened and converted King Lear, who refers to flattering courtiers as "gilded butterflies" and "poor rogues [who] talk of court news". Such men are not to be trusted, either in history or on the stage. Although most historians question the veracity of this anecdotal episode, seeing it as "apocryphal", the fact that the source for the story dates from only a century after Canute's own time suggests the possibility that there could be a core of fact at the heart of Henry of Huntingdon's account.

King Canute's reign, as noble as it was, would be eclipsed in terms of its virtue by the reign of his stepson, St. Edward the Confessor, who ruled England from 1042 until the fateful year of 1066.

Edward's reputation for holiness was acknowledged during his reign. He was an accessible ruler, being receptive

---

[14] Henry of Huntingdon, *The Chronicle of Henry of Huntingdon* (London: Andesite Press, 2017), 199.

to the needs and requests of his subjects and demonstrating great generosity to the poor. He was said to have received mystical visions and to have cured people of scrofula with the laying on of his hands. He strengthened links with the papacy, sending bishops to Leo IX's Councils in 1049 and 1050 and receiving papal legates in 1061. The most ambitious project he undertook was the founding of Westminster Abbey, which would become and has remained the place for the coronation of the kings and queens of England. It was completed and consecrated shortly before his death and became his place of burial, his tomb and relics being undisturbed to this day, having survived the ravages of the Reformation with its iconoclastic destruction of England's shrines to her saints.

St. Edward's death in 1066 would sound the death knell for Anglo-Saxon England, precipitating rival claims to the English throne and leading a few months later to the Norman Conquest. Both sides claimed Edward's blessing on their respective claims, and both sides, the victorious Normans and defeated Anglo-Saxons alike, would venerate him as a saint. In 1102, his body was found to be incorrupt, adding considerably to the reverence in which he was already held. He would be the accepted patron saint of England until the crusaders brought back their devotion to St. George, the warrior saint who would eventually displace Edward as the country's patron. Shakespeare's devotion to the saint was expressed in *Macbeth* when Edward's sanctity and his miraculous powers of healing are contrasted with the Machiavellian evil of the Scottish king.

Although it would seem apt to bring down the curtain on Anglo-Saxon England with the death of St. Edward the Confessor in 1066, only a few short months before the Battle of Hastings would bring Anglo-Saxondom to a definitive end, the final and climactic moment in the 650-year history of the Anglo-Saxons, and its greatest blessing, was a Marian apparition during St. Edward's reign.

In 1061, a widow and Lady of the Manor, Richeldis de Faverches, received a vision of Our Lady at Walsingham in the East Anglian county of Norfolk. In answer to a prayer that she might be permitted to honour the Virgin with some special work, she was led by the Blessed Virgin "in spirit" to Nazareth and shown the little house of the Holy Family, then preserved beneath the Basilica of the Annunciation. Our Lady then commanded Richeldis to build a replica of the holy house in Walsingham as a memorial of the great joy of the angelic salutation, promising that "all who sought her there might find succour".[15] Richeldis did as she was commanded, and Walsingham quickly became one of the most popular pilgrimage sites, not only in England but in the whole of Christendom. For over four centuries, pilgrims flocked to Our Lady's shrine from all over Europe—kings, aristocrats, and common people alike—so that the Walsingham Way was likened to the Milky Way, with each of the countless stars of the galaxy representing each of the countless pilgrims who flocked to Our Lady's shrine. An account of the history of the shrine, published in the mid-fifteenth century, tells of the many wonders and miracles reported by pilgrims and ends with a glorious hymn of praise to the Virgin, "England's celestial Queen", through whose singular blessing England is called the "Holy Land, Our Lady's Dowry".[16] And so it was that Anglo-Saxon England died in a blaze of glory, sanctified with a heavenly kiss from the Queen of Heaven herself,

---

[15] H.M. Gillett, *Famous Shrines of Our Lady* (Westminster, Md.: Carroll Press, 1950), 46–47.

[16] Ibid., 47–48.

which might be seen as Our Lady's blessing on the reign of the saintly King Edward. Such was the pyrotechnic climax, in which the England of the Anglo-Saxons, like a super nova, burned brightest as it passed away.

Chapter Five

Tyrannical Kings and Heroic Resistance

England's on the anvil—hear the hammers ring—
  Clanging from the Severn to the Tyne!
Never was a blacksmith like our Norman King—
  England's being hammered, hammered, hammered into line!

—Rudyard Kipling, from "The Anvil"

What are we to make of the Norman Conquest? Was it a good or bad thing for England? For Hilaire Belloc, it was an unmitigated blessing, serving to integrate England more fully into the Europe of the faith; for J. R. R. Tolkien, a scholar of Anglo-Saxon, it was an unmitigated disaster. This difference of opinion between two Catholic scholars was evident in an account of Tolkien's reaction to a talk given by Belloc to the Catholic chaplaincy at Oxford University, as recalled by the Jesuit Fr. Martin D'Arcy:

> In his talk Belloc came out with one of his pet themes: that the Anglo-Saxons were utterly unimportant in the history of England.... Well, Tolkien disagreed profoundly with Belloc on the question of the Anglo-Saxons. He was sitting just in front of me, and I saw him writhing as Belloc came out with some of his more extreme remarks. So during the interval, I said to him, "Oh, Tolkien, now you've got your chance. You'd better tackle

55

him." He looked at me and said, "Gracious me! Do you
think I would tackle Belloc unless I had my whole case
very carefully prepared?" He knew Belloc would always
pull some fact out of his sleeve which would disconcert
you! Now, that was a tremendous tribute from probably
the greatest authority in the world at the time on that
particular subject.[1]

Although Belloc and Tolkien had much in common,
not least of which was their shared and impassioned Catholic faith, it is intriguing that they should differ so profoundly on the importance of the Anglo-Saxons. Belloc's
view of history, for the most part astute and penetrative,
was always skewed by a less-than-balanced Francophilia
and an almost shrill Germanophobia. This was evident
in his dismissive disregard of the contribution to Christian culture of the Germanic tribes of England prior to
the Norman Conquest and his lauding of the Conquest
itself as having brought England into the fullness of Christendom, which was always, for Belloc, inseparable from
the influence of France. In contrast, Tolkien considered
Anglo-Saxon England to have been almost idyllically
Christian, a perspective coloured by his love for the Old
English language and its beauty.

Irrespective of which side we might prefer, the inescapable fact is that the Normans defeated the Anglo-Saxons at
the Battle of Hastings on October 14, 1066, thereby precipitating the Norman Conquest of England. It should be
added, however, that the Anglo-Saxon forces under King
Harold Godwinson bowed out in a blaze of veritable glory,
as is told in the Norse epic *King Harald's Saga*, which tells

[1] Martin D'Arcy, *Laughter and the Love of Friends: Reminiscences of the Dis-
tinguished English Priest and Philosopher* (Westminster, Md.: Christian Classics,
1991), 112–13.

of how Harold of England defeated the legendary warrior, King Harald Hardradi of Norway, at the Battle of Stamford Bridge in the north of England on September 25, only three days before the Norman army landed on the south coast, 240 miles to the south. King Harold could not possibly have heard of the Norman invasion until October 1 at the earliest, at which point he and the remnant of his exhausted army marched south, gathering additional forces as they went, arriving at Hastings by the morning of October 14. It was, therefore, a battle-weary and physically exhausted army which faced the invading Normans, a factor, no doubt, in the Anglo-Saxon defeat.

"The Norman Conquest brought England into line with all the rest of Christendom," wrote Belloc, "and merged English life in that of Western civilization more thoroughly than it had been since the Danish invasions had begun."[2] Insofar as this can be said to be true, it was brought about by the ruthless and relentless will of William the Conqueror, now William I, who set about restructuring the hierarchy of the English Church, replacing almost every Anglo-Saxon bishop with men of his own choosing, almost all of whom were from the continent. William's reorganization of the hierarchy was intended to bring the Church in England under the king's own sway, a feudalization of the Church which raised the secular power above that of religion, portending ill. As early as 1067, William had issued a decree asserting royal power over the making of canon law and asserted his own authority over any ecclesiastical disciplinary actions concerning his barons and officials. Well might those living in England at the time have questioned the price to be paid for merging

[2] Hilaire Belloc, *A Shorter History of England* (London: George G. Harrap, 1934), 113.

English life with the rest of Christendom, and well might they have looked back wistfully on the rule of St. Edward the Confessor who saw himself as a servant of the Church and not as her master.

The foregoing being said, William also oversaw an astonishing increase in the building and renovating of churches. Over the next half century, the Normans rebuilt the Saxon cathedrals, abbeys, and churches, as well as building castles in almost every town to defend the Norman ascendancy from Anglo-Saxon insurgency. These Norman edifices, both ecclesial and military, still grace the English landscape to this day.

In the midst of William's restructuring of the hierarchy in his own image and his replacing of Anglo-Saxons with ecclesiastics from Europe, one Anglo-Saxon bishop escaped the purge. St. Wulstan of Worchester (or Worcester) survived the vicissitudes of the time, remaining in office until his death in 1095, almost thirty years after the Conquest. Consecrated as Bishop of Worcester in 1062, during the reign of St. Edward the Confessor, one can only assume that Wulstan was spared because of his undoubted and uncontested sanctity. Dom David Knowles, a monk of Downside Abbey, drawing on William of Malmesbury's twelfth-century account of St. Wulstan's life, which was itself based on the life written by Coleman, Wulstan's own chaplain, illustrates the daily life of this holy man of God:

> He heard two masses every day before saying his own, and when travelling recited the psalms, the litany of the saints, and the Office of the dead; he refused to enter an inn before he had visited the neighboring church. Whenever and wherever he heard of a death, he caused those about him to say an Our Father, while he himself recited three

psalms, and on every day but Sunday and the great feasts he had a mass of the dead celebrated. Out of devotion to our Lady he said her Office daily.[3]

St. Wulstan's love for the poor and sick, especially lepers, was legendary, as was his relentless opposition to the slave trade which existed in his day. The main slave market was in Bristol, a port in the southwest of England, at which young men and girls were brought to be sold and shipped as slaves to Ireland. He spent many months in the neighbourhood of Bristol, going to the town every Sunday to preach against the wickedness of trading in human flesh. It was due to his preaching and no doubt also to his prayers that this wicked trade was brought to an end.

By the end of his long life, the fame of his sanctity had spread far and wide. He received letters from Pope Urban II, from the Archbishop of Bari, and from the patriarch of Jerusalem. He received requests for prayers from King Malcolm III of Scotland and from Malcolm's wife, who would later be canonized as St. Margaret of Scotland.

Although he survived William's purge of the Anglo-Saxon hierarchy, preaching peace between the Anglo-Saxons and their Norman conquerors, St. Wulstan was very much a pre-Conquest Englishman. It is significant that the only saints mentioned by name in William of Malmesbury's account of his life are those three giants of the Anglo-Saxon Church, Bede, Dunstan, and Oswald, and equally significant that it was only at his Diocese of Worcester that we find the transcription of Anglo-Saxon homilies after 1066. Worcester remained a centre for Anglo-Saxon culture and thought until Wulstan's death,

---

[3] Maisie Ward, ed., *The English Way: Studies in English Sanctity from Bede to Newman* (Tacoma, Wash.: Cluny Media, 2016), 67.

and Coleman's account of Wulstan's life is the last great prose work in Old English (except for additions to the *Anglo-Saxon Chronicle*). Thereafter, the sun set on Old English as a literary language, its place being taken by Norman French. It was not until the age of Chaucer, three centuries later, that literary English would reemerge in its hybrid Gallicized form.

William the Conqueror's efforts to control the Church within his realm were continued by his son, William Rufus, who acceded to the throne as William II in 1087. In an act of arrogance mixed with avarice, this new William had decided to leave the office of Archbishop of Canterbury vacant after Archbishop Lanfranc died in 1089, thereby removing any possible rival to his power and accruing to himself all the Church revenues due to the archbishop. It was only the fear of death during an illness in 1093 which induced the king to relent and recant. Fearing for his soul, he appointed the great St. Anselm as archbishop. Pope Urban II confirmed the appointment, but William, having recovered from his illness, refused Anselm's request to go to Rome to receive the pallium from the pope. In response, Anselm defended the pope's authority in matters spiritual. "In the things that are God's I will tender obedience to the Vicar of St. Peter," he told the king; "in things touching the earthly dignity of my lord the King I will to the best of my ability give him faithful counsel and help."[4] After the pallium was delivered to England by a papal legate, the king demanded his royal "right" to bestow it on Anselm. Once again, the saintly archbishop showed the courage to defy the secular power, refusing to receive

---

[4] *Catholic Encyclopedia* (New York: Robert Appleton, 1909); quoted in Robert R. Reilly, *America on Trial: A Defense of the Founding* (San Francisco: Ignatius Press, 2020), 73.

the pallium from the king. St. Anselm's holiness earned the king's wrath. "Yesterday I hated him with great hatred," William II exclaimed, "today I hate him with yet greater hatred and he can be certain that tomorrow and thereafter I shall hate him continually with ever fiercer and more bitter hatred."[5]

William II's arrogance was superseded by his successor, Henry I, who made an audacious claim to spiritual authority surpassing the power of the papacy itself. Henry argued, through his advocate, that the king, upon his coronation, becomes "another Christ, and, through grace, takes on the character of Christ himself".[6] Invested with such self-proclaimed power, King Henry demanded the right to consecrate bishops. St. Anselm once again, and with great courage, resisted the overreaching ambition of the secular power, and once again the saint's will prevailed. In 1107, Henry finally forswore his "right" to consecrate bishops.

In spite of the ongoing tension between church and state, this was a time of great spiritual flourishing. During the twelfth century, 126 new churches were built in London alone, along with thirteen chapels in monastic houses within the city. Abbeys were founded near the city walls at Bishopsgate and Aldgate, and in 1123, the priory of St. Bartholomew was founded just outside the city's northwest wall. The crusader knights of St. John of Jerusalem arrived at Clerkenwall in the middle of the twelfth century, as did another order of crusaders, the Knights Templar, who built a chapel, a replica of the Church of the Holy Sepulchre in Jerusalem, which still stands to this day.

[5] *Eadmer's History of Recent Events in England*, trans. Geoffrey Bosanquet (London: Cresset Press, 1964), 53; quoted in Reilly, *America on Trial*, 73.

[6] "The Norman Anonymous Tract on Christian Kingship"; quoted in Reilly, *America on Trial*, 73.

Far from the hustle and bustle of London, the twelfth century was also a time in which holy hermits, such as St. Godric, lived the simple life in self-built huts in the wilds of northern England, and in which holy monks, such as St. Aelred of Rievaulx, led a revival of monastic life, inspired by the Cistercian movement in France, of which the Englishman Stephen Harding was the founding light. It was also a century in which Englishmen were making their mark in Rome. Robert Pullen, who settled in Rome after teaching Scripture at Oxford University, became the first-ever English-born cardinal in 1144;[7] eight years later, another Englishman, Nicholas Breakspear, became the first, and so far only, English pope, taking the name of Adrian IV.

Considering the ongoing and perennial tension between church and state, brought to the fore by the power-hungry kings of the Norman Ascendency, it is worth quoting at length a work of political philosophy, *Policraticus*, published in 1159 by John of Salisbury, which states that all political power is under God and that all political rulers are therefore subject to God:

> Jurists declare that "the prince's pleasure hath the force of law"; but this maxim is false.... His power comes of God, and is still God's although it is exercised by a deputy. Thus we have the dependence of the royal power on the Divine Law clearly enunciated; and as the interpreter of that law we have the Church.... The prince will always prefer the advantage of others to his private will, and will not seek his own good but that of others. It is in this that the difference between the prince and the tyrant partly consists,

---

[7] Some sources mention an Englishman named Ulric (or Wilfrid) who is said to have been created cardinal around 1100, forty-four years prior to Pullen, but nothing is known of him beyond these passing references.

and so whilst the prince is to be honoured and revered, it is lawful to deceive and honourable to kill a tyrant, if he cannot be otherwise restrained.

Continuing in this strident tone, John called a tyrant an "image of depravity ... [who] spring[s] from evil and should be cut down with the axe wherever he grows". Furthermore, it was imperative that the Christian not be complicit in the tyranny of the secular ruler: "If [the prince] is resistant and opposes the divine commandments, and wishes to make me share in the war against God, then, with unrestrained voice I must answer back that God must be preferred before any man on earth."[8] These powerful words, which resonate strongly with respect to the perennial struggle for religious liberty in the face of secular tyranny, were especially resonant to the times in which John of Salisbury was writing.

John of Salisbury was a friend of Adrian IV (Nicholas Breakspear), staying with the recently elected pope for several months in 1155. Seven years later he became secretary to Thomas Becket, the newly consecrated Archbishop of Canterbury, a friendship which would bring him into renewed conflict with King Henry II, who, like his predecessors, was seeking to impose his royal will on the affairs of the Church. In 1166, Thomas Becket wrote to the king, reminding him that "you have not the power to give rules to bishops, nor to absolve or excommunicate anyone, to draw clerks before secular tribunals, to judge concerning churches and tithes, to forbid bishops to adjudge causes concerning breach of faith or oath, and many other things of this sort."[9] It was this letter which placed the king and

[8] Quoted in Reilly, *America on Trial*, 81.
[9] James Bruce Ross and Mary Martin McLaughlin, eds., *The Portable Medieval Reader* (New York: Viking Press, 1949), 246–50.

archbishop at loggerheads, with neither willing to compromise. In his frustration at the impasse, King Henry allegedly exclaimed, "Will no one rid me of this turbulent priest?" In obedience to what they perceived to be the king's will, four knights burst into Canterbury Cathedral on December 29, 1170, and butchered Thomas Becket as he knelt in prayer. His last words, before the fatal blows were struck, were the prayers of a saint: "To God and Blessed Mary, to the patron Saints of this Church and St. Denis I commend myself and the cause of the Faith."[10]

Hilaire Belloc was in no doubt of the historical importance of St. Thomas' martyrdom, which was the consequence of what he called the saint's "heroic resistance".[11] The principle for which St. Thomas suffered martyrdom was as clear as it was noble:

> That the Church of God is a visible single universal society, with powers superior to those of this world, and therefore of right, *autonomous*. That principle is the negation of the opposite ... the principle that the divine and permanent is subject to the human and passing power. St. Thomas died for the doctrine, the truth, that the link with eternal things must never be broken under the pressure of ephemeral desires, that the control of eternal things cannot, in morals, be subjected to the ephemeral arrangements of men.[12]

Having stated the principle for which St. Thomas of Canterbury laid down his life, Belloc proceeds to an appraisal of the historical significance and importance of the saint's "heroic resistance", which struck a blow for religious liberty against the encroachments of secular tyranny, the impact of which would reverberate down the centuries:

[10] Quoted in Ward, *English Way*, 125.
[11] Ibid., 105.
[12] Ibid., 103.

Those few moments of tragedy in the North Transept of Canterbury had done what so many years of effort had so far failed to do. The whole movement against the autonomy of the Church was stopped dead. The tide ran rapidly backward—within an hour St. Thomas was a martyr, within a month the champion not only of religion but of the common people, who obscurely but firmly knew that the independence of the Church was their safeguard. A tale of miracles began, and within a year the name of St. Thomas of Canterbury was standing permanently above and throughout Christendom. Everywhere there were chapels and churches raised to his name, and then came the great uninterrupted pilgrimages to his shrine year after year, until it rivalled St. James of Compostela, becoming the second great center in the West and loaded with gems and gold and endowment.[13]

[13] Ibid., 125–26.

Chapter Six

Merrie England

They called thee Merry England, in old time;
A happy people won for thee that name
With envy heard in many a distant clime;
And, spite of change, for me thou keep'st the same
Endearing title, a responsive chime
To the heart's fond belief.

—William Wordsworth, from
"They Called Thee Merry
England, in Old Time"

The horror felt throughout Christendom by the martyrdom of Thomas Becket forced Henry II to relinquish the
powers he had claimed over the Church. Furthermore,
on May 21, 1172, he performed a ceremony of public
penances for his role in Becket's martyrdom, solemnly
swearing to restore all property to the Church that he had
confiscated or otherwise acquired unjustly, promising not
to obstruct any appeals to Rome by the clergy and promising to provide money for two hundred knights for the
Crusades. Thereafter, King Henry was more careful and
circumspect in his efforts to enrich himself at the expense of
the Church. In 1185, when the abbot of Abingdon Abbey
died, Henry bestowed the abbey to Thomas of Esseburn,
who, in turn, proposed giving the abbey and all its wealth

and possessions to the king. In response, the prior and the other Benedictine brothers of the abbey appealed the decision and won a significant victory for religious liberty. The court declared that the "customary rights [of the abbey's Benedictine community] have been established reasonably and wisely, that nothing excessive could be found in them, and that the lord king, neither wishes nor dares to go against customs in some measure, so ancient, and so just as to change anything respecting them."[1]

If Henry II, chastened by the international condemnation of his excesses, had learned his lesson, albeit reluctantly and under compulsion, the same could not be said of King John, who has justifiably been enshrined by legend as the wicked antagonist to the noble outlaw Robin Hood. In 1205, King John attempted to install his own candidate as Archbishop of Canterbury in defiance of the pope, Innocent III, who had already appointed Stephen Langton as the bona fide archbishop. The pope warned the king that it was dangerous to "fight against God and the Church in this cause for which St. Thomas, that glorious martyr and Archbishop, recently shed his blood".[2] Unmoved by either the pope's cautionary words or the lessons of history, the king refused to accept Langton. The pope responded by placing England under an interdict. John reacted angrily and arrogantly, seizing church property; the pope promptly excommunicated him. The stand-off between king and Church dragged on for some time before King John finally capitulated, accepting Langton as archbishop in 1213.

[1] Charles Howard McIlwain, *Constitutionalism: Ancient and Modern* (Ithaca, N.Y.: Cornell University Press, 1947), 65.

[2] Nicholas Schofield and Gerard Skinner, *The English Cardinals* (Oxford: Family Publications, 2007), 23.

King John's troubles were only beginning, however, because he now faced a rebellion of his own barons. Acting as mediator between the king and the rebellious aristocracy, Archbishop Langton hearkened back to Anglo-Saxon England and the reign of St. Edward the Confessor as providing a practical political model for thirteenth-century England, as well as the Coronation Charter granted by Henry I in 1100. These negotiations led to King John's reluctant signing of the Magna Carta in 1215, limiting the power of the monarchy and laying the foundations for the English legal system. Archbishop Langton had helped draft the Magna Carta and was the first witness to sign it. Such was his role in this historic event that the political philosopher Ernest Barker has called Langton the "father of English liberty".[3]

Archbishop Langton travelled to Rome shortly after the signing of the Magna Carta and was in the Eternal City at the time of the Fourth Lateran Council, which was convened in November 1215. It is interesting to conjecture whether he might have met his fellow English prelate, Robert de Curzon, whom Innocent III had created a cardinal in 1212, who was also in Rome for the Council. Curzon has the distinction of being the only English cardinal to die on a battlefield. He joined the Fifth Crusade in 1218 and died in February the following year ministering to the crusaders during the siege of Damietta, a port at the mouth of the Nile. He did not live to see St. Francis of Assisi, who arrived in Damietta a few months later on his dangerous mission to convert the sultan.

---

[3] Robert R. Reilly, *America on Trial: A Defense of the Founding* (San Francisco: Ignatius Press, 2020), 75.

In 1220, Archbishop Langton presided at the solemn and joyful celebration of the fiftieth anniversary of Thomas Becket's martyrdom. To mark the occasion, the saint's relics were moved to a magnificent new shrine in the cathedral's Trinity chapel. The celebration has been described as "one of the most spectacular events of thirteenth century England".[4] Immersing himself in the festive spirit, Archbishop Langton provided barrels of free wine at each of the city's gates, ensuring that pilgrims from all directions and from all parts of England and Christendom would receive a merry welcome as they arrived.

It was perhaps largesse of this sort which earned mediaeval England its reputation for being "merry". It is an England in which daily life beat in rhythm with the heart of the liturgical year, an England evoking visions of villages coming together on feast days at fairs and other festivities, honouring the saints with rambunctious levitas, as well as solemn gravitas. It is an England in which Robin Hood and his Merry Men fight tyranny with Christian charity, and ill will with good spirits. It is an England evoked idyllically by Tolkien in his depiction of the Shire and its simple rustic inhabitants, who "love peace and quiet and good tilled earth" and who laugh, eat, drink, and are always ready for the slightest excuse for a party.[5] This is the stuff of myth and legend, of course, but such "stuff" can grow and flourish only from seeds of truth planted in fertile cultural soil. The song of Merrie England is sung by the unsung people, the ordinary folk in village and farm, who are not mentioned in history books. They do not make history

[4] Schofield and Skinner, *English Cardinals*, 24.

[5] J. R. R. Tolkien, from the Prologue to *The Lord of the Rings* (London: HarperCollins, 2004), 1.

but they *are* history. It would, therefore, be remiss of any history of True England if those who are its true heart are not evoked and honoured:

> Let not Ambition mock their useful toil,
>   Their homely joys, and destiny obscure;
> Nor Grandeur hear with a disdainful smile
>   The short and simple annals of the poor.[6]

This spirit, especially as it must have been present in the English guildsmen and craftsmen who built the great cathedrals, was praised with eloquence by the historian James J. Walsh in his history of the thirteenth century:

In these old medieval days England used to be called Merrie England and it is easy to understand that workmen would be profoundly merry at heart, when they had the consciousness of accomplishing such good work. Men must have almost tardily quitted their labor in the evening while they hoped and strove to accomplish something that would be worthy of the magnificent building in which so many of their fellow workmen were achieving triumphs of handicraftsmanship. . . . This represents the ideal of the workman's life. . . . The picture of the modern workman by contrast looks vain and sordid. . . .

It would be idle to say that these men who knew how to make beautiful things for these cathedrals were not conscious of the perfection of the work that they were accomplishing. The very fact that each in his own line was achieving such beautiful results must have stamped him as thoroughly capable of appreciating the work of others. The source of pleasure that there must have been therefore, in some twenty towns in England alone, to see their Cathedral approaching completion, must have been of itself a joy far beyond anything we can imagine as possible

---

[6] Thomas Gray, from "Elegy Written in a Country Churchyard".

for the workman of the present day. The interest in it was supreme and was only heightened by the fact that it was being done by relatives and friends and brother workmen ... and that whatever was done was redounding first to the glory of the Lord to whom they turned with so much confidence in these ages of faith.[7]

Perhaps the most important development in the Church in the thirteenth century was the founding of the two great mendicant orders, the Dominicans and the Franciscans. Archbishop Langton encouraged the establishment of houses by both orders in England, and the arrival of the friars added to the spiritual riches of the flourishing Christian culture. By 1261 there were around six hundred Dominicans in England, heralding something of a golden age for the Dominican Order. In 1272, Robert Kilwardby was appointed Archbishop of Canterbury by Pope Gregory X, the first English Dominican to hold such high office. Four years later, he presided at the translation of the body of St. Richard of Chichester, who had died in 1253 and had been canonized in 1262, to a new shrine behind the high altar of Chichester Cathedral. King Edward I and his queen were both in attendance in a show of pomp and circumstance in reverence to a saint reminiscent of the celebrations at Canterbury more than half a century earlier. As for the king himself, he was a great admirer of the Dominicans, with friars of the order being his preferred choice as royal confessors. In 1278, Robert Kilwardby was made a cardinal by Pope Nicholas III.

Moving into the fourteenth century and to the age of Chaucer, we find the life and work of the Church interwoven with the very fabric of daily life. Throughout the

[7] James J. Walsh, *The Thirteenth: Greatest of Centuries* (New York: Catholic Summer School Press, 1924), 126–27.

country, it was the Church which taught the children, fed the poor, and cared for the sick. The Church was also at the heart of the social life of the people, with local guilds staging mystery plays to celebrate significant dates and seasons of the liturgical year. Especially popular were plays and pageants associated with the newly established Feast of Corpus Christi on the Thursday after Trinity Sunday. Instituted by the Church in 1311, this special feast in honour and adoration of the Blessed Sacrament became one of the most popular of all Christian festivals. It was celebrated in every town, from one end of the country to the other, with processions of religious organizations from church to church and from shrine to shrine. The fact that the feast fell in summer, when days were warm and at their longest, added to the festive atmosphere.

The local craft guilds played a major role in the pageantry of these processions, especially the new guilds of Corpus Christi, which were formed to provide candles for eucharistic processions. In common with many towns, King's Lynn in Norfolk was blessed with a Corpus Christi guild which had been established in 1349, during the dark days of the Black Death. The sight of the Blessed Sacrament being hurried through the plague-ridden streets to the dying, "with only a single candle of poor wax burning in front of it, whereas two torches of the finest beeswax are hardly sufficient", had scandalized those who saw it. This prompted the founding of the guild, which was still active eighty years later when the fifteenth-century mystic Margery Kempe recorded the veneration accorded to the Blessed Sacrament as a priest bore it through the streets of King's Lynn on his way to minister to the dying, the townsfolk falling on their knees as he passed.[8]

---

[8] Eamon Duffy, *The Stripping of the Altars* (London: Yale University Press, 1992), 101.

From around 1347 until 1350, England and the whole of Christendom were struck by the Black Death. This deadly pandemic of bubonic plague would be the most devastating in history, killing tens of millions of people. In the words of Hilaire Belloc, it "tore through the living structure of Christendom like some horrible weapon tearing through the living flesh and organism of a man."[9] It is estimated that between a third and a half of the population was killed by the plague. Whole monastic communities were wiped out. The University of Oxford, which was essentially a clerical institution at the heart of ecclesiastical life, was especially hard hit, shrinking to only a third of its pre-pandemic size. And yet, in spite of such devastation, the country sprang back to life. The mystery plays once again became a part of the festive life of the people, as is clear from late fourteenth-century sources; the Church continued to provide the people with schools, hospitals, and relief for the poor.

In 1363, King Edward III appointed Simon Langham, a Benedictine abbot, as Lord Chancellor of England. Langham's opening speech to Parliament made history as the first ever to be given in English, a sign that the vernacular tongue of the nation was gaining acceptance, almost three centuries after the Norman Conquest had excluded it from the affairs of court. For those three centuries, as the historian Christopher Dawson wrote, "Latin was the language of learning, and French the language of society. English became the speech of the peasants, the mark of the simple and uneducated."[10] As late as the beginning of the fourteenth century, the English chronicler Robert of

[9] Hilaire Belloc, *How the Reformation Happened* (London: Jonathan Cape, 1928), 48.

[10] Maisie Ward, ed., *The English Way: Studies in English Sanctity from Bede to Newman* (Tacoma, Wash.: Cluny Media, 2016), 163.

Gloucester affirmed the marginalization of English within the higher echelons of English society: "If a man does not know French he is little esteemed, but low-born people hold still to English and their own tongue."[11] This reemergence of English, in its Gallicized "Middle" English form, would be confirmed in the following decades by the literary flourishing of Geoffrey Chaucer and William Langland, the latter of whom, the author of *Piers Plowman*, has been described by Christopher Dawson as "the Catholic Englishman par excellence, at once the most English of Catholic poets and the most Catholic of English poets" and as "a man in whom Catholic faith and national feeling are fused in a single flame".[12] According to Dawson, Langland "saw Christ walking in English fields in the dress of an English laborer",[13] and it is to Langland that we have the earliest literary references to Robin Hood. A contemporary of both Langland and Chaucer was the anonymous poet who wrote *Sir Gawain and the Green Knight*, which drew on the Arthurian legends and which represented a revival of the ancient Anglo-Saxon alliterative verse, as distinct from the modern Renaissance style favoured by Chaucer.

Returning to affairs of state, all was well between the king and Simon Langham, who became Archbishop of Canterbury in 1366 until the pope, Blessed Urban V, made Langham a cardinal in 1368. In a fit of outrage that he had not been consulted, King Edward III considered that Langham had ipso facto forfeited the see of Canterbury, taking the opportunity to seize for himself the substantial revenues attached to the see. Langham went into exile and never returned to England, even though he and the

---

[11] Ibid.
[12] Ibid., 161.
[13] Ibid.

king were subsequently reconciled. Following his death in 1376, Langham's body was returned to his native land and is now buried in Westminster Abbey, the only cardinal, or indeed archbishop, ever to be interred in the prestigious abbey's hallowed grounds.

As was illustrated graphically in Chaucer's *Canterbury Tales*, written in the final two decades of the fourteenth century, healthy merriment could deteriorate all too easily into drunkenness, debauchery, and other manifestations of decadence. In the General Prologue to the *Tales*, Chaucer introduces us to a menagerie of miserable sinners, seasoned with a handful of saints. There is the less-than-holy Prioress, too prim and proper for her own good, who seeks the pleasures that opulence affords, and the worldly Monk, whose wealth makes a mockery of his vow of poverty and whose heretical theology makes a mockery of his orthodox pretensions. Even worse are the lecherous Friar and the corrupt Pardoner, the latter of whom makes a living selling fake relics to the gullible faithful. We also meet the shady Merchant, the pleasure-seeking Franklin, the avaricious Physician, the formidable and self-serving Wife of Bath, and the utterly uncouth Miller, amongst others. And yet there are also noble souls, such as the conscientious Clerk, or student, who prefers poverty and a life of learning over the comforts of the world, and the poor Parson, who exemplifies the calling of a good and holy priest, as well as the Parson's brother, the Ploughman, who, living in peace and perfect charity, loving God above all, is the epitome of a truly holy layman. In Chaucer's time, as in our own, the saints are always outnumbered by the sinners and yet it is the saints who season the culture, like leaven, helping it to rise from the secular gutter.

One such saint, epitomizing the simplicity of spirit exemplified by Chaucer's Parson, was St. John of Bridlington,

prior of St. Augustine's monastery in Bridlington in Yorkshire from 1362 until his death in 1379. Known for his utter
fidelity in small things as well as great, he was a beacon
of hope and inspiration at a time in which monastic slack-
ness was commonplace. Greatly loved during his lifetime,
he was invoked in prayer following his death. Miracles
were reported at his tomb, and he was canonized in 1401.
The famous English victory under Henry V at Agincourt
in 1415 was attributed to his intercession.

A contemporary of St. John of Bridlington was Julian of
Norwich, a mystic and anchorite who, in 1373, received
a number of mystical visions centred on the Holy Trinity
and the Passion of Christ. Living a solitary life walled up
in a cell attached to the wall of St. Julian's church in Norwich, from which she presumably took her name, she
spent a solitary life of prayer meditating upon the visions
she had received. These meditations and reflections were
written down and were subsequently published as *Reve-
lations of Divine Love*, the earliest surviving book in the
English language authored by a woman. From her cell
Julian could see into the church through a small window,
enabling her to see Mass being celebrated and to receive
Communion. The cell, which had evidently become
a place of pilgrimage in the century or so following
her death, was destroyed during the iconoclasm of the
English Reformation.

From the peace and seclusion of her cell, Julian would
have been relatively untouched by the political unrest of
the times, culminating in the Peasants' Revolt of 1381,
which raged in the neighbourhood of Norwich and
throughout large parts of the rest of the country. In Hilaire
Belloc's description of events, the rebels in Norfolk were
"thoroughly defeated largely through the military temper
of the Bishop of Norwich, who fought a battle with the

insurgents and won it".[14] Farther south in London, the peasants murdered the Archbishop of Canterbury after he had sought refuge in the Tower of London and looted and ransacked his palace in Lambeth. It should be stated, however, that the rebellion was emphatically not a rising against the Church but against the government, which had sought to impose an unjust poll tax to pay for the wars in France and which was sanctioning the abuse of peasant labour under England's feudal laws. Far from being directed against the Church, priests were among the ringleaders of the rebellious peasants in Hertfordshire and Essex. The Archbishop of Canterbury, Simon Sudbury, was a victim of the mob because he had recently been appointed Lord Chancellor by the king and was seen, therefore, as a representative of the government. Although the rebellion was crushed, with around fifteen hundred rebels being executed in its aftermath, it achieved one of its principal aims in the effective ending of the feudal practice of forced labour, or serfdom. Thereafter, England's rural population would begin to enjoy the fruits of their own labour in ways that had never been possible in earlier centuries. As Hilaire Belloc explained in *The Servile State*, the economy of England was evolving, seemingly naturally and inexorably, into a system rooted in private property ownership, not merely for the feudal lord but also for the peasant, the possession of which fostered both economic and political freedom:

> If at the end of the fourteenth century, let us say, or at the beginning of the fifteenth, you had visited some squire upon his estate in France or in England, he would have

[14] Hilaire Belloc, *A Shorter History of England* (London: George G. Harrap, 1934), 200.

told you of the whole of it, "These are my lands." But
the peasant ... would have said also of his holding, "This
is my land." He could not be evicted from it. The dues
which he was customarily bound to pay were but a frac-
tion of its total produce. He could not always sell it, but it
was always inheritable from father to son; and, in general
... the slave had become a free man for all the ordinary
purposes of society. He bought and sold. He saved as he
willed, he invested, he built, he drained at his discretion,
and if he improved the land it was to his own profit.[15]

In addition, as Belloc also explained, a host of other
institutions contributed to the widespread possession of
private property. Most important were the guilds which
oversaw the practice of industry in the towns. A guild
was "a society partly cooperative, but in the main composed of private owners of capital whose corporation was
self-governing".[16] Above all else, the guild guarded private property ownership amongst its members, working
to prevent the monopolization of ownership in too few
hands and the consequent proletarianization of those dispossessed by such concentrations of ownership. "There
was a period of apprenticeship at a man's entry into a
guild, during which he worked for a master; but in time
he became a master in his turn. The existence of such
corporations as the normal units of industrial production,
of commercial effort ... is proof enough of what the
social spirit was which had also enfranchised the laborer
upon the land."[17]

Although Belloc might be accused of romanticizing the
economic enfranchisement of the people of England in
the early fifteenth century, his general argument is sound

---

[15] Hilaire Belloc, *The Servile State* (Indianapolis: Liberty Classics, 1977), 78.
[16] Ibid., 78–79.
[17] Ibid., 79.

enough. As time went on, a greater proportion of the population was being enfranchised in terms of individual ownership of private property. England was moving towards a society "in which the determinant mass of families were owners of capital and of land [and] in which production was regulated by self-governing corporations of small owners [and] in which the misery and insecurity of a proletariat were unknown".[18] This process of progressive enfranchisement of the people of England would continue until Henry VIII's "Reformation" transformed the country into a secularized plutocracy.

If the Peasants' Revolt had been primarily directed against the government, another revolt was very much an attack upon the Church. In 1381, the same year as the Peasants' Revolt, John Wycliffe was dismissed from the University of Oxford for his attacks upon theological orthodoxy. In the same year, Adam Easton, a Benedictine priest who would be made a cardinal by the pope, published the *Defensorium ecclesiasticae potestatis*, a condemnation of Wycliffe and his heretical ideas. Wycliffe attacked the papacy, the priesthood, and the religious life and is rightly seen as a forerunner of the Protestant revolt 130 years later. Although he died in 1384, his followers, known as Lollards, continued to spread his ideas. In 1414, a Lollard revolt led by Sir John Oldcastle against both the Church and the king was defeated after a brief battle at St. Giles' Fields in London. Shakespeare would immortalize and lampoon Sir John Oldcastle as the feckless and drunken buffoon, John Falstaff, in several of his plays.

The limited success of the Lollards was due to the passionate and impassioned Catholic culture of the people which was made manifest throughout the late fourteenth and fifteenth centuries in the aforementioned mystery

---

[18] Ibid., 81–82.

plays. These were performed to mark the liturgical year in towns across the country, and probably, in one form or another, in just about every town of any size from the Scottish border in the north to the English Channel in the south. Even allowing for the loss of so many histor-ical records due to the vicissitudes of time, it is known from the fragmentary surviving evidence that mystery plays were performed regularly in Bath, Beverley, Bristol, Brome, Canterbury, Chester, Coventry, Ipswich, Leices-ter, Lincoln, London, Newcastle, Northampton, Nor-wich, Wakefield, Worcester, and York. The Chester cycle contains twenty-four separate plays; the Wakefield cycle, thirty-two plays; the Coventry cycle, forty-two plays; and the York cycle forty-eight plays.[19] Although these plays were usually local affairs, produced by the guilds, some had gained such a reputation that they attracted visitors from farther afield. The cycle of mystery plays produced at Coventry, perhaps the most famous in England, were graced with royal visits on several occasions.

As for the plays themselves, the full cycle covered the entire spectrum of salvation history from the fall of Lucifer to doomsday and could take three days to perform. It is worth listing the plays as a means of illustrating the depth of theological understanding which was present amongst the general population in the fifteenth century:

The Fall of Lucifer
The Creation and Fall of Man
Cain and Abel
Noah and the Flood
Abraham and Isaac
Moses

---

[19] Peter Happé, ed., *English Mystery Plays* (London: Penguin Classics, 1976), 10.

The Prophets
The Nativity—Annunciation, Suspicion of Joseph, Shepherds, Purification, Magi, Flight into Egypt, Massacre of the Innocents
The Baptism
The Temptation
Lazarus
The Passion—Conspiracy, Judas, Last Supper, Caiaphas, Condemnation, Crucifixion, Lament of Mary, Death
The Resurrection and Ascension
The Assumption and Coronation of the Virgin
Doomsday

The plays were performed on pageant carts, which were so expensive to make and maintain that several guilds would bear and share the financial burden. These were essentially mobile theatres, containing several stage sets, as well as a closed space to serve as a dressing room. Since some of the plays called for an upper level from which angels might descend, one can only imagine the ingenuity and craftsmanship that their construction must have demanded. Guild accounts show considerable expenditure on paint and carpentry.

This coming together of the townsfolk in all parts of the country to stage dramatic re-presentations of the key episodes of salvation history formed an integral part of the cultural and religious life of the people of England in the fourteenth and fifteenth centuries. As such, the mystery plays exemplify the integration of faith and culture into a seamless unity, expressive of the very soul of the nation.

Having surveyed a "Merrie England" of faith and festivity, albeit smeared with sin and suffering, let's now turn to England's love affair with the Blessed Virgin Mary, without which England would be neither "true" nor "merrie".

Chapter Seven

Our Lady's Dowry

"Though I give this land to Our Lady,
That helped me in Athelny,
Though lordlier trees and lustier sod
And happier hills hath no flesh trod
Than the garden of the Mother of God
Between Thames side and the sea."

—G. K. Chesterton,
from *The Ballad of the White Horse**

The great devotion of the people of England to the Blessed Virgin is evident in the fact that there were shrines of Our Lady in every county and diocese throughout the country. Some of these were expressions of purely local piety, others were of more than local importance, and some, such as the shrine of Our Lady of Walsingham, were of international renown. Edmund Waterton in his seminal volume *Pietas Mariana Britannica*, published in 1879, attests to the ubiquitous character of the Virgin's presence in shrines across the length and breadth of the land; and, as H. M. Gillett attests, even Waterton's extensive research is far from exhaustive.[1]

---

* These words, though written by Chesterton, are spoken by Alfred the Great.

[1] H. M. Gillett, *Famous Shrines of Our Lady* (Westminster, Md.: Carroll Press, 1950), 44.

As for Walsingham's place in Merrie England's history, as previously mentioned, it was said that there were so many pilgrims on the Walsingham Way, heading for the shrine, that they resembled the numerous stars in the Milky Way. Other romantic souls even suggested that the Milky Way itself pointed towards Walsingham. Certainly, the presence of Our Lady of Walsingham serves as a backdrop to the whole of English history as the Milky Way forms the backdrop to the night sky.

Such was Walsingham's prestige throughout the whole of Christendom that Miguel Cervantes, in Spain, writing sixty-seven years after the shrine's destruction, was moved to write that there was an "infinite number of little birds, hopping from branch to branch, all naturally singing *Walsingham* [a song made popular by pilgrims to the shrine]".[2]

It seems that pilgrimages to Walsingham began as soon as news spread of the apparition in 1061. A house of Augustinian Canons was established in the vicinity of the shrine within a century of the apparition, the first prior of which served from 1153 until 1173; and even though so much of the documentary evidence has not survived, it is possible to deduce from the few remaining fragments the various paths which pilgrims would have trudged to Christendom's principal Marian shrine. We know that a hostel for poor pilgrims had been established prior to 1224 by William de Bec on the path, near Billingford, from Norwich to Walsingham. This would have been one of the busiest of the pilgrimage routes, not merely because Norwich was the second largest city in England, after London, during the Middle Ages, but because this would probably have been the preferred route of pilgrims arriving from overseas. The other major pilgrimage route

[2] Ibid.

on the Walsingham Way would obviously have been from London.

Although Walsingham enjoyed the undisputed place of honour, England was awash with other manifestations of the nation's love for the Mother of God. This was evident in the many Cistercian abbeys founded in the twelfth century, almost all of which were dedicated to Mary. These included the abbeys at York, Waverley, Budwas, Hailes, Kirkstall, Tintern, Fountains, and Furness. Many of these were founded in fulfilment of vows to Our Lady, and the abbey in Tintern possessed a miraculous image of the Virgin, which became an object of great devotion and a shrine which received papal blessing.

In 1194, the Yorkshire town of Doncaster acquired by Charter the rights of an annual three-day fair on the "Vigil, Feast and the Morrow" of the Feast of the Annunciation.[3] This feast, one of many similar fairs throughout the country, was held every year for several centuries until it was suppressed during the Reformation. May was another month in which England celebrated her love for the Blessed Virgin. The May Day celebrations heralded the coming of Mary's month. There was the crowning of Mary as the Queen of the May and maypole dancing on the village green. Many of these traditions survived in broken and fragmented form, in spite of attempts by the Puritans to crush England's festive spirit. And yet, as H. M. Gillett observed, the Queen who had been the very purpose of the celebrations had been forgotten: "Without knowing why they did so, children continued to choose the prettiest maid among them to be crowned by way of substitute for the true May Queen, the real Fairy Princess of their dreams.

---

[3] H. M. Gillett, *Shrines of Our Lady in England and Wales* (London: Samuel Walker, 1957), 98.

All unbeknown to themselves ... they were but carrying on the English tradition of love for Our Lady."[4]

A crowning of a different sort occurred in 1246, when King Henry III gave twenty marks for the making of a golden crown to be set on the head of the statue of Our Lady of Walsingham at England's premier Marian shrine. This was but one of many gifts that Henry III made to the shrine to which he went on pilgrimage in person many times. Another king who showed great devotion to Our Lady of Walsingham was Henry III's eldest son, Edward I, who attributed an escape from death to the Virgin's intercession. "On account of this miracle," wrote Thomas of Walsingham in his early fifteenth-century chronicle *Historia Anglicana*, "ever afterwards he heartily honoured Our Blessed Lady of Walsingham, to whose favour he ascribed this escape from danger."[5] Edward I would make no fewer than twelve personal pilgrimages to Walsingham. Almost every other English monarch would follow in his pilgrim footsteps to Our Lady's shrine, right up until its destruction during the reign of Henry VIII.

Further proof of Edward I's devotion to the Virgin is evident in his pilgrimage to Glastonbury in 1278, England's oldest Marian shrine. King Edward and his queen, Eleanor, stayed for the whole of the Easter Octave. On Easter Sunday, Mass was sung in the royal presence by the Dominican Archbishop of Canterbury, Robert Kilwardby. Two days later, the king and his court assembled to witness the opening of what was accepted as the tomb of King Arthur and Queen Guinevere. The bodies were then transferred, amidst much pomp and ceremony, to an ornate tomb before the high altar of the abbey church.

[4] Ibid., 286.
[5] Ibid., 300–301.

In Aylsford in Kent on July 16, 1251, according to tradition,[6] St. Simon Stock, a Carmelite monk, was blessed with a vision of the Blessed Virgin, holding a scapular, which is the source of the devotion to the brown scapular commonly practiced by Catholics worldwide to this day. In 1287, the Synod of Exeter decreed that an image of Our Lady should be placed prominently in every church of the diocese and that the Feast of Our Lady's Conception (now the Feast of the Immaculate Conception) should be observed as a holy day of obligation throughout the diocese. In 1328, the Diocese of Exeter having blazed a trail, the Feast of the Conception became a day of obligation throughout the whole of England. At the end of the fourteenth century, the English cardinal Adam Easton worked tirelessly for the promotion of the Feast of the Visitation of the Blessed Virgin Mary, and it is thought that he might even have composed the Office of this feast.[7]

Throughout the fourteenth century, Walsingham continued to wax as a place of Marian pilgrimage, attracting royalty and noblemen from far-flung corners of the British Isles and beyond. In 1361, King Edward III granted £9 towards the expenses of the Duke of Brittany, a prisoner of war, so that he might make a pilgrimage to Walsingham with all due decorum. Three years later, he gave safe conduct to King David II of Scotland to make a pilgrimage to Our Lady's shrine, accompanied by twenty knights; one of several pilgrimages to Walsingham; and also to Canterbury, that the Scottish king undertook. King David's father, Robert the Bruce, was also said to have been given safe conduct to Walsingham, shortly before his death in

[6] The first mention of the apparition is in the late fourteenth century, over a century later, which has caused a degree of scepticism with respect to its historical authenticity.

[7] Nicholas Schofield and Gerard Skinner, *The English Cardinals* (Oxford: Family Publications, 2007), 47.

1329.[8] Such were the numbers arriving from continental Europe that there was a fixed scale of charges for pilgrims visiting Walsingham from Flanders, as the representatives of those unable to make the pilgrimage in person.

Back in London, in 1369, Edward III gave to "John Bulwick, 10 marks per annum, to celebrate daily before the image of Our Lady, the Blessed Mary, in this Chapel of Our Lady, near the King's Chapel of St. Stephen, Westminster."[9] According to the fourteenth-century chronicler Jean Froissart, this particular image of the Virgin, known as Our Lady of Pewe, "wrought great miracles and splendid favours, to which the kings of England were wont to turn, always in confidence and hope".[10] It was before this image that the fourteen-year-old king, Richard II, knelt and prayed prior to riding out to meet Wat Tyler and his rebels during the Peasants' Revolt in 1381. As Froissart wrote:

> The king went to Westminster and heard Mass in the church there, and all his lords with him.... And beside this church there was a little chapel with an image of Our Lady.... There the king made his devotions before this image; and having made his offerings to it, he then mounted and rode off to meet the rebels.[11]

A similar account is recorded by the historian John Strype:

> On the coming of the rebels and Wat Tyler, the ... King went to Westminster, to the High Altar there, and offered, then confessed himself to an anchorite; then betook

[8] Gillett, *Shrines of Our Lady in England and Wales*, 302.
[9] Ibid., 336.
[10] Ibid., 333.
[11] Ibid., 344.

himself to the Chapel of Our Lady of Pewe, there said his devotions, and went to Smithfield to meet the rebels.[12]

According to legend, it was at this time that the king dedicated England as "Our Lady's Dowry", offering the nation to her as England's "protectress", seeking deliverance for himself and his kingdom from the Peasant's Revolt. This moment is depicted with great beauty in the Wilton Diptych, one of the finest examples of late mediaeval art, in which King Richard kneels before the Virgin and Child, who are surrounded by angels, one of whom holds aloft a St. George's Cross flag. The king is presented to the Madonna and Child by three saints: St. John the Baptist (the king's personal patron) and by the two patron saints of England, St. Edward the Confessor and St. Edmund the Martyr. (It was not until the Reformation that St. George emerged definitively as England's patron.) Although it is often presumed that this dedication by the king is the origin of England's being known as Our Lady's Dowry, the title was already in common usage and was probably connected to the deep devotion of the people of England to Our Lady of Walsingham. Eamon Duffy stated that "Englishmen were encouraged to think of their country as being in a special way 'Mary's Dowry', a notion propagated ... by the custodians of the shrine at Walsingham."[13] In around 1350, a mendicant preacher stated in a sermon that "it is commonly said that the land of England is the Virgin's dowry."[14] Writing around fifty years later, the Archbishop of Canterbury, Thomas Arundel, discussing Mary and the Incarnation,

---

[12] Ibid.

[13] Eamon Duffy, *The Stripping of the Altars* (London: Yale University Press, 1992), 256.

[14] Nigel Saul, *For Honour and Fame: Chivalry in England, 1066–1500* (London: Random House, 2011), 208.

wrote that "we English, being ... her own Dowry, as we are commonly called, ought to surpass others in the fervour of our praises and devotions."[15] By the reign of Henry V, two decades later, the title *dos Mariae* (dowry of Mary) was being applied to England in Latin texts. On the eve of the Battle of Agincourt in 1415, according to the contemporary chronicler Thomas Elmham, English priests prayed for victory to "the Virgin, protectress of her dower".[16]

Such was the devotion to the Virgin that other Marian shrines, apart from Walsingham, were graced with royal visits. The shrine to Our Lady of Doncaster in Yorkshire was visited by Henry Bolingbroke in July 1399, a few months before his coronation as Henry IV, and Edward IV went on pilgrimage to the shrine in 1470. A little farther north in Knaresborough, still in Yorkshire, a shrine to the Virgin was carved out of a cliff face, becoming known as the Chapel of Our Lady of the Crag. In the south of England, on the bank of the River Thames, the shrine to Our Lady of Caversham had already existed for centuries when, in 1439, the Countess of Warwick, bequeathed "a crown of gold made from my chain, and other broken gold in my cabinet, weighing 20lbs" for Our Lady's statue.[17] In the same will, the countess bequeathed to Our Lady of Walsingham, "a tabernacle of silver, of the same *timbre* as that of Our Lady of Caversham".[18] H.M. Gillett imagines what the shrine at Caversham and its statue must have looked like after the receipt of these generous bequests:

> We can visualize ... the statue of Our Lady of Caversham set in a silver tabernacle—the equal of one that was thought

[15] Sarah Jane Boss, *Mary* (London: Continuum, 2004), 118.
[16] Saul, *For Honour and Fame*, 209.
[17] Gillett, *Shrines of Our Lady in England and Wales*, 81.
[18] Ibid.

worthy of Our Lady of Walsingham, and crowned with a superlative crown of gold, the like of which can hardly have been equaled at that time at any shrine in Europe.[19]

Positioned at one of the relatively few bridges crossing the Thames, the shrine of Our Lady of Caversham was ideally situated to be a popular pilgrimage site. Gillett imagines that the shrine was "thronged day after day" with pilgrims from every part of England, "regardless of season ... rich and poor alike":

> Courtiers from Windsor, scholars from Oxford, religious from Notley, Reading, and a score of other monasteries, merchants from the north finding their way to southern markets, countryfolk going to the fairs at Reading and St. Giles of Oxford; all these and countless others found their way to the feet of the Blessed Mother of God in her Caversham shrine.[20]

As for the common people, Marian devotion was widespread throughout the fifteenth century, as is evident in the beautiful Marian poetry that survives from this time, such as "I Sing of a Maiden" which ends with the wonderful lines: "Mother and Maiden, was never none but she, / Well may such a lady God's mother be."[21] Prayers in Latin, such as the *Salve Regina* and the *Ave Maria*, were part of the daily piety of the people, as were prayers and meditations on the Joys of Mary: the Annunciation, Nativity, Resurrection, and Ascension as well as her own coronation as Queen of Heaven. These "were familiar to every man, woman, and child from their endless reproduction in

---

[19] Ibid., 81–82.

[20] Ibid., 82.

[21] The spelling has been modernized for the sake of clarity.

carving, painting, and glass".[22] The Joys of Mary were also a central part of the Corpus Christi mystery plays.

Dovetailing with the popular devotion to Mary's Joys were devotions to her Sorrows. The cult of the Sorrows of the Virgin, or the Mater Dolorosa, found expression in the words of the *Stabat Mater*, evoking the Virgin's grief at the Crucifixion of her Son, and in the multifarious visual representations of the *Pietà*, depicting the Virgin's cradling of the dead Christ. Every parish church in the country contained images of the Mater Dolorosa on the rood screens across the chancel arch, in which the Virgin and the Beloved Disciple are shown flanking the Crucified Christ.

We will end this brief survey of the Marian devotion of Merrie England by placing ourselves before the image of Our Lady of Pewe at the chapel in Westminster at which Richard II had declared England to be Our Lady's Dowry amidst the mayhem of the Peasants' Revolt. It is now 1483, a century later, and England is ruled by another Richard— Richard III—whose reign would mark the beginning of the end of Merrie England. Richard III had his rival Earl Rivers executed in 1483 at Pontefract in Yorkshire, the site of another Marian shrine. In his will, Earl Rivers bequeathed his body to Our Lady of Pontefract, his hair shirt to Our Lady of Doncaster, and his heart to Our Lady of Pewe, stipulating that it be carried to "Our Lady of Pue adjoining to St. Stephen's College at Westminster, there to be buried by the advice of the Dean and his brethren".[23] Well may the unjustly executed earl have sought to have his heart buried close to a shrine to Our Lady which was of such spiritual importance to successive kings and queens of the realm. "The Chapel of St. Mary de Pewa is a place of

[22] Duffy, *Stripping of the Altars*, 257.
[23] Gillett, *Shrines of Our Lady in England and Wales*, 346–47.

great devotion within the Palace of Westminster," stated a Deed of Foundation, dated July 28, 1480, "more fit for this sacrifice to be offered, where by the frequent attestation of miracles it is evident that the prayers of the devout faithful are more effectively heard; that it abounds in indulgences, as well for the living as for the dead."[24]

The shrine of Our Lady of Pewe would be destroyed only a few short decades later, as would the shrines of Our Lady all over the land, razed to the ground by Henry VIII in the Tudor Terror that he would unleash on the people and faith of England.

[24] Ibid., 347.

Chapter Eight

Prelude to Tyranny

Presumption and vainglory,
Envy, wrath, and lechery,
Couvetise and gluttony,
Slothful to do good,
Now frantic, now starke wood.
Set up a wretch on high
In a throne triumphantly,
Make him a great estate
And he will play checkmate
With royal majesty.

> —John Skelton,
> from "Why Come Ye
> not to Courte?"

These lines of verse by the Tudor poet John Skelton refer to Cardinal Wolsey, but they are at least as applicable to Wolsey's master, Henry VIII, whose egocentric rule of England presaged disaster. We will begin, however, with Henry's father, Henry VII, whose seizure of the throne in 1485 established the Tudor dynasty.

Shortly after his coronation, Henry VII travelled through the north of England as a means of establishing his authority in those parts of the country, especially Yorkshire, in which he was distrusted and disliked in equal measure. Arriving in Yorkshire, he made a pilgrimage to the shrine of Our Lady of Doncaster, hearing Mass at the Lady shrine itself. One can imagine that he would have petitioned the Virgin to intercede for him as he sought to heal the wounds of the Wars of the Roses, a series of civil wars fought between the houses of Lancaster and York over the preceding thirty years. Henry had inherited the Lancastrian claim to the throne, but he still had to deal with those who upheld the rival claims of the House of York. In order to heal the wounds, or at least secure the peace, Parliament had petitioned him to marry Elizabeth of York, thereby uniting the two houses. A key figure in arranging the marriage was the Bishop of Ely, John Morton, who had fled England after earning the enmity of Richard III but had returned after Henry's accession to the throne.

In 1486, after Morton had been appointed Archbishop of Canterbury, he became one of the king's most trusted advisers, as was illustrated in his being appointed Lord Chancellor in 1487. In 1493, at Henry VII's request, Pope Alexander VI, the notorious Borgia pope, made Morton a cardinal, a dubious distinction perhaps. It was surely significant, however, that the future Pope Paul III, who would convene the Council of Trent, was made a cardinal on the same day, proof that the hand of Providence writes straight with crooked lines.

It was at Morton's palace in Lambeth that the twelve-year-old Thomas More arrived in 1490 to serve as a page. Two years later, Morton nominated his bright young page for a place at the University of Oxford, thereby launching More on his brilliant but costly rise to fame. In a quasi-autobiographical section of his book *Utopia*, More reminisced about the two years he spent as the archbishop's page:

During my stay I received a lot of kindness from the Most
Reverend John Morton.... He was a person that one
respected just as much for his wisdom and moral character
as for his great eminence.... He had the sort of face that
inspires reverence rather than fear. He was quite easy to
get on with, though always serious and dignified.... He
also had a quite remarkable intellect, and a phenomenal
memory.... Apparently the King had great confidence in
his judgment, and at the time of my visit the whole country seemed to depend on him.[1]

Thomas More's firsthand account of his own memories of Archbishop Morton contrast dramatically with the
account offered over a century later by Francis Bacon,
who wrote that Morton was "in his nature harsh and
haughty" and was "envied by the nobility and hated of
the people". Adding insult to injury, Bacon also ascribed
to Archbishop Morton an egregious and avaricious principle of tax assessment that he called "Morton's Fork",
which involved "persuading prodigals to part with their
money because they did spend it most, and the covetous
because they might spare it best".[2] This view was contradicted by the Italian chronicler Polydore Vergil, a contemporary of Archbishop Morton whose *Anglica Historia*
was written by 1513. Vergil commented that it was clear
from the increased taxes imposed by the king following
the archbishop's death that Morton had actually served as a
restraining force upon the king's avarice. Seen in the light
of Morton's contemporaries, there can be little doubt that
Francis Bacon's historical revisionism is an example of the

[1] Thomas More, *Utopia*, trans. Paul Turner, rev. ed. (London: Penguin
Books, 2003), 21–22.
[2] Nicholas Schofield and Gerard Skinner, *The English Cardinals* (Oxford:
Family Publications, 2007), 73–74.

calumnious nature of what Hilaire Belloc called the "enormous mountain of ignorant wickedness" that constituted "tom-fool Protestant history".[3]

Archbishop Morton died in September 1500 and was buried close to the shrine of Our Lady of the Undercroft in the crypt of Canterbury Cathedral. Meanwhile, in London, the queen was continuing the tradition of previous monarchs in honouring the Virgin at what might be called the "royal" shrine of Our Lady of Pewe in Westminster. The queen made an offering to the shrine on the eve of the Annunciation in 1502; on December 8 of the same year, she made a further offering, "upon the Conception of Our Lady, to Our Lady of Pyewe".[4]

In the following year, the foundations were laid for a new Lady Chapel in Westminster Abbey, replacing the more modest one built during the reign of Henry III in the thirteenth century. Apart from his desire to honour the Mother of God, the king also planned to be buried in this new chapel, desiring, like Archbishop Morton, to be laid to rest under the prayerful protection of the Virgin. This magnificent edifice, in which the king and queen would indeed be buried, as would many later monarchs, is now known simply as the Henry VII chapel, bereft of its purpose of being a magnificent shrine to the Virgin.

In 1505, Henry VII would confirm the mediaeval charter, dating from 1194, bestowing upon Doncaster the right to hold an annual three-day fair on the "Vigil, Feast and the Morrow" of the Annunciation. Life, it seemed, was going on much as it had for centuries. In the following

---

[3] Hilaire Belloc to Hoffman Nickerson, September 13, 1923, Belloc Collection, Boston College; quoted in Joseph Pearce, *Old Thunder: A Life of Hilaire Belloc* (San Francisco: Ignatius Press, 2002), 230.

[4] H. M. Gillett, *Shrines of Our Lady in England and Wales* (London: Samuel Walker, 1957), 349.

year, the king heard Mass at the magnificent King's College Chapel in Cambridge, which was still under construction. He was on his way to Walsingham, following in
the footsteps of numerous kings before him. All appeared
to be as it should be and as it had ever been. And yet troubles were afoot. In the crowds who witnessed the king's
arrival in Cambridge was a seventeen-year-old student
by the name of Thomas Cranmer. We don't know
what the precocious young man thought or felt as he
watched the pomp and circumstance of the king's train
pass through the streets; but we do know that he was
unimpressed with the scholastic philosophy which he
was being taught by his professors, most of whom had
lost the vibrancy of the intellectual life that had characterized the previous centuries and were merely going
through the motions in a manner that lacked motivation
or purpose. Dead to the living tradition that had animated Christendom since the time of Christ, the young
man wanted something different. In the decades ahead,
he would share the responsibility for unleashing the
"something different" which would devastate England.

Upon his death in 1509, Henry VII bequeathed to the
shrine of Our Lady of Walsingham a gilt image of himself,
kneeling in prayer. His young son, Henry VIII, who was
only seventeen when he ascended the throne, emulated
his late father's generosity by bestowing on the shrine a
magnificent collar of rubies, as well as providing the fund-
ing for new stained glass windows for the outer chapel in
which the holy house of the apparition was enshrined.

Considering the munificence of various monarchs across
the centuries, not to mention the generosity of countless pilgrims, it was not surprising that Erasmus should be
impressed by the beauty he encountered upon his arrival
at Walsingham in 1512, even if his descriptions are barbed

with satire. He described the priory church as "graceful
and elegant", commenting that the famous statue of the
Virgin was not to be found within it. "She cedes it, out
of deference to her Son. She has her own church, that
she may be on her Son's right hand."[5] "Well might Erasmus have felt dazzled at all he saw," wrote H. M. Gillett,
"for there, glistening in the semi-dark fragrance of the
Holy Chapel was a spectacle which vied with anything
that could be found in Our Lady's other holy shrines on
the continent."[6]

In 1517, Cardinal Wolsey wrote to the king, telling him
that he was setting out on a pilgrimage to Walsingham and
from thence to the shrine to Our Lady of Grace in Ipswich
in fulfilment of a vow and in hope of a cure for a stom-
ach ailment. As for the king himself, his *Book of Payments*
records gifts between 1511 and 1519 to various shrines,
including Walsingham, Doncaster, and Our Lady of Pewe
in Westminster, in payment for candles and Masses to be
said, especially for the repose of the Holy Souls.[7]

The faith and piety of the king were reflected in the
faith and piety of the people. "The English were reckoned to be a devout people," wrote the historian Gerard
Culkin. "Foreigners remarked that daily Mass was always
well attended, and that the people were much attached to
such devotions as the rosary and the Little Office of Our
Lady."[8] Most of the books published in these early days
of printing were devotional works, and there were innumerable religious guilds and fraternities across the length
and breadth of the country. Even the smallest villages had

[5] Ibid., 302.
[6] Ibid., 304.
[7] Ibid., 349–50.
[8] Gerard Culkin, *The English Reformation* (London: Sands, 1955), 7.

their own guilds, as Eamon Duffy shows in his masterful history of the period. The village of Bressingham in Norfolk had two guilds: the Guild of St. John the Baptist and the Guild of St. Peter, the first of which was large, owning a herd of thirty cows, a guildhall, and having its own chaplain, and the latter of which was much more modest, meeting in guild-holders' houses and owning only two small parcels of land bequeathed by a brother in the 1460s.[9] These guilds were responsible for much of the furnishing of local churches, as were other groups of "bachelors", "young men", "maydens", and "wyves". In the Cornish parish of St. Neot, in 1523, the "wives of the western end of the parish" donated a stained glass window depicting the Pietà; in 1528, the "young men" of the parish donated a stained glass window depicting the legend of St. Neot.[10]

A vision of what life would have been like in England in 1520 is offered by Ronald Hutton, professor of history at Bristol University who writes of "a land crowded with parish churches blazing with colour and filled with carvings, statues, veils, hangings, side-chapels and paintings on walls and screens".[11]

> Every church would have at least three (and up to 20) side altars dedicated to saints other than the one who was patron of the main church: figures of transcendent humanity as well as sanctity, whom ordinary people could make into friends and patrons.... Each parish would have three to twelve guilds ... which all but the poorest could

[9] Eamon Duffy, *The Stripping of the Altars* (London: Yale University Press, 1992), 151.

[10] Ibid., 150.

[11] Ronald Hutton, "I'm Not a Catholic, but I'd Have Liked to Live in Catholic England", *Catholic Herald*, August 21, 2020. This and the following quotes by Hutton are from this source.

afford to join and which provided the benefits of both a
social club and an insurance company.

There were the holy wells scattered across the landscape, often places of physical beauty and healing power
as well as sanctity. Pilgrimage provided abundant opportunity, given the great number of shrines spread around
the nation, for a vacation (often with friends) as well as
an opportunity to obtain divine help and work out spiritual problems. The relics in these places embodied a
proportionately huge number of exciting stories, of miracle, heroism and edification. Almost a thousand religious
houses preserved their own works of art and libraries full
of manuscripts.

The many feast days in the liturgical year "fostered a
lay festive culture of plays, pageants, parades, church ales,
village revels, may-poles, Morris dances, Christmas games,
wassails and midsummer bonfires". It was no wonder that
"people nostalgic for this age of colour, innocence, local-
ism and rampant creativity" should coin the expression
"Merrie England" to describe it. In addition, Professor
Hutton continued, the circles around John Colet, John
Fisher, and Sir Thomas More pursued the truths of faith
and reason with intellectual vigour and rigour, infusing
their discussions with a profound knowledge of classical
Greece and Rome.

If all appeared to be well in England, the same could not
be said of parts of continental Europe. Martin Luther had
begun his revolt against the Church in 1517, and his ideas
were gaining traction in Germany. By around 1520, in
Cambridge, Thomas Cranmer and his circle were meeting
to read and discuss Luther's work. In the following year,
King Henry VIII wrote a response to Luther's book *On
the Babylonian Captivity of the Church*. The king's response,
the *Assertio Septem Sacramentorum*, was, as its title affirms, a

defense of the Catholic doctrine of the sacraments, which Luther had denied, and of the supremacy of the see of Rome. Within a year, in one of the great ironies of history, Pope Leo X bestowed upon Henry VIII the title of Defender of the Faith as a token of his gratitude for Henry's staunch and vigorous defence of the Church against Luther's heresies.

Thomas More, a friend and favourite of the king, would write in the *Dialogue of Comfort against Tribulation* that "it is hard for any person either man or woman, in great worldly wealth and much prosperity, so to withstand the suggestions of the devil and occasions given by the world, that they keep themselves from the deadly desire of ambitious glory." These words should be borne in mind as we consider the fall from grace of Henry VIII.

Although Thomas More was close to the king, he was under no illusions with respect to the king's character. After his son-in-law, William Roper, had congratulated him on his receiving the king's favour, having observed the king enfolding his arms affectionately round More's neck, More replied that he had "no cause to be proud thereof, for if my head would win him a castle in France … it should not fail to go".[12] This was in 1525. By 1529, he had won the favour of the king to such an extent that, following the fall of Cardinal Wolsey, More was appointed to the position of Lord Chancellor. Having little option but to accept, he must have felt that the king had handed him a poisoned chalice, one which might well cost him his life. He was already in a precarious position because he had expressed to the king his opposition to the king's plans to have his marriage with Catherine annulled. It was true that

[12] Claude Williamson, ed., *Great Catholics* (London: Nicholson and Watson, 1938), 156.

Henry, having appointed More as his chancellor, had told him that he would not force his conscience on the issue of the marriage, telling him that he must first look to God and after God to the king; yet, even so, More could not feel confident that his opposition to the king's plans would be tolerated for long.

As it became clear that the pope would not bend to the king's will on the matter of the annulment, Henry began to listen to the Machiavellian promptings of the anti-Catholic Thomas Cromwell that, as the king, he should free himself from the will of Rome by making himself the head of the Church in England. Such a suggestion was reinforced by the anti-clericalism of Parliament. "Now with the Commons is nothing but 'Down with the clergy'," Bishop John Fisher complained, "and this, meseemeth, is for lack of faith only."[13]

The king and his allies in Parliament began a war of attrition against the Church, encroaching upon her rights and eyeing with increasing envy and avarice the land and wealth she possessed. In 1530, John Fisher, along with two other bishops, appealed to Rome against the English Parliament's increasing usurpation of the rights of the Church. Henry responded with the issuing of an edict making all appeals to Rome illegal. Fisher and the other bishops were arrested but later released. When, in February 1531, the king sought to force the clergy of England to recognize him as "Supreme Head of the Church in England", Fisher succeeded in having this modified by the addition of the words "so far as God's law permits", a get-out clause respecting the religious conscience of the clergy which Henry would not tolerate for long.

---

[13] James Gairdner, *The History of the Church in the Sixteenth Century* (London: Macmillan, 1902), 104.

On May 15, 1532, the Catholic hierarchy of England surrendered. In what became known as "the submission of the clergy", the hierarchy of the Church in England placed itself under the will and pleasure of the king. On the following day, Thomas More resigned as chancellor. For More, the king's triumph had changed the very nature of England, destroying the very legal system on which she stood which had held the king as having authority *sub Deo et lege* (under God and the law). Having declared himself head of the Church in his realm, Henry, like the Caesars of old, had effectively declared himself divine, above the laws of either God or man. He was a law unto himself who could and would do as he willed. "We shall soon see a worse than Nero on the throne," wrote William Cobbett. "We shall soon see him laying all law prostrate at his feet; and plundering his people, down even to the patrimony of the poor."[14] With such a "Nero" on the throne, the stage was set for the beginning of the Tudor Terror.

[14] William Cobbett, *A History of the Protestant Reformation* (Sevenoaks, Kent: Fisher Press, 1994), 35.

Chapter Nine

The Tudor Terror

O, how wretched
Is that poor man that hangs on princes' favours!
There is, betwixt that smile we would aspire to,
That sweet aspect of princes, and their ruin,
More pangs and fears than war or women have;
And when he falls, he falls like Lucifer,
Never to hope again.

—William Shakespeare,
from *The Life of King Henry the Eighth*

In June 1532, displaying a courage that was sadly lacking in the rest of England's bishops, John Fisher preached publicly against the king's plans to divorce Catherine. In January of the following year, the king secretly went through a form of marriage with Anne Boleyn, who was now pregnant. Two months later, Thomas Cranmer became Archbishop of Canterbury. A week later, Fisher was arrested. It seems that the king and Cranmer wanted Fisher out of the way so that he could not speak out publicly against the granting of the king's divorce, which Cranmer pronounced in May, or the coronation in early June of Anne Boleyn, who was now six months pregnant. Bishop Fisher was released two weeks after the coronation, with no charges being made against him.

The new creed of Machiavellianism, which dominated English affairs during the years of the Tudor Terror, was evident in an exchange between Henry VIII's henchman, Thomas Cromwell, and Reginald Pole, later to become Cardinal Archbishop of Canterbury under Mary Tudor. Cromwell recommended that Pole read Machiavelli's book *Il Principe* rather than Plato's *Republic* were he to desire a better understanding of realpolitik. Cromwell then expounded upon his own Machiavellian views, explaining that the king's inclinations should be studied and then furthered, without sacrificing the appearance of religion or virtue.[1] Although Pole promised to read Machiavelli at Cromwell's urging, he chose principle over principalities. When the king offered to make him Archbishop of York if he would agree to support the annulment of his marriage, he refused the offer and went into exile.

In a further example of the king's and Cranmer's ruthless Machiavellianism, John Fisher was accused in March 1534, along with Thomas More and others, of alleged complicity in the so-called treason of Elizabeth Barton, known as the Holy Maid of Kent, who had claimed to have had a vision of the place in hell reserved for Henry if he divorced Catherine and married Anne Boleyn. Dispensing with the formality of any trial, Parliament found Fisher and others guilty of the charge. Fisher's punishment was the forfeiture of all his personal estate and imprisonment at the king's pleasure. He was subsequently granted a pardon on payment of a fine of £300. The poor hapless "Holy Maid" was not so fortunate. In April, she was hanged for treason, along with five of her associates, four of whom were priests. Her head was then severed and placed on a spike

---

[1] Claude Williamson, ed., *Great Catholics* (London: Nicholson and Watson, 1938), 175.

on London Bridge as a warning to any others who might be tempted to question the actions of the king. A year later, the heads of John Fisher and Thomas More would suffer the same grisly fate. In the words of historian Richard Rex, "the execution of the Holy Maid and her companions was one of the many ways in which judicious use of judicial terror ... was employed to secure compliance with the English Reformation."[2]

In the same month in which More and Fisher had been arrested for their alleged involvement with the Holy Maid, Parliament passed the First Succession Act, a law which compelled all those called upon to do so to take an oath of succession, acknowledging any children from the marriage of Henry and Anne to be legitimate heirs to the throne. Failure to do so would be considered an act of treason, punishable by death.[3] John Fisher refused the oath and was imprisoned in the Tower of London on April 26, 1534. Two weeks earlier, Thomas More had also refused the oath.

It was from his prison cell in the Tower that More saw the abbot of the London Charterhouse and three other monks passing below his window on their way to meet a martyr's death, chanting praises to the Lord as they went. Like More and Fisher, they had refused the oath. "These blessed fathers be now as cheerfully going to their deaths as bridegrooms to their marriage," More exclaimed to his daughter.[4]

William Cobbett, never one to mince his words or pull his polemical punches, was brutally candid in his description of this "judicious use of judicial terror":

---

[2] Richard Rex, "The Execution of the Holy Maid of Kent", *Historical Research* 64 (1991): 220.

[3] Technically they were guilty of misprision of treason, which, at the time, was itself considered to be treason and therefore a capital offence.

[4] Philip Caraman, ed., *Saints and Ourselves* (London: Catholic Book Club, 1953), 76–77.

The work of blood was now begun, and it proceeded with steady pace. All who refused to take the oath of supremacy,—that is to say, all who refused to become apostates,—were considered and treated as traitors, and made to suffer death accompanied with every possible cruelty and indignity. As a specimen ... let us take the treatment of John Houghton, prior of the Charterhouse in London, which was then a convent of Carthusian monks. The prior, for having refused to take the oath, which, observe, he could not take without committing perjury, was dragged to Tyburn. He was scarcely suspended when the rope was cut, and he fell alive on the ground. His clothes were then stripped off; his bowels were ripped up; his heart and entrails were torn from his body and flung into a fire; his head was cut from his body; the body was divided into quarters and parboiled; the quarters were then subdivided, and hung up in different parts of the city; and one arm was nailed to the wall over the entrance into the monastery![5]

As news of the horrific and heroic deaths of these holy monks reached them, John Fisher and Thomas More must have reflected grimly on what awaited them, if they continued to refuse to conform to the king's new tyranny. What must More have thought and felt when visited by Margaret, his beloved daughter, who was pregnant with his grandchild? How could his paternal heart not break as he looked upon her? "He may be called almost the patron saint of family life," Christopher Hollis wrote. "Of his [family] life there we have so many and such vivid pictures, and his happiness came to him so largely from it. His happiness was thus a happiness that does not differ in kind from that that is offered to every normal man and woman,

[5] William Cobbett, *A History of the Protestant Reformation* (Sevenoaks, Kent: Fisher Press, 1994), 37.

and it is this very fact which heightens the horror and the grandeur of his final end. He stepped out to that end from just such a life as our own."[6]

In comparing More's imprisonment and passion with that of John Fisher's, we see the palpable difference between the laity and the priesthood. More has a loving wife and children for whom he is responsible and who are his dependents. Fisher, on the other hand, has taken a vow of celibacy; acting *in persona Christi*, he chose the Bride of Christ (the Church) as his spouse. More has, therefore, more of an excuse for having divided loyalties. We can understand the temptation to equivocate with his conscience in order to succor his family. He is, therefore, to be praised and venerated all the more for having resisted it. A priest, however, is not in this awkward position. He has the Church as his Bride and is called to lay down his life for her. This absence of divided loyalties is one of the strongest arguments for priestly celibacy. It is, therefore, tragic, and an indictment of the weakness and cowardice of the Church's hierarchy, that John Fisher was the only English bishop to defy the king. He serves, therefore, in his day and ours as a potent symbol of the self-sacrificial duty of the bishops of the Church in all ages to resist the spirit of the world, the spirit of the age, and to remain true to the Body of Christ, serving the Heilige Geist (Holy Spirit) and not the zeitgeist.

What must More have thought and felt when he heard that the king was parceling out his property, pillaging his wealth and his family's inheritance, showing no more respect to the property rights of the citizens of the state than he would later show to the property rights of the Church? More heard that his land in Oxfordshire had been

---

[6] Christopher Hollis, *St. Thomas More* (London: Burns & Oates, 1961), 31.

given by the king to Sir Henry Norris, a courtier who had promoted the cause of Anne Boleyn, and that his land in Kent had been given to George Boleyn, Anne's brother. Meanwhile, like a circling crow or vulture, the Duke of Suffolk, Henry's brother-in-law, was waiting to move into More's family home in Chelsea as soon as More was dead. "A deadly grief unto me," More wrote to his daughter Margaret when the news of the theft of his property had reached him, "and much more deadly than to hear of my own death ... is that I perceive my good son, your husband and you, my good daughter and my good wife and mine other good children and innocent friends in great displeasure and danger of great harm thereby."[7]

It was ironic that Henry Norris and George Boleyn were not destined to enjoy their inheritance at More's expense, both losing their lives only a year after More's own death. George Boleyn was found guilty of incest with his sister, Anne, and Norris was convicted of committing adultery with her. Both men were also condemned for treason and were imprisoned in the Tower before being executed on Tower Hill on May 17, 1536, possibly on the very same block on which More himself had been martyred only ten months earlier. The ill-fated Anne Boleyn lost her head on the same block only two days later. Needless to say, most historians agree that the so-called plot surrounding Anne, together with the accusations of incest and adultery, were cynically fabricated by Henry in order to rid himself of another unwanted wife. If Henry was now proving Lord Acton's adage that power tends to corrupt and absolute power tends to corrupt absolutely, the situation in England following Henry's revolution, masquerading as a "reformation", proved the other adage that revolutions devour

[7] Ibid., 207.

their own children. Whether saints or sinners, conscientious objectors or inconscionable courtiers, nobody was safe from the Machiavellian machinations of the king.

Bishop John Fisher, aging and ailing, was so weak on the morning of the execution that he had to be carried from his cell. As to the execution itself, we have an eyewitness account of his final words, spoken from the scaffold. "Christian people," Fisher declared to the crowd gathered on Tower Hill, "I am come hither to die for the faith of Christ's Catholic Church."[8]

Although Fisher's last moments epitomized the dignified courage which had characterized his life, there was nothing dignified in the manner that his body was treated following his death. Presumably on Henry's orders, the decapitated corpse was stripped naked and left on the scaffold for the rest of the day. In the evening, it was removed unceremoniously to a nearby churchyard, where it was dumped, still naked, into a rough grave. There was no funeral prayer. Fisher's head was stuck upon a pole on London Bridge, where it remained for two weeks, its ruddy and apparently incorrupt appearance exciting much attention.

It was now Thomas More's turn to face the executioner's axe.

Three days after the martyrdom of John Fisher, Henry ordered preachers to denounce the treasons of Sir Thomas More from their pulpits. Since More's trial for treason wasn't due to start until a week later, on July 1, the king's orders signified, if such signification were necessary, that the trial was already a foregone conclusion and that only one verdict would be tolerated. The parallels with the justice system in other secularist tyrannies, such as the show trials in the Soviet Union under Josef Stalin, are clear enough.

---

[8] Maisie Ward, ed., *The English Way: Studies in English Sanctity from Bede to Newman* (Tacoma, Wash.: Cluny Media, 2016), 212.

The case against More was flimsy at best, based on the duplicitous and mendacious evidence of Richard Rich, one of the most disreputable figures in English history; it broke down completely under the sharp-witted cross questioning of the defendant. Yet, as Christopher Hollis reminds us, "evidence or no evidence, no jury was brave enough to bring in a verdict against the Crown in the days of Tudor terror."[9] After only about fifteen minutes of deliberation, if indeed any real deliberation took place, the jury returned its predestined "guilty" verdict.

Before sentence could be passed, More reminded the judge presiding at the trial, Thomas Audley, who had succeeded him as Lord Chancellor, that it was customary, following the jury's verdict, for a defendant to have the opportunity to address the judge before sentencing. His words echo down the centuries as a perennially pertinent iteration of Catholic political philosophy:

> Forasmuch, my lords, as this indictment is grounded upon an Act of Parliament directly repugnant to the laws of God and His Holy Church, the supreme government whereof, as any part thereof, may no temporal prince presume by any law to take upon him, as rightfully belonging to the See of Rome, a spiritual pre-eminence by the mouth of Our Saviour Himself, personally present upon the earth, only to St. Peter and his successors, bishops of the same see, by special prerogative granted, it is therefore in law among Christian men insufficient to charge any Christian man.[10]

The law, in short, was unlawful. More proceeded to say that Henry's law also contradicted the Magna Carta which had stipulated that the Church in England shall be

[9] Hollis, *St. Thomas More*, 231.
[10] Ibid.

free from secular jurisdiction, having "her whole rights and liberties inviolable". The king, therefore, had no right according to either the laws of Christendom (international or universal law) or the laws of England (the Magna Carta) to pass the Act of Supremacy, which invested what amounted to divine right in the king himself; therefore, his subjects had no responsibility to obey such laws but, on the contrary, a moral duty to oppose them. When the Lord Chancellor endeavoured to argue with him, More reiterated his position. "I am not bound, my Lord, to conform my conscience to the counsel of one realm against the general counsel of Christendom."[11]

Mounting the scaffold on July 6, 1535, More turned to Edmund Walsingham to request his help ascending the steps to his place of execution. "I pray you, Mr. Lieutenant," he quipped, retaining his sense of humour to the last, "see me safe up and for my coming down, I can shift for myself."[12] From the scaffold itself, moments before his head was severed from his shoulders, he proclaimed to the gathered crowd of Londoners that he died "the king's good servant, but God's first".

More's head was taken to London Bridge, where the severed head of John Fisher was still on gory display. Fisher's head was removed from its place and thrown into the Thames. More's head was then put in its place.

Hollis described More and Fisher as "the two most learned men in England" and their deaths as the killing of learning, as well as the killing of justice, laughter, and holiness.[13] With such a sweeping judgement, we can only partly agree. Whether More and Fisher were indeed

---

[11] Ibid., 232.

[12] From William Roper's *Life of Sir Thomas More* (1626); quoted in Hollis, *St. Thomas More*, 237.

[13] Hollis, *St. Thomas More*, 239.

peerless in learning is perhaps a moot point; but their deaths did not kill learning, which continued "of a sort" (to quote Belloc),[14] nor laughter, which would reemerge uproariously in the comedies of Shakespeare, nor holiness, which always defies the grave, the blood of the martyrs being the seed of the Church. It did, however, kill justice or at least seriously weaken it. The king's usurpation of the religious rights of the Church, and therefore the religious liberties of his subjects, set in motion a process of secular nationalism that would lead to the rise of the sort of secularism which ripens into secular fundamentalism. When the state gets too big for its boots, trampling on religious liberty, it is not long before the boots become jackboots, trampling on the defenceless and the weak, and piling up the bodies of its countless victims.

The final word on the legacy of John Fisher and Thomas More, and the final judgement (under God) on why we should see them as heroes, is given by G. K. Chesterton, a man who proves in his very self that the killing of More and Fisher did not kill learning, laughter, or holiness. In an essay on Thomas More, Chesterton goes to the heart of what separates the pride of a king from the humility of a saint:

> Henry always wanted to be judge in his own cause; against his wives; against his friends; against the Head of his Church. But the link which really connects More with that Roman supremacy for which he died is this fact: that he would always have been large-minded enough to want a judge who was not merely himself.... There is this true relation between the martyr and the doctrine for which he died; that he died, not only defending the Pope, but defying the sort of man who wants to be Pope.[15]

[14] Hilaire Belloc, "Lines to a Don", stanza 2.
[15] Ward, *English Way*, 221.

Reginald Pole, from the safety of his exile in Italy, expressed the shock and anger of all of Christendom in his condemnation of Henry VIII's outrageous attacks upon the Church. Warning the king of the danger to both his soul and his kingdom, he exhorted him to return to the unity of the Church. He then compared Henry to Nero and Domitian in the manner of Henry's ruthless persecution of Christians and labelled him a greater enemy to Christendom than Islam. Last but not least, he expressed disbelief at the enormity of Henry's slaying of the recent martyrs, More, Fisher, and the Carthusians:

> Is it possible? Could you slay men like these, who by your own judgment in former days, and by the judgment of all, were held in the highest esteem for innocence, virtue and learning, and that for no other reason than they would not violate their conscience by assenting to your impious laws?[16]

One can imagine Henry's fury upon receipt of such strident criticism of his royal majesty. In response, he invited Pole to England to discuss the matter. Understandably, Pole remained in Italy, remarking in his response to the king's invitation that, like the fox, he had seen many animals going into the lion's cage, but none coming out again.[17] One can only imagine the extent of Henry's rage upon his learning, in December 1536, that Pole had been made a cardinal by Pope Paul III.

In January 1536, Queen Catherine died, having spent the last years of her life effectively under house arrest at Kimbolton Castle. "For the gentle, simple and dignified Queen

---

[16] Nicholas Schofield and Gerard Skinner, *The English Cardinals* (Oxford: Family Publications, 2007), 111.

[17] Williamson, *Great Catholics*, 177.

Catherine all men felt sympathy," wrote Hilaire Belloc. "They were familiar through portraiture and report with her broad smiling presence, her fair features—never beautiful but most pleasing—her admitted goodness." In addition, Belloc continued, "her misfortunes [had] endeared her to the English people. She had borne child after child to her husband and had suffered disappointments, for all those children save one had died in infancy or had come still-born, and her miscarriages were known."[18] William Cobbett was as effusive in her praise as he was withering in his condemnation of her abusive husband:

> She had been banished from court. She had seen her marriage annulled by Cranmer, and her daughter and only surviving child bastardized by act of parliament; and the husband, who had had five children by her ... had had the barbarity to keep her separated from, and never to suffer her, after her banishment, to set her eyes on that only child! She died, as she had lived, beloved and revered by every good man and woman in the kingdom, and was buried, amidst the sobbings and tears of a vast assemblage of the people, in the Abbey-church of Peterborough.[19]

If Cobbett was angered by Henry's treatment of Catherine, he was positively apoplectic with respect to Henry's destruction of England's monasteries and convents, which were "seized on, first and last, taken into the hands of the King, and by him granted to those who aided and abetted him in the work of plunder".[20] The plunder, which Cobbett called an "act of monstrous tyranny",[21] was made

---

[18] Hilaire Belloc, *Cranmer* (London: Cassell, 1931), 52–53.
[19] Cobbett, *History of the Protestant Reformation*, 28–29.
[20] Ibid., 48.
[21] Ibid., 65.

possible by the passage of an Act of Parliament in March 1536 for the suppression of the monasteries and the passing of all property and wealth owned by these religious communities into the hands of the king and his heirs. It is to this pillaging and "act of monstrous tyranny" that we now turn.

Chapter Ten

Pillage and Pilgrimage

And the eyes of the King's Servants turned terribly every way,
And the gold of the King's Servants rose higher every day.
They burnt the homes of the shaven men, that had been quaint
*   and kind,*
Till there was no bed in a monk's house, nor food that man could
*   find.*
The inns of God where no man paid, that were the wall of the
*   weak.*
The King's Servants ate them all. And still we did not speak.

— G. K. Chesterton, from "The Secret People"

The destruction of England's monasteries was carried out in two phases. First, the smaller religious communities were closed under the pretext of "reform", and then, once the appetite for plunder had been awakened in the avaricious hearts of the aristocracy, the larger abbeys and monasteries, with their richer pickings, were plundered. A total of between eight and nine hundred religious institutions were seized throughout the country, with the thousands of nuns and monks being ejected unceremoniously.

In terms of realpolitik, Henry would not have been able to get his hands on the wealth of the Church without bribing the nobles with a promise of a share of the plunder. Had the aristocracy not been bought in this way, they would no doubt have rebelled in defiance of the king and in defence of the Church. It was, therefore, in appealing to the baser appetites of the ignoble nobility that Henry succeeded in sacking the Church and removing her power from his realm. This was the sense in which G. K. Chesterton speaks of the eyes of the King's Servants turning terribly every way, seeking for hordes of other men's gold, and it is in this sense that he speaks of the gold of the King's Servants rising higher every day.

What Henry unleashed, once the pillaging began, was a feeding frenzy of greed, which he could no longer assuage or control. He complained to Thomas Cromwell, whom he had put in charge of overseeing the dissolution of the monasteries, that "the cormorants, when they have got the garbage, will devour the dish." Cromwell reassured him that there were more rich pickings in the larger abbeys that had not yet been pillaged. "Tut, man," the king replied, "my whole realm would not staunch their maws."[1] By the time that the dissolution of the monasteries was complete, the king was not much wealthier than he had been before the debauch began. Even worse, from his perspective, was the realization that he had inadvertently compromised his own position of power by creating a new secular plutocracy, a new class of "lords of the manor", which owned the huge tracts of land that had previously belonged to the Church and the wealth and power associated with such ownership.

As for the monasteries themselves, it is only possible to offer a few examples of the tragedy of the plunder and of the heroism of the monks and nuns.

In August 1535, Thomas Cromwell's inquisitors arrived at Glastonbury, hoping to find evidence of corruption

---

[1] William Cobbett, *A History of the Protestant Reformation* (Sevenoaks, Kent: Fisher Press, 1994), 70.

which would serve as the pretext for the abbey's dissolution. They were disappointed. "There is nothing notable: the brethren be so straight kept that they cannot offend."[2] Such innocence was no defence in the Tudor reign of terror, and it was inevitable that Glastonbury would go the way of every other monastery in the land. When the elderly abbot, Richard Whiting, refused to surrender the abbey to the king, he was arrested and imprisoned in the Tower of London. It was said that "a written book of arguments in behalf of queen Catherine"[3] was discovered in the abbey when it was searched, incriminating evidence in a time of totalitarian madness. Such evidence was hardly needed. Abbot Whiting's fate was sealed. Thomas Cromwell, serving as judge and jury ahead of any trial, wrote that "the Abbot of Glaston [is] to be tried at Glaston and also executed there with his accomplices."[4] It is not known whether any formal fallacy of a trial was ever actually held, but the preordained sentence for treason was carried out in Glastonbury as Cromwell had stipulated. Abbot Richard Whiting and two other monks were dragged on a hurdle to the Tor, the hill overlooking the abbey, where they were hanged, disemboweled, beheaded, and quartered. The abbot's head was stuck on a pike above the entrance to the abbey for all to see. His quarters were boiled in pitch and then displayed in the nearby towns of Wells, Bath, Ilchester, and Bridgewater. Abbot Richard Whiting was seventy-eight years old when this act of barbarism was inflicted upon him, a

---

[2] H.M. Gillett, *Shrines of Our Lady in England and Wales* (London: Samuel Walker, 1957), 153.

[3] Gilbert Huddleston, *The Catholic Encyclopedia*, vol. 13 (New York: Robert Appleton, 1912), s.v. "Blessed Richard Whiting".

[4] From Thomas Cromwell's manuscript "Remembrance"; quoted in Gillett, *Shrines of Our Lady in England and Wales*, 154. The spelling has been modernized for the sake of clarity.

mark of the merciless Machiavellianism of the king and
his "good servants".

With the brutal execution of these three monks, the
curtain fell on England's oldest Marian shrine, which
dated from the first century and which, according to
legend, had been founded by St. Joseph of Arimathea as
early as A.D. 63. A few years later, in the reign of Edward
VI, Glastonbury would be granted by the boy king to his
uncle, Edward Seymour, who had recently made himself
the first Earl of Somerset, and who, as Lord Protector of
the Realm and Governor of the King's Person, had probably "granted" himself Glastonbury Abbey and its lands.
And so, in a few short years, Glastonbury had passed from
the possession of selfless men worshipping the Lord to
a self-serving man who had made himself an earl. The
absurdity of the situation is more farcical than tragic, more
bathos than pathos. There is, however, a hopeful and
ultimately triumphant postscript to the story of Glastonbury. Abbot Richard Whiting and his two companions
would be beatified by Pope Leo XIII in 1888. And thus,
wrote H. M. Gillett, Our Lady of Glastonbury, as Queen
of Martyrs, "was presented with jewels infinitely more
precious than any sapphire, with which her crown might
be adorned".[5]

The abbots of the monasteries at Reading and Colchester also embraced martyrdom but most of the other abbots
chose a more comfortable option. The seventy-second and
last abbot of St. Augustine's Abbey in Canterbury, the first
Benedictine abbey to be founded in England, surrendered
the abbey with all its possessions to the king's commissioners in 1538, accepting a generous annual pension for
his "loyalty". Henry VIII then turned the abbey into a

[5] Gillett, *Shrines of Our Lady in England and Wales*, 155.

palace for Anne of Cleves, the fourth of his wives. And yet even these so-called "voluntary surrenders" were acts of coercion. As William Cobbett quipped, they were the sort of voluntary surrender "which men make of their purses when the robber's pistol is at their temple or his blood-stained knife at their throat".[6]

The dissolution of the monasteries had a significant impact on London, changing the political and commercial hub of the nation from a complex interweaving of religious and commercial activity to an avowedly secular metropolis. There were thirty-nine religious houses in London at the time of the dissolution, of which twenty-three were within the single square mile that comprised the city itself. "Almost overnight," wrote Simon Jenkins, "the City and its surrounding land saw a transfer of ownership and wealth on a scale not witnessed even during the Norman Conquest." The vast bulk of this property "passed to aristocrats, merchants and cronies of the monarch".[7] The king claimed for himself York Place on the river, which had been the possession of Cardinal Wolsey, having previously claimed Wolsey's Hampton Court as his royal palace. Other church property was given to the aforementioned Edward Seymour, soon to become the king's brother-in-law, who demolished it in order to build a personal palace for himself. Other church land in the city went to the Duke of Norfolk, the Earl of Bedford, and the Earl of Dorset. Holy Trinity Priory at Aldgate was given to the Lord Chancellor, Thomas Audley, who had been the judge at the trial of Thomas More.

Of the eight or nine hundred monasteries, priories, and other religious institutions destroyed at this time, around

[6] Cobbett, *History of the Protestant Reformation*, 70.
[7] Simon Jenkins, *A Short History of London* (London: Viking, 2019), 45.

150 were nunneries, a little more than half of which were Benedictine. Some of these were of great antiquity, such as those at Barking, Romsey, and Wilton, which had been established from the earliest days of Anglo-Saxon Christianity, almost a thousand years earlier.

Except for the Holy Maid of Kent, the nuns of England were spared the death penalty. The government was generally reluctant to make martyrs of women, though there were exceptions, and the convents were less powerful and of less consequence than the monasteries. The nuns were simply dispossessed of their convents and dispersed into the general community, with or without adequate pensions, presumably returning to their families. It seems from the surviving evidence that most of them continued to live according to their vows, as far as this was possible. In diverse places, small groups were found living together, trying to live their former observance, as discretely as the hostile times demanded. The last prioress of the Benedictine convent at Thetford in Norfolk, Elizabeth Hothe, was discovered in 1553 to be living in Norwich on the same miserly annual pension of £5 which she had been granted fifteen years earlier. Reportedly now being a hundred years old, she had "nothing to live upon but the same pension, and is reputed a good and catholic woman".[8]

The thousands of monks and nuns made homeless by the avarice of the king and his partners in plunder were not, by any means, the only people to suffer. It was the poorest who suffered most as the richest became richer still. The monasteries were the centres of charity, dispensing help to the sick, disabled, and the destitute, as well as providing education.

---

[8] Benedictines of Stanbrook, *In a Great Tradition: Tribute to Dame Laurentia McLachlan, Abbess of Stanbrook* (London: John Murray, 1956), 69.

All of this disappeared overnight, leaving the weakest and most vulnerable without any recourse for help. In London, as the monasteries disappeared, "the poor, sick, blind, aged and impotent ... were lying in the street, offending every clean person passing by with their filthy and nasty savours."[9] Nor was the problem restricted to London. Throughout the country, the monasteries had exercised hospitality to waifs and wayfarers and generosity to the poor. They educated the young and were far more generous as landlords than the new secular lords of the manor would prove to be. Everybody but the king and his partners in crime were victims of the pillaging of the Church. "Here was a breach of Magna Charter in the first place," wrote William Cobbett, "a robbery of the monks and nuns in the next place, and, in the third place, a robbery of the indigent, the widow, the orphan and the stranger."[10]

The charity of the monasteries was replaced with the brutality of the state. As the country swarmed with beggars, bereft of any means of assistance, laws were passed which made war on the weak and defenceless. The persevering beggar was punished by having part of his ears severed and, should this not prove a sufficient deterrent, he would be put to death if convicted of begging again. Such was the compassion Henry VIII exhibited to the poor whom his own avarice had left bereft of any option but to beg.

The horrors that befell the people of England following the dissolution of the monasteries provoked even Protestants to consider it a crime and a disgrace. Robert Crowley, the Protestant printer, poet, and polemicist, was no friend of the Church, and yet, as these lines of verse

---

[9] Jenkins, *Short History of London*, 46.
[10] Cobbett, *History of the Protestant Reformation*, 68.

illustrate, he was distressed by the consequences of Henry's avaricious debauch:

> As I walked alone
> and mused on things,
> That have in my time
> been done by great kings,
> I bethought me of abbeys,
> that sometime I saw,
> Which now are suppressed
> all by a law.
> O Lord, (thought I then)
> what occasion was here
> To provide for learning
> and make poverty clear.
> The land and the jewels
> that hereby were had
> Would have found godly preachers
> which might well have led
> The people aright
> that now go astray
> And have fed the poor
> that famish every day.[11]

In similar fashion, the Protestant historian Paul Henri Mallet wrote of how "the monks softened ... the ferocious manners of the people, and opposed ... the tyranny of the nobility, who knew no other occupation than war and grievously oppressed their neighbours. On this account the government of monks was preferred to theirs.... It was an unusual saying, that it was better to be governed by the bishop's crozier than the monarch's scepter."[12]

[11] Kenneth Baker, ed., *The Faber Book of English History in Verse* (London: Faber & Faber, 1988), 115.

[12] Quoted in Cobbett, *History of the Protestant Reformation*, 244–45.

As the pillage and plunder continued, it was not the case, as Chesterton implied, that the people of England "did not speak". They rose in anger in a rebellion that became known as the Pilgrimage of Grace. Apart from the widespread dismay at the dissolution of the monasteries and its harmful consequences, there was a general disdain for Thomas Cranmer and other heretic bishops, and an equal disdain for Thomas Cromwell and the malevolent and self-serving courtiers with whom the king had surrounded himself. There is no doubt, however, that the king's attack on the Church was the spark that lit the fuse of open revolt. The monasteries were at the very core of the social fabric and social welfare of local communities, and the people rightly perceived the destruction of the monasteries as an attack upon their own way of life. There were also rumours that the king's "reformation" would lead to the closure of parish churches, and the stripping of their wealth, which had been supplied by the generosity of local guilds and by the financial sacrifice of local people.

At the beginning of October 1536, a sermon in the parish church of Louth in Lincolnshire sparked the uprising. Within a week, a people's army had occupied Lincoln. The rising spread to the north, the whole of Yorkshire rising in protest. According to the historian Gerard Culkin, the rising of the north of England in protest at the king's "reformation" was "the most serious threat to his throne ... in all the long years of his reign".[13] Thousands of men from all parts of Yorkshire and beyond descended on York to join the people's army which had assembled there under the leadership of Robert Aske, a London attorney. Under his guidance, the revolt became a pilgrimage for the

[13] Gerard Culkin, *The English Reformation* (London: Sands, 1955), 46.

restoration of religion and religious liberty. The pilgrims wore a badge depicting the Five Wounds of Christ and swore an oath to exalt and defend the Church. Aske composed a proclamation, itemizing the purpose and demands of the Pilgrimage, which was presented to the king.

Henry was alarmed by the uprising and had every reason for being so. The Duke of Norfolk, whom Henry had appointed to deal with the uprising, warned him that the royal forces, numbering only eight thousand men, were no match for the forty thousand rebels who now included in their ranks "all the flower of the North". Furthermore, and of even greater concern, the duke reported that the king's own troops "think their quarrel to be good and godly".[14] Faced with such unwelcome news, the king had little option but to negotiate. On December 5, the Duke of Norfolk, as the king's representative, met the leaders of the Pilgrimage at Doncaster and received the list of their demands. The first demand was for the suppression of heresy, the second was for the restoration of the pope's authority in spiritual matters, and the third was for the restoration of the suppressed abbeys. Gerard Culkin states that these principal demands of the Pilgrimage served as proof "that there was no popular support for Henry in his quarrel with the Pope once he began to attack Catholic teaching [and] that the people understood and disapproved of what Henry had done when he made himself Pope in England".[15] As for Robert Aske, who had taken up residence at the friary which housed the shrine to Our Lady of Doncaster, he stated that "every man grudged the Supremacy." Then he added, speaking for himself, that he was willing to die,

[14] Ibid., 46–47.
[15] Ibid., 48.

"unless the bishop of Rome was head of the Church in England as heretofore".[16]

Powerless to put down the Pilgrimage of Grace by military means, Henry employed that other weapon of the cynical machiavel: the power of the lie. Promising concessions and a general pardon for all who had taken part in the Pilgrimage, Henry persuaded the good-natured but gullible Aske to order the rebels to disperse and disarm. As soon as the tens of thousands of "pilgrims" had returned home, Henry moved his troops into the north of the country. He was now in a position to force his own will on the people. Robert Aske was executed in York on July 12, 1537, and a further two hundred or so would suffer a similar fate. The king then stepped up his war on the remaining abbeys, accusing the abbots and monks of complicity in the Pilgrimage and executing them as traitors. The abbots of Jervaulx and Fountains and the prior of Bridlington were executed at Tyburn. With the popular uprising defeated by the king's dissimulation, deception, and broken promises, the Church was now utterly defenceless. By 1540, every remaining monastery and religious house in England had been destroyed, its wealth passing into the hands of the ignoble nobility. "The carcass being thus laid prostrate," wrote William Cobbett, "the rapacious vultures who had assisted in the work flew on it and began to tear it in pieces. The people here and there rose in insurrection against the tyrant's satellites; but deprived of their natural leaders, who had for the most part placed themselves on the side of the tyranny and plunder, what were the mere common people to do?"[17]

[16] Ibid.
[17] Cobbett, *History of the Protestant Reformation*, 71.

The long-term effect of the dissolution of the monasteries would be nothing less than seismic in terms of its
indelible and devastating impact on the very sociopolitical
structure of England. It led to the erosion of the power of
the common people but also, and ironically, the erosion
of the power of the monarchy. "Nothing that the Crown
let go ever went back to the Crown," wrote Belloc, "and
year after year more and more of what had once been the
monastic land became the absolute possession of the large
landowners."[18] The landed gentry, which already possessed
between a quarter and a third of the nation's property, both
land and capital, "the soil and the ploughs and the barns
of a village", now possessed the land previously owned by
the monasteries, tipping the scale decisively in their favour
in terms of economic and political power. "They became
at a blow the owners of *half* the land! In many centers of
capital importance they had come to own *more* than half the
land."[19] This new class of landed aristocrats became "the
economic masters of the rest of the community", transforming England from being a monarchy, in which the
power of the king had been limited by law, into a self-
serving plutocracy which was a law unto itself:

> Thus the main consequence of the dissolution of the mon-
> asteries was the impoverishment of the Crown and the
> great increase in economic power of the landed classes.
> These from the next generation onward became more
> and more important as against the declining power of the
> King; at the end of a century the landed gentry of England
> were to destroy that kingly government, and were to take
> over power.[20]

[18] Hilaire Belloc, *The Servile State* (Indianapolis: Liberty Classics, 1977), 92.
[19] Ibid.
[20] Hilaire Belloc, *A Shorter History of England* (London: George G. Harrap,
1934), 278.

Having destroyed the monasteries, the plunderers turned their attention to the numerous shrines to the Blessed Virgin and the saints which had been a central part of English life for more than a thousand years. Henry took a sadistic pleasure in destroying the shrine in Canterbury to St. Thomas Becket, the saint who had faced down the power of the king, stripping the magnificent shrine of its many treasures. The same fate awaited the many Marian shrines around the country, as this report sent to Thomas Cromwell by one of his minions demonstrates:

> In my most humble manner I have me commended unto your good Lordship ascertaining the same that I have pulled down the image of Our Lady of Caversham, whereunto was great pilgrimage. The image is plated over with silver and I have put it in a chest fast locked and nailed up, and by the next barge that cometh from Reading to London it shall be brought to your Lordship. I have also pulled down the place she stood in, with all other ceremonies, as lights, shrouds, crutches, and images of wax hanging about the Chapel, and have defaced the same thoroughly in eschewing of any further resort thither.[21]

In another letter, the same correspondent informed his master of the property attached to the shrine: "At Caversham is a proper lodging where the Canon lay, with a fair garden and an orchard meet to be bestowed upon some friend of Your Lordship's in these parts."[22]

It was inevitable that the avaricious eyes of the king and Cromwell would eventually fall on the shrine of Our Lady of Walsingham, the place of pilgrimage which was the very heartbeat of the England which saw itself as Our Lady's Dowry. This heart needed to be broken and then

---

[21] Gillett, *Shrines of Our Lady in England and Wales*, 83.
[22] Ibid., 85.

ripped out so that the destruction and desecration of Merrie England could be complete.

Cromwell met with initial resistance as he turned his
attention to England's most important shrine to the Virgin.
"The initial attempt to sweep away the ancient sanctuary
which meant so much to English hearts had met with sharp
protest," wrote H. M. Gillett.[23] In the naïve belief that it
was still possible to reason with the king, the leaders of the
protest, Nicholas Mileham, the subprior of Walsingham,
and his chief ally, George Guisborough, had petitioned
Henry and, in consequence, were charged with treason
and sentenced to death, being butchered in front of the
very gates of Walsingham Priory. Nine others shared the
same fate, being slaughtered and quartered in other parts of
Norfolk. The people looked upon these martyrs as heroes,
but they were powerless to stop the pillaging of the shrine
which followed. On July 14, 1538, the image of Our Lady
of Walsingham was taken from the shrine, together with
all the wealth which surrounded it. The image was taken
to London and was burned at Cromwell's house in Chelsea, together with the images of Our Lady of Ipswich and
Our Lady of Pen-Rhys, as well as statues from several
other Marian shrines.

It is difficult to contemplate the desolation that this desecration of England's holiest shrine must have engendered
in the hearts of the Catholic faithful who still constituted
the vast majority of the population. It was captured best,
perhaps, in the words of a poem, sometimes called "A
Lament for Walsingham", which is believed to have been
written by St. Philip Howard, Earl of Arundel, who was
destined to die a martyr's death during the reign of Elizabeth I.

[23] Ibid., 95.

In the wracks of Walsingham
Whom should I choose
But the Queen of Walsingham
to be my guide and muse.

Then, thou Prince of Walsingham,
Grant me to frame
Bitter plaints to rue thy wrong,
Bitter woe for thy name.

Bitter was it so to see
The seely sheep
Murdered by the ravenous wolves
While the shepherds did sleep.

Bitter was it, O to view
The sacred vine,
Whilst the gardeners played all close,
Rooted up by the swine.

Bitter, bitter, O to behold
The grass to grow
Where the walls of Walsingham
So stately did show.

Such were the worth of Walsingham
While she did stand,
Such are the wracks as now do show
Of that Holy Land.

Level, level, with the ground
The towers do lie,
Which, with their golden glittering tops,
Pierced once to the sky.

Where were gates are no gates now,
The ways unknown
Where the press of peers did pass
While her fame was blown.

Owls do scrike where the sweetest hymns
Lately were sung,
Toads and serpents hold their dens
Where the palmers did throng.

Weep, weep, O Walsingham,
Whose days are nights,
Blessings turned to blasphemies,
Holy deeds to despites.

Sin is where Our Lady sat,
Heaven is turned to hell,
Satan sits where Our Lord did sway—
Walsingham, O farewell!

Chapter Eleven

A Protestant Puppet

What should I say?
Since Faith is dead,
And Truth away
From you is fled?
Should I be led
With doubleness?

—Sir Thomas Wyatt,
from "A Revocation"

Still desperate for a male heir, Henry became betrothed to Lady Jane Seymour on May 20, 1536, a day after the execution of his second wife, Anne Boleyn. After a betrothal of only ten days, Henry and Jane Seymour were married. In October of the following year, the queen gave birth to the future Edward VI. She died several days later from complications arising from the long and difficult labour. According to the historian Sir Richard Baker in his *Chronicle of the Kings of England*, the queen "had her body ripped up to preserve the child".[1] Although later biographers give less credence to such a gruesome scenario, Henry's history of desperate measures to secure a male heir, coupled

[1] Quoted in William Cobbett, *A History of the Protestant Reformation* (Sevenoaks, Kent: Fisher Press, 1994), 43.

with his brutal treatment of anyone who crossed his will, renders it more than plausible that he would have been willing to sacrifice the mother for the child.

One of the most egregious examples of Henry's heartless cruelty to those whom he had once held in high regard is his treatment of Lady Margaret Pole, mother of Cardinal Pole. Lady Margaret was a direct descendant of the royal house of Plantagenet, the dynasty that had ruled England for 331 years, from 1154 until 1485. She was a niece of both Edward IV and Richard III. Held in high favour by Catherine of Aragon, she became godmother and later governess to the princess Mary. As for the king, he had once held Margaret Pole in the highest favour, describing her as the most saintly woman in England.[2]

All was well until Henry decided to divorce Catherine. A staunch Catholic, Lady Margaret opposed the divorce and refused to acknowledge Anne Boleyn as queen. Seeking to live a peaceful life and not wishing to be pressured to compromise her principles, she retired from court to Warblington Castle, her moated home on the Sussex coast. She might have been left alone had it not been for her son's vociferous condemnation of Henry's attacks upon the Church, issued in 1536 from the safety of his exile in Rome. Reginald Pole's *Unitate Ecclesiae* had infuriated the king, a fury which was heightened still further by Pole's being made a cardinal by the pope. Unable to get his hands on Cardinal Pole, he exacted his revenge by turning on Pole's family, warning the French ambassador that he intended to kill the lot of them.[3] Lady Margaret's

---

[2] Peter Stanford and Leanda de Lisle, *The Catholics and Their Houses* (London: Harper Collins, 1995), 4.

[3] Ibid., 5.

son Geoffrey and her son-in-law Henry, Lord Montague, were arrested, as was Montague's cousin, the Marquis of Exeter. In 1539, Geoffrey was pressured into turning king's evidence, which was sufficient to condemn his confreres to death.

Nor were the children of the condemned men spared. Lord Montague's son was imprisoned in the Tower of London, never to be seen again, and the Marquis of Exeter's son spent his entire childhood and adolescence in the Tower, not being released until Mary became queen in 1553. Those visiting the Tower of London can still see the pathetic inscriptions carved by these two children on their dungeon walls.

As for Geoffrey, his life was spared as a reward for his treachery. "[A] pariah with the blood of his family on his hands, ... he spent the rest of his life wandering around Europe demented with remorse."[4]

Finding his lust for vengeance unassuaged by the arrest and subsequent execution and imprisonment of the male members of Cardinal Pole's family, the king ordered the arrest of the "most saintly woman in England", the godmother of his daughter. With unremitting courage, Margaret Pole refused to confess to any "Catholic plot" against the king and insisted that she was guilty of no wrongdoing. Since her innocence or otherwise was of no concern to Henry, she was condemned without trial and imprisoned for two years in the Tower of London, in the same place in which her grandson was also confined. Struggling with the chill and damp of her cell, and "tormented by the severity of the weather and insufficient clothing", she was finally led to the executioner's block

[4] Ibid.

on the morning of May 27, 1541. She was now sixty-seven years old. It was said that, when asked to lay her head upon the block, she had refused. "No," she is said to have replied, "my head shall never bow to tyranny: it never committed treason; and if you will have it, you must get it as you can."[5] According to traditional accounts, the executioner, who was young, inexperienced, and drunk, had to chase the old lady round the scaffold, lunging at her clumsily with his axe, striking her with the blade half a dozen times before completing his grotesque task. Since, however, the execution was carried out in private, within the Tower, there were no witnesses to confirm or deny such stories. "Though it might make a colourful story for Beefeaters to tell impressionable tourists," wrote Nicholas Schofield and Gerard Skinner, "the truth is that Lady Margaret died with dignity despite the fact that the novice headsman 'hacked her head and shoulders almost to pieces'."[6]

Even after he had killed the old woman, who had been a close friend and confidante of his first wife and a second mother to his daughter, Henry's desire for vengeance against Cardinal Pole was still not satisfied. Ignoring Margaret Pole's desire to be buried in a beautiful chantry she had prepared at Christchurch Priory, he insisted that she be buried in the Tower of London. He then seized her property, including Warblington Castle, bestowing it upon his "true servants".

If Henry had hoped that his spleen-venting vengeance would cause Cardinal Pole to collapse in an apoplexy

---

[5] Cobbett, *History of the Protestant Reformation*, 46.

[6] Nicholas Schofield and Gerard Skinner, *The English Cardinals* (Oxford: Family Publications, 2007), 112.

of remorse and regret having dared condemn the king's attacks upon the Church, he was to be disappointed. The cardinal's response was dignified by the faith that he and his mother professed: "Until now I had thought God had given me the grace of being the son of one of the best and most honoured ladies in England ... but now he has vouchsafed to honour me still more by making me the son of a martyr.... Let us rejoice, for we have another advocate in heaven."[7] Cardinal Pole's judgement was confirmed more than three hundred years later, in 1886, when Pope Leo XIII beatified Lady Margaret Pole as a martyr. As for the cardinal himself, he declared that if his own slaughter could bring about the king's conversion, he would desire it at once.[8]

Henry VIII died in January 1547, bringing to an end one of the most draconian periods in all of history. His lamentable legacy was summarized candidly and succinctly by Hilaire Belloc:

> Henry ruled by terror during all the later part of his life.... Men yielded to new and dreadful powers abominably exercised for coercion, and very nearly all—all save a handful of heroic monks and the two shining examples of Fisher and More—became abject. Cranmer's complete abandonment of all morals and dignity under the effect of the terror is so extreme as to be grimly comic. Cromwell's is pitiful, falling at last to a whining letter squealing for life and begging to kiss once more the royal hand and smell its heavenly savour.[9]

[7] Claude Williamson, ed., *Great Catholics* (London: Nicholson and Watson, 1938), 180.

[8] Ibid.

[9] Hilaire Belloc, *Wolsey* (London: Cassell, 1930), 273–74.

Belloc's appraisal of Henry's legacy, as candid as it is, pales beside the unremitting fervor of William Cobbett's condemnation of his reign:

All law and justice were laid prostrate at the feet of a single man, and that man a man with whom law was a mockery, on whom the name of justice was a libel, and to whom mercy was wholly unknown.

It is easy to imagine that no man's property or life could have security with power like this in the hands of such a man. Magna Charter had been trampled under foot from the moment that the Pope's supremacy was assailed. The famous act of Edward the Third, for the security of the people against unfounded charges of high treason, was wholly set aside. Numerous things were made high treason which were never before thought criminal at all. The trials were for a long while a mere mockery, and at last they were altogether, in many cases, laid aside and the accused were condemned to death, not only without being arraigned and heard in their defence, but in numerous cases without being apprised of the crimes or pretended crimes for which they were executed. He spared neither sex nor age if the parties possessed, or were suspected of possessing, that integrity which made them disapprove of his deeds. To look awry excited his suspicion, and his suspicion was death. England, before his reign so happy, so free, knowing so little of crime ... now saw upwards of sixty thousand persons shut up in her jails at one and the same time.... His people, deserted by their natural leaders, who had been bribed by plunder or the hope of plunder, were the terrified and trembling flock; while he, the master-butcher, fat and jocose, sat in the palace issuing orders for the slaughter, while his high priest, Cranmer, stood ready to sanction and to sanctify all his deeds.[10]

[10] Cobbett, *History of Protestant Reformation*, 44–45.

Such is the enormity of Henry VIII's destructive and tyrannical impact, and such is the sheer grossness of his "achievement", that Cobbett's splenetic pouring forth of his scorn at the king and his diabolical work does not seem the least out of place or hyperbolic. For Cobbett, Henry was "the most unjust, hard-hearted, meanest and most sanguinary tyrant that the world had ever beheld, whether Christian or heathen", a judgement that is too shrill, indubitably, but not unwarranted. Who, at any rate, will step forward in Henry's defence, even in the presence of such a sweeping and over-the-top appraisal of his place in history? Even if Cobbett goes too far, we are not minded to contradict him, even as many other tyrants, probably even worse, come to mind.

And he continues. The England which Henry had "found in peace, unity, plenty and happiness, he left torn by factions and schisms". His Machiavellian realpolitik had "laid the foundations of immorality, dishonesty and pauperism", the bitter harvest of which would be reaped by the English people for centuries to come.[11] Nor was Cobbett the only nineteenth-century author to write so scathingly of Henry VIII. Charles Dickens was equally strident in his condemnation: "The plain truth is, that he was a most intolerable ruffian, a disgrace to human nature, and a blot of blood and grease upon the History of England."[12]

Having bid a less than fond farewell to Henry VIII, we will now turn our attention to what Cobbett referred to as "the reigns of his unhappy, barren, mischievous and miserable children, with whom, at the end of a few years, his house and his name were extinguished forever".

---

[11] Ibid., 83.
[12] Quoted in Kenneth Baker, ed., *The Faber Book of English History in Verse* (London: Faber & Faber, 1988), 115.

Upon Henry's death, Cardinal Pole wrote to Pope Paul III in the optimistic and premature hope that it might now be possible to restore England to communion with the Holy See. The pope appointed him as legate, and Pole wrote to the Privy Council, requesting that he be received in the pope's name. The Council refused to even read the letter, signifying the contempt and hostility which would characterize the reign of Edward VI, Henry's only male heir, in its relationship with the Church. If anything, the war on the Church was even more vicious during the reign of Edward than it had been during the reign of his father. Since the new king was only nine years old, the government was run by what the historian Gerard Culkin called "a band of unscrupulous adventurers who ruled in the name of the boy king".[13]

During the six years of Edward's rule, the Mass was abolished, the altars destroyed, and a new Protestant liturgy, including a new profession of faith, was imposed upon the people of England. Ironically, considering Henry's famous defence of the seven sacraments of the Church in his riposte to Luther, his *Assertio Septem Sacramentorum*, all but two of the sacraments would be abolished during the reign of his son. Encouraged by the government, "foreign Protestants swarmed into the country"[14] and were given key posts in the universities. All of this was enacted by the clique who ruled in the king's name without any consultation with either the English people or the English Church. Any who opposed this revolution masquerading as "reform" were sent to the Tower or scaffold, or both. Stephen Gardiner, the Bishop of Winchester, was sent to prison for refusing to teach the Protestant doctrines

---

[13] Gerard Culkin, *The English Reformation* (London: Sands, 1955), 1.
[14] Ibid., 2.

now mandated by Thomas Cranmer, the Archbishop of Canterbury—the remainder of the bishops, with a few noble exceptions, being as craven under Edward as they had proved themselves to be under Edward's father.

Amidst the religious "reform", the pillaging of the churches continued. We have already mentioned how the Earl of Somerset, abusing his authority as Lord Protector of England, had awarded Glastonbury Abbey to himself, and this spirit of self-enrichment and self-empowerment animated an Act of Parliament in November 1547 which assigned all chantries and free chapels to the Crown. With the monasteries and abbeys already devoured by the avaricious feeding frenzy, the cormorants were now picking the last meat from the bones of the Church's wealth, as Henry himself had predicted.

Another law, or "injunction", promulgated in 1547, condemned "wandering to pilgrimages", kissing of relics, the praying of the Rosary, the burning of candles, and other "such like superstition". Religious processions were banned, as were all remaining relics, images, pictures, and paintings in churches, which were "monuments of feigned miracles, pilgrimage, idolatry and superstition". The destruction was to include any images "in glass windows". This went even beyond the practice in avowedly Protestant jurisdictions overseas, such as Zwingli's Zurich, in which stained glass windows were permitted to remain untouched on the not unreasonable assumption that people did not kneel before images in windows to venerate them. The ringing of bells was forbidden during religious services, "except one bell in convenient time to be rung or knolled before the sermon".[15]

---

[15] Eamon Duffy, *The Stripping of the Altars* (London: Yale University Press, 1992), 450–52.

In December 1547, a royal proclamation was issued which forbade any public discussion of the doctrine of the Eucharist "till the king, by the advice of his council and clergy, should define the doctrine, and what form of words might safely be used about it".[16]

As for the treatment of the poor, who had been plunged into penury by the destruction of the monasteries and the charitable support the monasteries had offered, Edward was even more tyrannical than his father. An Act of Parliament passed at the beginning of his reign sanctioned the punishment of beggars through the branding of them with a red-hot iron and by making them slaves for two years, during which time they could be forced to wear an iron collar and be fed on nothing but bread and water. The condition of the poor was made worse by the new plutocracy's stealing of the common land. This land, held in common by each village, enabled the poor to graze livestock, the keeping of which was a key component of the rural economy. The seizure of these commons and their enclosure for use as private farmland by the new lords of the manor, squatting luxuriously on the property they had stolen from the Church, had calamitous consequences for the common folk who now had no land on which to keep the livestock on which they depended for sustenance.

The English people, mindful of the ruthless and deadly punishment that awaited any outward sign of dissent, tolerated the tyranny in sullen silence. It was, however, the introduction of the new Protestant service at Whitsuntide in 1549 and the consequent definitive banning of the Mass which finally caused the people to rise in anger. The imposition of an unwanted Protestantism and the banishment

---

[16] Culkin, *English Reformation*, 67.

of the Mass, the sacrificial heart of Christian worship, was met with active opposition across the country. In London, Bishop Bonner protested and was deposed and imprisoned. Dissent and resistance were rife in the universities, at Oxford and Cambridge, but it was in the west of the country that the most spirited resistance arose. The people of Devon and Cornwall likened the new state-imposed Protestant service to a "Christmas game", a mere mummery,[17] and rose in violent rebellion. Demanding the withdrawal of the new service and the restoration of the Mass, the Catholic insurgents succeeded in having the Mass restored in the west of the country. Similar popular risings happened in other parts of England.

"The people rose everywhere," wrote Hilaire Belloc, "save in the north."[18] Although the north of England was the most Catholic part of the country, the people of the north could still remember the brutal suppression of the Pilgrimage of Grace only twelve years earlier, "and the dreadful massacres which had followed its repression". After that earlier rising, which was in defence of the monasteries, the north had been put under martial law. "There had been hangings in every village, and a general butchery by the Royal troops before the regular executions began."[19] Belloc continues:

Elsewere than in the north, save within striking distance of the government in London, the explosions were universal. The populace rose in Sussex as in Somerset; in the Midlands, Leicestershire, Worcestershire, Rutlandshire, Warwickshire; in Suffolk as in Surrey, in Hampshire and Berkshire, even in Hertfordshire within a day's ride of

[17] Ibid., 71.
[18] Hilaire Belloc, *Cranmer* (London: Cassell, 1931), 247.
[19] Ibid.

London, even in Essex where they were so near to the power of the government.

They were unorganized, they had no leaders, for the gentry were united against them—being now the possessors of the Church loot and the authors of the new thefts of commons and guild property and the rest. In Buckinghamshire [the rebels] became formidable; in Oxfordshire they were very nearly successful; but the most important centres were those in which they did manage to get someone who could organize them.[20]

The rebels of the west, who rose on the day after the imposition of the new Protestant service, were under the leadership of Sir Humphrey Arundel. With a force of between seven thousand and ten thousand men, they attempted to take the city of Exeter before being defeated by a much better armed royal army. In Norfolk, the rebels were led by a local landowner, Robert Kett. Beginning as a protest against the enclosure of common land, it quickly became part of the general rising of the people against the tyranny being imposed by the new plutocracy and its Protestant allies. Kett and his army of some sixteen thousand men encamped on Mousehold Heath, near Norwich, and then marched upon and took the city itself. In early August, the rebels defeated an army sent by the government, led by the Marquess of Northampton, but were finally defeated by a royal army under the Earl of Warwick.[21]

Hilaire Belloc attributed the victory of the government to "the presence on English soil of well-trained foreign

[20] Ibid.

[21] Such is the ignorance of history and the ingrained anti-Catholicism of contemporary culture that the poet Keith Chandler, in his poem about Kett's Rebellion, writes of the victors calling for "a Thanksgiving Mass" to celebrate the defeat of the rebels.

mercenaries, Italian and German, taking government pay
and willing to obey any orders for the cutting down of
English men and women, to whose lives they were naturally indifferent. It was with the aid of these," Belloc continued, "and of its artillery, that the government at last
obtained the victory."[22]

Once again, the English had risen against the imposition
of the state religion and once again the government had
seen itself on the brink of collapse. It saved itself, once
again, through the merciless suppression of all dissent. In
Oxfordshire, dozens of priests were hanged from the stee-
ples of their own churches for their complicity in the rising of the people in defence of the Mass. Sir Humphrey
Arundel was executed at Tyburn, and Robert Kett was
hanged for treason from the walls of Norwich Castle. It
is estimated that almost half of those who rose against the
government in Devon and Cornwall were killed—almost
four thousand people, both armed and unarmed, put to
the sword by the foreign mercenaries. These merciless
mercenaries also slaughtered three thousand of those who
had followed Kett in Norfolk, with a further three hundred of his followers subsequently being hanged. Parliament passed laws in the wake of the uprisings making it
a crime to organize political meetings and even to speak
publicly about changing the law. Further laws were passed
in which the newly enriched landed gentry gave themselves the right to enclose all the common land, attaching
the heaviest penalties to any future resistance to this theft
of the people's commonly held inheritance.

Ironically, having used his troops to put down the rebellion of the English people, the Earl of Warwick turned his
forces on the government itself, overthrowing the regime

---

[22] Belloc, *Cranmer*, 248.

of the Earl of Somerset, who would later be executed. He ruled the country as a de facto dictator, with the king as his puppet, from the end of 1549 until the death of Edward VI in 1553. This change of ruler made little difference to the people of England, however, who were simply being governed by a new anti-Catholic tyrant.

Even as the Earl of Warwick was plotting to seize control of the English government, an Englishman of a very different ilk was at the conclave in Rome to elect a successor to Pope Paul III, who had died in November 1549. Cardinal Pole stood in very high favour in the conclave. At the third scrutiny, he received twenty-six votes. Two more would have sufficed to make him pope. Eventually, Cardinal Del Monte was elected, taking the name of Julius III. Pole's humble acceptance of the will of the conclave was exemplified in his comment that "the Lord did not require this particular ass."[23]

Back in England, the Earl of Warwick, now elevated in noble rank to the Duke of Northumberland, sought to consolidate his power through the forging of an alliance with the extreme Protestants, even though he himself seemed to have no particular religious affiliation and would die on the scaffold in 1553 professing himself a Catholic. One of the first actions of his government was the passing of an Act ordering the confiscation and destruction of the old Catholic service books, intending thereby to destroy even the memory of the Mass and to make efforts at Catholic restoration more difficult. As with all totalitarian regimes, the burning of books and the smothering of all memories of the past and its traditions were necessary prerequisites for the new revolutionary order. A further Act ordered the destruction of all religious images

---

[23] Williamson, *Great Catholics*, 181.

that had somehow escaped the earlier waves of destruction and desecration. Then, in 1551, a commission was
appointed to make inventories of the church plate, altar
vessels, vestments, and jewels in every church in the country. These were then confiscated, becoming the property
of the Crown, "to be employed unto his Highness' use".[24]
Having gorged themselves on the flesh of the monasteries
and abbeys, and having picked the bones of the chantries
and the free chapels, the cormorants now set to feasting
on the wealth of every parish church in the land. Apart
from impoverishing every church in England, aesthetically
as well as financially, this act of daylight robbery left the
secular clergy in a state of utter poverty.

Bishops were deposed and imprisoned for their opposition to the government's sacrilegious policy, and others were "persuaded" to resign. The sees of Durham,
Westminster, and Gloucester were suppressed, and their
wealth and revenue confiscated. The see of Lincoln was
left vacant for a year, enabling it to be plundered all the
more easily. The puppet king, at the behest of his "Protector", appointed new bishops whose only qualification was
complete acquiescence in the tyrannical acts of England's
dictator. Nicholas Ridley, Bishop of Rochester, was promoted to Bishop of London and immediately ordered the
destruction of all the altars in his diocese. Consider this
man in relation to St. John Fisher, who had been Bishop
of Rochester only twenty years earlier, and consider how
England had fallen in the wake of Henry's megalomaniacal
war on the Church.

Bishop John Hooper, an apostate monk who was fanatical in his advocacy of Protestant "reform", was made
Bishop of Gloucester and, later, Bishop of Worcester;

---

[24] Culkin, *English Reformation*, 74.

Bishop Myles Coverdale, another apostate monk whose Protestant spin on the New Testament had been too much even for Henry VIII to tolerate, was made Bishop of Exeter; and Bishop John Ponet, who succeeded Ridley as Bishop of Rochester, was not merely one of the most vocal of the Protestant "reformers" but was also a bigamist, whose marriage to a butcher's wife while the butcher was still alive caused scandal even in such a scandalous age.

In such a "reformist" culture, it was no surprise that Archbishop Cranmer's revised Prayer Book should be imposed on the whole country by the Act of Uniformity in 1552. Far more overtly Protestant than the earlier version, it essentially forced upon an unwilling population the heretical doctrines of John Calvin.

In the months following the imposition of the new Prayer Book, the "reformers" also published a new catechism and a revision of canon law, the latter insisting on the duty of the monarch to maintain uniformity of religion by punishing dissent with death, and also legalizing divorce in defiance of both the words of Christ and the teaching of the Church.

As for the ordinary people of England, they treated all of this with contempt. It was the work of the tyrants who had stripped them of the faith of their fathers and which had plunged them into depths of poverty, through the removal of the monasteries, their safety net in times of hardship or sickness; through the enclosure of the common land, the foundation of their economic sustenance; and through the destruction of the guilds, their guarantor of economic independence and cultural cohesion. What had any of this "reform" to do with the ordinary people of England? It was the work of the machiavels and the plutocrats who had made themselves rich on the pickings of the Church and the vulnerability of the poor.

There was hope, however, in the fact that the boy king, a fanatical Protestant under the "protection" of fanatical Protestants, was clearly on the point of death. His father, the tyrant Henry, had stipulated that Edward's half-sister Mary should be heir to the throne should Edward have no issue. Mary was known to be a devout Catholic. It was hoped that all would be well when she became queen.

Chapter Twelve

Mary Tudor

Enter Queen Mary, with a prayer-book in her hand, like a nun.
MARY: Thus like a nun, not like a princess born,
Descended from the royal Henry's loins,
Live I environ'd in a house of stone.
My brother Edward lives in pomp and state;
I in a mansion here all ruinate.
Their rich attire, delicious banqueting,
Their several pleasures, all their pride and honour,
I have forsaken for a rich prayer-book.
The golden mines of wealthy India
Are all as dross compared to thy sweetness:
Thou art the joy and comfort of the poor;
The everlasting bliss in thee we find.
This little volume enclosed in this hand,
Is richer than the empire of this land.

—John Webster, from *Lady Jane Grey*

If it is true that history is written by the victors, there can be few more egregious examples of the distortion of history by the victorious party than the way in which the two Tudor queens of England, Mary and Elizabeth, have been portrayed in what Hilaire Belloc derided as "tom-fool Protestant history".[1] Belloc lamented that "most people are still steeped in that false official history which warps all English life,"[2] which was why he embarked upon the "weary work [of] fighting this enormous mountain of ignorant wickedness".[3] In similar vein, though writing a century earlier, William Cobbett waxed indignant in the face of this Whig propaganda masquerading as history:

We are now entering upon that reign the punishments inflicted during which have furnished such a handle to the calumniators of the Catholic Church, who have left no art untried to exaggerate those punishments in the first place, and in the second place to ascribe them to the Catholic religion, keeping out of sight all the while the thousand times greater mass of cruelty occasioned by the Protestants in this kingdom.[4]

Cobbett distanced himself from all acts of cruelty, irrespective of who perpetrated them, stating that he had no intention of defending "all the punishments inflicted ... in the reign of Queen Mary", but, "as to the Queen herself, she was one of the most virtuous of human beings."[5] On this account he was outraged that England's "official" history speaks of "Bloody Mary" and "Good Queen Bess",

[1] Hilaire Belloc to Hoffman Nickerson, 13 September 1923, Belloc Collection, Boston College; quoted in Joseph Pearce, *Old Thunder: A Life of Hilaire Belloc* (San Francisco: Ignatius Press, 2002), 230.

[2] Hilaire Belloc—Elizabeth Belloc Correspondence, Special Collection, Georgetown University, Washington, D.C.; quoted in Pearce, *Old Thunder*, 229.

[3] Belloc to Nickerson, 13 September 1923; quoted in Pearce, *Old Thunder*, 230.

[4] William Cobbett, *A History of the Protestant Reformation* (Sevenoaks, Kent: Fisher Press, 1994), 98.

[5] Ibid.

failing to mention that "for every drop of blood that Mary shed Elizabeth shed a pint."[6]

Although Henry VIII had decreed that Mary should succeed Edward, were Edward to die without a direct heir, the boy king's "protector", the Duke of Northumberland, persuaded him to override the will of his father by making a will bequeathing the throne to the heirs of Henry's sister, the Duchess of Suffolk. This meant that Lady Jane Grey, a fervent Protestant, would inherit the kingdom, becoming queen instead of Mary. It so happened that the "protector" had married his second son to Lady Jane Grey a few months earlier, ensuring the continuation of his own power and influence following the ailing king's death.

Three weeks after Edward VI's will became law, Mary and Elizabeth were summoned to court. Sensing their half-brother's treachery, neither princess obeyed the royal command. It probably saved their lives. Two days later, on July 6, 1553, Edward died, having reigned for six years. He was only fifteen.

On July 8, Nicholas Ridley, Bishop of London, gave a sermon denouncing Mary as being illegitimate and, on the following day, Jane Gray was proclaimed queen. The people of England, still resoundingly Catholic in sympathy, were outraged, proclaiming Mary to be the true queen. The Privy Council, fearful of the populist uprising, switched allegiance and proclaimed Mary to be queen. The Duke of Northumberland, who was on his way with a contingent of soldiers to Framlingham Castle in Suffolk to arrest Mary, heard of the Privy Council's decision and had little option but to surrender. His act of treason would cost him his head.

[6] Ibid., 99.

Having been proclaimed queen behind the walls of Framlingham Castle, her erstwhile prison, Queen Mary set off for London. Passing through Suffolk and Essex, she was "greeted on the road with the strongest demonstrations of joy at her accession".[7] The cheering throngs thickened as she approached London, where she was joined by Elizabeth, the two half-sisters, riding on horseback, entering the city together in triumph, accompanied by a popular spirit of triumphalism. The houses of the city were decorated, the streets strewn with flowers. Mary was crowned, "in the most splendid manner and after the Catholic ritual",[8] by the same Bishop Gardiner who had been deprived of the bishopric of Winchester for opposing Cranmer's "reforms" and who was a prisoner in the Tower of London at the time of Mary's accession to the throne. "The joy of the people was boundless," wrote Cobbett. "It was a coronation of greater splendor and more universal joy than ever had before been witnessed."[9]

Considering that the people of England had risen in insurrection only three years earlier in defence of the Mass and in protest at the Protestant tyranny, one can only imagine the sense of sheer relief and joy with which the people celebrated what they must have hoped and believed was a restoration of Merrie England after twenty years of madness.

Eamon Duffy shows how the accession of Mary was greeted in the small parish of Morebath in Devon, which had been stripped of all its wealth by the plutocratic and Protestant pillage and had been plunged into debt in consequence. We are told that Mary's accession was "pure

[7] Ibid.
[8] Ibid., 100.
[9] Ibid.

joy" for the priest of the parish and that "his parishioners rallied to the restoration of Catholicism."[10] A general meeting of the parish was called to settle accounts
with those who had loaned the parish money following
its impoverishment at the hands of the plunderers. Many,
including the priest himself, accepted less than they had
originally loaned. "Parishioners who had acquired Catholic ornaments during the years of spoil now brought
them again, some asking for reimbursement, others giving them as gifts."[11] One parishioner gave back an image
of the Blessed Virgin. Others returned paintings, books,
and parts of the dismantled rood-loft. Fr. Trychay, the
parish priest, wrote that "like true and faithful Christian
people, this was restored to this church by the which
doings it showeth that they [acted] like good Catholic
men."[12] It is not difficult to imagine that these scenes
of joy at the restoration of the faith of their fathers, was
repeated by the faithful in the vast majority of parishes
throughout the length and breadth of the land.

Duffy offers other telling snapshots of England's joyous response to the restoration of true and traditional religious practice. In Melton Mowbray in Leicestershire, the
altar stones were restored immediately so that Mass and
"Dirige", traditional prayers for the dead, could be sung
for the soul of the recently deceased king, in whose reign
both the Mass and prayers for the dead were banned. A
holy irony indeed! It was also reported that, in "many
places of the realme", the Catholic gentry commanded
that Mass be celebrated once more "with a decent order as

---

[10] Eamon Duffy, *The Stripping of the Altars* (London: Yale University Press, 1992), 501.

[11] Ibid.

[12] Ibid. In this and the following quotes from Duffy, the spelling has been modernized for easier comprehension.

hath been used before time". But since, at the beginning
of Mary's reign, "there was no act, statute, proclamation or
commandment set forth for the same", many clergy "durst
not be bold to celebrate in Latin, though their hearts were
wholly inclined that way".[13] Such trepidation was indicative of the way in which the clergy of England had been
terrorized during the reigns of Henry and Edward, living
in fear of reprisal should they act unilaterally without formal government consent. All such trepidation evaporated
on August 18, when Mary issued a proclamation announc-
ing her desire for Catholic restoration.

Eamon Duffy, a trained and restrained historian who is
not prone to the visceral and vituperative rhetoric to which
William Cobbett so often succumbed, wrote nonetheless
that the queen's proclamation "opened the floodgates" for
the restoration of the traditional liturgy throughout the
country. Within three weeks of the proclamation, a contemporary source reported how the north of England had
returned almost overnight to the practice of the faith:

> There were very few parish churches in Yorkshire where
> Mass was not sung or said in Latin.... Altars were reedi-
> fied, pictures or images set up, the cross with the crucifix
> thereon ready to be borne in procession ... and all this
> came to pass without compulsion of any act, statute, proc-
> lamation or law.[14]

Although this was the typical response in most parts
of the country, those areas in which Protestantism had
gained a foothold were rent with division. London was
bitterly divided, as was the county of Kent. In the Kent-
ish parish of Adisham, the Catholic churchwarden accused

[13] Ibid., 527.
[14] Ibid., 528.

the Protestant minister and his assistant of being "heretic knaves [who] have deceived us with this fashion for too long".[15] Ignoring the swell of restorationist zeal, for which the churchwarden was the spokesman, the minister continued resolutely with the communion service which Cranmer had forced upon the country. There was increasingly bitter conflict between the two parties which involved the Protestant communion table being repeatedly dismantled and then reerected. Things came to a head on Holy Innocents Day (December 28) in 1554, when the Catholics in the parish invited a priest from a neighbouring parish to sing matins, Mass, and evensong according to the traditional Latin rite. When the Protestant minister tried to disrupt the Mass by preaching against transubstantiation, he was pulled down from the pulpit by his own parishioners and locked in a side chapel.

In spite of the overwhelming support of most of her subjects, Mary's efforts to restore England to the faith were beset with difficulties. As Cobbett explained, "The plunder had been so immense, the plunderers so numerous, they were so powerful, and there were so few men of family of any account who had not participated in deeds one way or another hostile to the Catholic Church, that the enterprise of the Queen was full of difficulty."[16] To put the matter plainly, the nobility of England were so compromised morally by their participation in the debauched feeding frenzy of the previous twenty years that very few felt the need or desire to repent and still less the need or desire to relinquish their ill-gotten gains.

Seeking to practice what she preached, and perhaps hoping to set a self-sacrificial example which others might

[15] Ibid.
[16] Cobbett, *History of the Protestant Reformation*, 101.

follow, Queen Mary resolved to keep none of the plunder
with which her father had sought to enrich himself and the
Crown. In November 1555, she relinquished the annual
income that the Crown received in tithes and other taxes
from the parish churches of England. This represented a
huge financial sacrifice on her part, estimated to be in the
order of £63,000 in the money of that day, which equates
to around $25 million in today's currency. Nor did she
stop there. She also restored all the church and abbey lands
which had been seized by the Crown during the reigns of
Henry and Edward, or at least what was left of such land
following the parcelling of it out to those who were the
kings' partners in crime. Apart from the reestablishment
of abbeys, monasteries, priories, and nunneries that this
facilitated, the queen also restored St. John's Hospital in
London and reestablished the Savoy Hospital for the poor,
liberally endowing both with a yearly revenue from her
own purse.

Explaining this relinquishing of the Crown's illic-
itly acquired wealth, Queen Mary said that she would
be "Defender of the Faith" in reality and not merely in
name, a quip which might be seen as a barbed reference
to the father who had so abominably treated her mother.
She told her own Privy Council that her conscience forbade her to retain any possessions gained by theft, con-
fessing that she valued her conscience "more than ten
kingdoms".[17] This astonishing generosity commanded the
respect of those who were otherwise her sworn enemies.
The seventeenth-century Protestant historian and polemicist Peter Heylyn, who was no friend of either Mary or
the Church, observed that it was "hard to say how far the
nobility and gentry might have done the like if the queen

[17] Ibid., 109.

had lived for some few years longer".[18] Such a view must be set against the outright possessiveness and selfishness of the nobility. Take, for instance, the Earl of Bedford, who was so scandalized by Mary's decision to restore stolen church property to its rightful owners, that he tore off the rosary which he wore at his belt and flung it in the fire, swearing that he loved his "sweet abbey" of Woburn more than all the fatherly counsels of Rome.[19] Such men, and there were many of his ilk, would constitute a powerful opposition to the queen's hopes for the restoration of England's faith.

The accession of Mary to the throne enabled Cardinal Pole to return to England after twenty years in exile. He returned as papal legate and would become Archbishop of Canterbury in 1556, the successor to the deposed and disgraced Thomas Cranmer. What followed was a bloody stain on Mary's reign and on Cardinal Pole's otherwise admirable reputation. Prompted by Mary's own Privy Council, which was determined to restore the faith by the same violent means by which it had been oppressed, the queen and the cardinal acquiesced in the burning of heretics.

William Paget, a member of Mary's Privy Council, estimated that Protestants comprised only one-twelfth of the population of England.[20] They were, however, more powerful than their numbers suggested and were concentrated in the centres of power in London and South East England. They constituted a vociferous and vituperative minority who were content with nothing but the overthrow of Mary's "papist" government and the establishment of Protestantism throughout the realm, irrespective

---

[18] Quoted in ibid.

[19] H. F. M. Prescott, *Mary Tudor* (London: Macmillan, 1953), 316.

[20] Hilaire Belloc, *A Shorter History of England* (London: George G. Harrap, 1934), 298.

of the will of either the monarch or the vast majority of her subjects. There could be no peace and no coexistence between the warring parties. Such was proven by the Protestant response to Mary's attempts, in the first years of her reign, to show a degree of tolerance towards dissenters. Only three of those who had conspired against her accession to the throne were executed for treason. The rest were pardoned, much to the consternation of her own advisers who saw her tolerance as folly. Furthermore, and in spite of Protestant calls for revolution, she published a declaration in which she promised a conciliatory approach to religious conflict pending Parliament's decision on resolving the crisis. Nobody was punished for holding dissenting religious views in the first eighteen months of her reign. The only arrests were of those who were guilty of inciting violent disorder.

Almost eight hundred Protestants went into voluntary exile to the Protestant strongholds in Germany and Switzerland, from whence they openly plotted Mary's destruction and the imposition of Protestantism on an unwilling population. "While the government carefully refrained from prosecuting religious dissent," wrote Gerard Culkin, "the Protestant preachers, and still more their leaders among the exiles on the continent, were deliberately stirring up sedition in England."[21]

Culkin contextualized the situation in a candid and balanced way, which is lacking in most historical studies of Mary's reign:

It should not be forgotten that the idea of religious toleration was altogether foreign to the mind of the time. Neither in England nor abroad did Catholics or Protestants believe

[21] Gerard Culkin, *The English Reformation* (London: Sands, 1955), 92–93.

it to be either possible or desirable for two conflicting religious faiths to exist together in the same country. The Protestants in England no more desired mere toleration for themselves than they were prepared to concede it to their opponents. They wanted only a Protestant victory. If this could be achieved by violent means—and that seemed to be the only solution as long as Mary lived—then they were ready for violence.[22]

From the very beginning of Mary's reign, long before the commencement of any government persecution, England was flooded with anti-Catholic propaganda and violent attacks on the queen and her government. There was no suggestion that the Protestants were willing to compromise. It was all out war. Although it is probable that the princess Elizabeth, as Mary's heir, was privy to at least some of the anti-Catholic plots, her guilt has never been definitively established.

In those areas of the country in which Protestantism had a significant presence, and especially in London, there were sporadic acts of violence. A dagger was thrown at a priest who was preaching from the pulpit of St. Paul's Cathedral. Thomas Flower, an apostate monk, attacked a priest during the distribution of Communion at Mass at St. Margaret's Church in Westminster, the priest's blood splattering the consecrated hosts. "In the face of such outrages," wrote Gerard Culkin, "the government had no choice; it must either act or be destroyed."[23] Faced with "treason, sedition, and every kind of violence and disorder", the government had to choose between the rigorous imposition of order or seeing the country reduced to a state of anarchy. In choosing the former path, the stage

[22] Ibid., 93.
[23] Ibid.

was set for the bloody persecution of Protestants for heresy, which would see around three hundred people being burned at the stake. According to H. F. M. Prescott, this was "the panic reply of a social and political order threatened by a force which seemed determined on nothing short of anarchy".[24]

None of this excuses burning people at the stake, but it does at least point to the very difficult position in which the queen and her government found themselves. They had no choice but to act and to act decisively. The problem was, however, that they overreacted in acting decisively in the way that was chosen. This overreaction provided the source material for John Foxe's *Book of Martyrs*, published in 1563, which would prove to be what Gerard Culkin calls "probably the most effective piece of propagandist writing which has ever appeared in England".[25] Purporting to give a factual account of the sufferings of the Protestant martyrs during Mary's reign, it is full of inaccuracies, not all of which are the result of genuine error, and, indeed, sheer fabrication. These defects notwithstanding, Foxe's book has formed the bedrock foundation for the anti-Catholic prejudice animating most interpretations of this period of English history ever since. Ever after, Mary Tudor would be tainted with a "bloody" reputation as indelible as Lady Macbeth's. Her sister, however, would suffer no such fate, her own sins being washed white by the whitewashing of her reputation by later generations of propagandists, masquerading as historians.

Mary Tudor died on November 17, 1558, on the same date that St. Elizabeth of Hungary had died more than three hundred years earlier. Although both of royal blood,

[24] Prescott, *Mary Tudor*, 305.
[25] Culkin, *English Reformation*, 96.

nobody would be reckless enough to ascribe to Mary a canonized place with the saints. She was, however, a devout adherent to the faith that she shared with the saints and spent her life trying to serve God in a genuinely self-sacrificial spirit. The same could not be said of her half-sister, Elizabeth, who, having nothing in common with her Hungarian namesake except the Christian name they shared, would spend her life sacrificing others on the altar of her self-serving ambition. It is to this truly bloody queen that we now turn our attention.

Chapter Thirteen

Bloody Bess

The Queen was in her chamber, her sins were on her head,
She looked the spirits up and down and statelily she said:—
"Backwards and forwards and sideways though I've been,
Yet I am Harry's daughter and I am England's Queen!"
And she faced the looking-glass (and whatever else there was)
And she saw her day was over and she saw her beauty pass
In the cruel looking-glass, that can always hurt a lass
More hard than any ghost there is or any man there was!

—Rudyard Kipling, from "The Looking-Glass"

The cold queen of England is looking in the glass.

—G. K. Chesterton, from "Lepanto"

As chance or providence would have it, Cardinal Pole died only a few hours after the death of the queen whom he had so faithfully served. Although Pole would be vilified by historians for his role in Mary's persecution of Protestants, Ernest C. Messenger was closer to the truth when he wrote that "there can be little doubt that Reginald Cardinal Pole was one of the noblest of men, and one of the greatest Archbishops that sat in the Chair of St. Augustine".[1] One of Cardinal Pole's last acts was to send a

---

[1] Claude Williamson, ed., *Great Catholics* (London: Nicholson and Watson, 1938), 186.

message to Princess Elizabeth, which was almost certainly an exhortation to Elizabeth to stay true to the Catholic faith that she had professed during her sister's reign. Elizabeth, however, would have other priorities ordered in accordance with her own power-hungry ambition.

As for Elizabeth's faith, she had been a Protestant during the reign of Edward and a Catholic during the reign of Mary. To all outward appearances, her conversion had seemed genuine enough. She went to Mass publicly and had her own confessor and a Catholic chapel in her house. On her deathbed, Mary had asked Elizabeth for an honest avowal of her religious opinions and was assured by Elizabeth of her fidelity to the faith. Rather than disavow her Catholic faith, she told her half-sister, she would pray that the earth might open its maw and swallow her. She made similar assurances to the Duke of Feria, the Spanish envoy who informed King Philip that Elizabeth's accession would make no alteration in matters of religion in England.

Matters were complicated by the fact that Elizabeth was illegitimate by law. Her father's marriage to her mother was considered invalid because Henry's divorce from his first wife, Catherine of Aragon, was also considered invalid—its being contrived by Henry's own minions in defiance of the pope who had refused the divorce. If Henry and Anne Boleyn were not legally married, their child was illegitimate and devoid of any legal claim to the throne. To complicate matters still further, Henry had himself had a law enacted which declared his marriage to Anne Boleyn to be invalid, thereby rendering his daughter Elizabeth illegitimate and removing her claim to the throne. Although Henry had subsequently changed his mind, declaring Elizabeth to be second in line to the throne after Mary, in the event of his son failing to have any issue, the earlier law bastardizing Elizabeth had never been repealed. In addition, another Act of Parliament, passed in the reign of Edward VI, had reversed an earlier law which had declared Henry's marriage to his first wife illicit. Since the law now affirmed that Henry and Catherine of Aragon were indeed legally married, this meant that Henry's marriage to Anne Boleyn was null and void, Catherine still being alive and legally wedded to the king at the time of his "marriage" to Anne. In consideration of these convoluted circumstances, one is reminded of Walter Scott's admonishment: "O, what a tangled web we weave when first we practice to deceive!"[2]

When informed of Elizabeth's accession, it was no wonder that the pope responded that he could not recognize the hereditary right of a person not born in lawful wedlock. The pope's adherence to objective principle rather than subjective pragmatism would serve to push Elizabeth more assuredly towards the Protestant party. In William Cobbett's words, the pope's judgement "was of itself a pretty strong inducement [to become a Protestant] for a lady of so flexible a conscience".[3]

If Elizabeth were illegitimate and therefore ineligible to inherit the throne of England, the true queen was Mary, queen of Scotland, the nearest legitimate descendant of Henry VII. Clearly, if Elizabeth desired the throne but was considered a usurper in the eyes of the Catholic world, it was in her interests to align herself with the Protestants who had no scruples with respect to her legitimacy.

It did not take long for Elizabeth's true position to become manifest. In early December 1558, only about

---

[2] From *Marmion*, Canto VI.
[3] William Cobbett, *A History of the Protestant Reformation* (Sevenoaks, Kent: Fisher Press, 1994), 123.

three weeks after the coronation, the Bishop of Chichester was imprisoned for denouncing a Protestant whom the queen had sent to preach at Paul's Cross. Ten days later, the Bishop of Winchester, preaching at Mary's funeral service, had warned that the Protestant "wolves" were returning from Germany and Geneva, "full of pestilent doctrines, blasphemy and sedition, to infect the people".[4] He too was imprisoned for his act of candour.

On Christmas Day, the Bishop of Carlisle was ordered not to elevate the Host at Mass in the royal chapel. When the bishop refused to comply with the royal command, the queen ostentatiously left after the reading of the Gospel, thereby removing herself prior to the Consecration. In spite of this act of impiety, the queen had no sympathy for the extreme Protestants who had prospered and come to prominence during Edward's reign. Her own position, insofar as it can be discerned, appears to have been the sort of pragmatic anti-papal cafeteria "Catholicism" favoured by her father. The problem was that the Protestant faction now effectively controlled Parliament and the queen was aware that she could not govern the country without Parliament's consent and cooperation. Whether she liked it or not, she was at the mercy of the very "wolves" of which the Bishop of Winchester had warned her.

In 1559, an Act of Parliament restored to the Crown the royal supremacy which had been abolished during Mary's reign and restored Protestant worship throughout the land. The English bishops were vociferous in their opposition to these changes. Nicholas Heath, the Archbishop of York, warned that were England to "forsake and fly from the holy unity of Christ's Church ... leaping out of Peter's ship, we hazard ourselves to be overwhelmed

---

[4] Gerard Culkin, *The English Reformation* (London: Sands, 1955), 100.

in the waves of schism, sects and divisions".[5] The victory of the well-organized Protestant party in Parliament over the will of the bishops signified the decisive victory of the secular power over the power of the Church, and signalled to Elizabeth that the real political power resided with the Protestants, whom she sought to appease thereafter.

The Act of Supremacy, which came into force in May 1559, reestablished the anti-papal legislation that had been passed during the reign of Henry and repealed during the reign of Mary. As with the legislation under Henry, the Act repudiated any obedience to the papacy and severed England from the unity of the Church. Attached to the Act was the reimplementation of the anti-papal oath of 1536 acknowledging the queen to be "Supreme Governor in all matters ecclesiastical and spiritual". All clergy were required to take the oath, as were those taking degrees at the universities, all judges, justices, mayors, and other officials. The penalty for refusing the oath was at first the loss of office only, but four years later, it was increased to a loss of goods and imprisonment for a first offence, with a punishment of death for a second offence, refusal a second time being considered an act of treason.

A second law, the Act of Uniformity, which came into force in June 1559, abolished the Mass and the sacraments, and repudiated the doctrine of the Real Presence. It also made it an offence for any clergyman to refuse to per-form the Protestant service, punishable through the loss of a year's income and six months imprisonment. A third offence carried a life sentence. Any layperson who so much as voiced a criticism of the new Protestant service was to be fined a hundred marks, a huge sum, roughly equiva-lent to about $27,000 in today's currency. Furthermore,

[5] Ibid., 102.

attendance at the new state-imposed religion was made compulsory for everybody, irrespective of religious conviction or freedom of conscience. Failure to attend the Protestant service in the local parish church every Sunday was punishable by a fine.

The Act of Uniformity empowered the queen to appoint commissioners to travel the country administering the Oath of Supremacy to the clergy. All but one of the bishops who had already protested the injustice of the new laws refused to take the oath. They were duly deprived of their sees and subsequently imprisoned. Apart from the heroic stand of these noble bishops, the strongest resistance to the new tyranny came from the cathedral churches and the universities, especially Oxford. Seven deans, ten archdeacons, seven diocesan chancellors, and around sixty heads and fellows of colleges were deprived of their offices. Faced with such merciless resolution on the part of the government, most of the clergy submitted to the oath, though no doubt with severe misgivings. Of those who refused, many went into exile.

The people of England, still overwhelmingly Catholic, resented the new religion and found the compulsory attendance at its services a hateful and loathsome burden. It is this imposition of a state religion, against the will and contrary to the faith of the people, which sowed the seeds of cynicism towards religion, which would become a defining characteristic of the English people by the eighteenth century. Resistance continued in the form of an underground Church. The courageous minority of priests who had refused the oath and were deprived of their parishes, continued their ministry in secret, relying on the good will and generosity of the laity for their livelihood, having been deprived of their income. Other members of the clergy, having taken the oath and outwardly conforming, continued to minister the sacraments in secret. As for the Catholic laity, they now fell into three broad camps. There were those who conformed, grumbling about the imposition of the new Protestant service but making the best of a bad situation; there were those who became known as the "church papists", who outwardly conformed to the state religion but secretly received the sacraments of the Church whenever a priest was available to minister them; and there were the recusants, those who refused, in conscience, to attend the Protestant services and paid the government-imposed fines for their nonattendance.

There was so little enthusiasm in most of the country for the new religion that the Protestant communion service was very rarely celebrated, their being so few who were willing to receive the nonsacramental bread as a substitute for the Blessed Sacrament. In the Catholic heartland of the north, and particularly in Lancashire, the new religion was ignored as far as possible, through the connivance of the local magistrates who, sharing the Catholic faith of the people, turned a blind eye to the celebration of Mass.

Due to the necessary secrecy with which the priests of the underground Church conducted their ministry, there is little documentary evidence of their activities. It is only possible, therefore, to speak of those who were captured and imprisoned, relying on court records and other official documents. Take, for instance, the case of Henry Comberford, one of only eleven priests of the Diocese of Coventry, from a total of around 250, who had the courage to refuse the Oath of Supremacy. Travelling to Yorkshire, he ministered to the Catholics of the north for over ten years before his capture in 1570, along with two other priests who had similarly been deprived of their livings for refusing the oath. During the interrogation that followed his arrest, Fr. Comberford was recorded as affirming "the

Mass to be good, and saith that he will maintain the same until death".[6] Being imprisoned at first at Hull and later in York Castle, he continued to practise his priesthood behind bars, being described as "a great perverter of others",[7] which might be translated in nonsectarian terms as "a great converter of others". He died in 1586, after sixteen years of close confinement. His was a fate that would be shared by many others during the reign of Bloody Bess.

As for the fate of the recusant laity, the case of Sir Thomas Fitzherbert is typical of the hardships faced by those who had the courage of their convictions. He was locked up in the Fleet prison in London in 1561 for refusing to attend the compulsory Protestant services, finding himself incarcerated along with fellow recusants, the Bishop of Chester and the Dean of Saint Paul's. In 1563, the Protestant Bishop of London reported that Sir Thomas was offered his freedom "if he would be bound in the meantime to go orderly to the church, without binding him to receive Communion".[8] Much to the bishop's consternation, Sir Thomas refused. He continued to refuse for the next thirty years, spending most of his life in prison in consequence, with only occasional brief periods of freedom. At the time of his death, at the age of seventy-four in 1591, he had lost two-thirds of his lands in fines. A year earlier, his brother John had died in the Fleet prison for his own recusancy.

In *The Stripping of the Altars*, Eamon Duffy shows how parishes across the country put up a silent and ultimately futile resistance to the destruction and confiscation of images, statues, books, and vestments. It was only when

[6] Ibid., 116.
[7] Ibid.
[8] Peter Stanford and Leanda de Lisle, *The Catholics and Their Houses* (London: Harper Collins, 1995), 30.

the official government visitation arrived at each parish that the desecration and the renewal of the plunder took place, the people watching in powerless bewilderment as the heart of their faith was being ripped out before their eyes.[9] This war of attrition against the faith of the common people continued with the determination of the Protestant authorities to put an end to the performance of the mystery plays, which had been such a part of the communal and traditional life of Merrie England. At York and at Chester, the scripts were collected by the authorities for "revision" and not returned in time for the annual performances to be staged. The last cycle of mystery plays was performed in York in 1569 and in Chester in 1575. The last complete cycle was performed in Coventry in 1580, ending a tradition that stretched back to the Middle Ages. It seems likely that the young William Shakespeare, who lived with his recusant Catholic family in Stratford, only twenty miles from Coventry, would have attended the Coventry mystery plays, their annual performance being a manifestation of popular folk resistance to the war on the faith.

Faced with such relentless persecution at home, it was inevitable that those in exile should take up the leadership of the English Resistance. Many exiles had clustered in the French city of Douai and in the Flemish city of Louvain, both of which were just across the English Channel and out of Elizabeth's reach. Douai and Louvain were both university towns, so it was natural that they should be the destination for the heads and fellows of colleges who had refused to take the Oath of Supremacy; being deprived of their positions and their livelihoods, they should have chosen exile rather than imprisonment. During the first

[9] Eamon Duffy, *The Stripping of the Altars* (London: Yale University Press, 1992), 574–75.

ten years of Elizabeth's reign, over a hundred senior members of Oxford University alone had gone into exile, joining the English diaspora in Douai and Louvain. A printing press was set up at Louvain, and two houses of study nicknamed "Oxford" and "Cambridge" were established.

The person who would emerge as the leader of what might be called the English Church in exile was William Allen, former principal of St. Mary's Hall, Oxford (which was merged in 1902 with Oriel College). Allen was ordained a priest in 1565 and quickly became known as the author of various Catholic tracts in what would be a war of apologetics with the English Protestant regime. Fr. Allen wrote treatises defending the doctrines of purgatory and confession, and a further work defending the sacraments. In 1568, he founded the English College at Douai, which would play a major role in preserving the faith in England by training future priests.

In 1568, the year in which Fr. Allen founded the seminary in Douai, Elizabeth imprisoned the exiled Mary Stuart, Queen of Scots, an act which would precipitate the Northern Rebellion of the following year. As we have seen, Mary Stuart was not only a Catholic but was considered by many to be the rightful queen, Elizabeth being illegitimate. She was, at any rate, the undisputed heir to the throne until or unless Elizabeth married and had children. "Mary's arrival served to focus the forces of discontent in the country," wrote Gerard Culkin,[10] particularly in the Catholic heartland in the north of England. The northern earls rose in rebellion, marching south in the hope of rescuing Mary from her imprisonment in the midlands. Rallying under the banner of the Five Wounds, under which their fathers had fought for religious liberty during the

---

[10] Culkin, *English Reformation*, 117.

Pilgrimage of Grace, thirty-three years earlier, they called for the restoration of the Catholic faith to the people of England. Taking the northern city of Durham, the rebels restored the Mass, and then continued the march southward, restoring the Mass as they went. It was an impressive demonstration of the strength of Catholic allegiance in the north of the country, but militarily it was a disaster. Retreating before the advance of the royal army, the rebellion ended in disarray. As with Henry VIII's response to the Pilgrimage of Grace, Elizabeth showed no mercy. More than eight hundred people were hanged, including the priest who had said the first Mass in Durham. "Three hundred were put to death in Durham alone," wrote Hilaire Belloc, "every village which had sent even one man to the rising was visited with executions."[11]

On February 25, 1570, in the wake of the horrific reprisals meted out by Elizabeth's government, St. Pius V issued a papal bull, *Regnans in Excelsis* (Reigning on High), excommunicating Elizabeth, "the pretended queen of England and the servant of crime", and calling on the people of England to resist her tyrannical rule. In referring to Elizabeth as "the pretended queen", Pius was reflecting the general view that Elizabeth was not the rightful ruler of England but a usurper. He then proceeded to condemn Elizabeth for the "strong hand" with which she had sought to prohibit the practice of the "true religion". Witnessing "impieties and crimes multiplied one upon another [and] the persecution of the faithful," Pius declared that Elizabeth "and her adherents ... to have incurred the sentence of excommunication and to be cut off from the unity of the body of Christ". Going even further, the pope declared

<hr>

[11] Hilaire Belloc, *A Shorter History of England* (London: George G. Harrap, 1934), 319.

her "to be deprived of her pretended title to the aforesaid crown and of all lordship, dignity and privilege whatsoever", thereby releasing all "the nobles, subjects and people" of England from all oaths sworn to her.

It is the consensus among historians today that St. Pius' excommunication of Elizabeth had been an error of judgement, not least because it had hardened the queen's heart still further against her Catholic subjects and had led in consequence to an increase of the Elizabethan state's persecution of them. "It proceeded from insufficient understanding of the situation of English Catholics," wrote David Hugh Farmer; "it made their position much more difficult; it gave their opponents in the government a wonderful opportunity, exploited to the full, of accusing them of disloyalty and treason."[12] Farmer's judgement was echoed by Jessie Childs: "The irony of *Regnans in Excelsis* is that it did more damage to the English Catholic community than any Protestant proclamation could have done. Pope Pius V had issued it at the behest of the northern earls, but by the time it appeared in England, all that was left of the rebellion were the corpses, hanging 'for terror' in the marketplace."[13] According to another historian, Diarmaid MacCulloch, the example of Pius' bull of excommunication was employed almost four hundred years later to dissuade the pope from issuing an encyclical condemning Hitler: "Pius's action was so generally recognized as a political blunder that it was even remembered in the 1930s when the papacy considered how to react to Adolf Hitler's regime: discreet voices in the Vatican privately recalled the bad precedent, and behind the scenes

[12] David Hugh Farmer, *The Oxford Dictionary of Saints* (Oxford: Oxford University Press, 1987), 401.

[13] Jessie Childs, *Terror & Faith in Elizabethan England* (Oxford: Oxford University Press, 2014), 28–29.

it was a factor in preventing a public papal condemnation of Nazism."[14]

Intriguingly, St. Pius' excommunication of Elizabeth was viewed very differently by English Catholics in the early eighteenth century. "Elizabeth, Queen of England, whom the Protestants of this nation deservedly call the Bulwark of the Reformation, was solemnly excommunicated by our saint," writes an anonymous biographer of Pius V in the 1720s, "who united Spain and Portugal against her, and omitted nothing in his power that might excite the Catholic princes against her, and destroy her credit in the world for the interest of religion."[15]

This robust eighteenth-century defence of St. Pius V's position with respect to Elizabeth I is much more likely to have reflected the view of the persecuted Catholics of the sixteenth century than do the cold and distant judgement of twentieth- and twenty-first-century historians.

There is no doubt that Pius V's condemnation of Elizabeth raised the political temperature in England and led to increased persecution of England's Catholics. On the other hand, it clarified the political situation, enabling Catholics in England to come to terms with the grim reality of their position. One wonders, for instance, whether saints, such as Edmund Campion, Robert Southwell, or Margaret Clitherow, would have stepped forward to lay down their lives for Christ and His Church if Pope Pius had not drawn such a definitive line in the sand. Would the world be a better place if they had chosen tolerance of tyranny instead of heroic self-sacrifice even unto death? Would the world be a better place if Catholics had followed the

---

[14] Diarmaid MacCulloch, *Reformation: Europe's House Divided 1490–1700* (London: Allen Lane, 2003), 334.

[15] Anonymous, *The Lives of the Saints*, vol. 2 (London: Thomas Meighan, 1729), 241. The spelling has been updated for clarity of comprehension.

path of least resistance against the tyranny of secular rulers? Is fear of reprisals by a tyrant, be it Elizabeth or Hitler, grounds for remaining silent or grounds for a failure to act?

Irrespective of the judgement of history, for better or worse, with respect to Pius V's excommunication of "the pretended queen" of England, the judgement of the queen herself was that the "papists" must be made to pay for their allegiance to the pope of Rome. New penal laws were passed in 1571 making it punishable by death even to attend a private Mass, held in secret, and severe punishments were enacted for the mere possession of articles associated with Catholic worship and practice. For the remainder of Elizabeth's reign, her kingdom was destined to become a land of martyrs.

Chapter Fourteen

A Land of Martyrs

Why do I use my paper, ink and pen
And call my wits to counsel what to say?
Such memories were made for mortal men,
I speak of saints whose names shall not decay.
An angel's trump were fitter for to sound
Their glorious death if such on earth were found.

—St. Henry Walpole's epitaph on the
life and death of Edmund Campion

One of the earliest fruits of the scholarship emanating from the French city of Douai was the English translation of the Latin Vulgate Bible, the celebrated Douai-Rheims Version (also spelled Douay-Rheims). The Douai-Rheims New Testament was published in 1582, almost thirty years before the appearance of the King James Version. It was, however, in the provision of a new generation of "seminary priests" that Douai would play such a crucial role in the ongoing English Resistance. "Our students intended for the English harvest," wrote Fr. Allen, "are not required to excel or be great proficients in theological science ... but they must abound in zeal for God's house, charity and thirst for souls."[1] The first four priests were ordained in

[1] Nicholas Schofield and Gerard Skinner, *The English Cardinals* (Oxford: Family Publications, 2007), 119.

1573, sailing for England the following year. By 1580, a hundred newly ordained priests had been sent into "the English harvest". Fr. Allen was under no illusions with respect to the sacrifices that these young men, thirsty for souls, would face upon their return to enemy territory: "I could reckon unto you the miseries they suffer in night journeys in the worst weather that can be picked, peril of thieves, of waters, of watches, of false brethren."[2] Soon to be added to this list of perils was that of martyrdom, the college producing the first of its 160 martyrs in 1577 with the trial and execution of St. Cuthbert Mayne.

Another future martyr, St. Robert Southwell, wrote that it had become their duty,

> by the gentleness of [their] manners, the fire of [their] charity, by innocence of life and an example of all virtues, so to shine upon the world as to lift up the *Res Christiana* that now droops so sadly, and to build up again from the ruins what others by their vices have brought so low.[3]

The harvest was indeed proving bountiful, with young Englishmen flocking to Douai in ever-increasing numbers. In 1583, there were eighty new arrivals within six months. Many of these would later return as priests; no fewer than 450 would be sent from Douai by the end of Elizabeth's reign. These priests kept the faith alive, moving in secret from place to place, feeding the faithful, reconciling those who had lapsed, and making spectacular conversions. Elizabeth's government responded with an ongoing nationwide priest-hunt, aided and abetted by an efficient network of spies and informers. By the end of the queen's

[2] Ibid.
[3] Ibid.

reign, 126 priests would be executed for no other crime than their priesthood.

In 1579, the indomitable Fr. Allen transformed the moribund English Hospice in Rome into what became known as the Venerable English College, a seminary which trains men for the priesthood to this day. It was at this college on October 16, 1594, that Fr. Allen died, having been made Prefect of the English Mission in 1581 and cardinal in 1587. On his deathbed, he lamented that he should die in bed while "by his persuasion so many had borne imprisonments, persecutions and martyrdom in England."[4] His own unworthiness to die a martyr's death was seen by him as being what his sins deserved.

Typical of the courage of those families offering resistance to the war on the faith was the Ingleby family of Ripley Castle in Yorkshire. The Earl of Huntingdon referred to this most determined of recusant families as "a nest of traitors", stating in 1572 that the family was a mainstay of recusancy in the north of the country.[5] The head of the family, Sir William, took the pragmatic approach of outwardly conforming to the dictates of the new religion in order to avoid paying the crippling fines for recusancy, while simultaneously encouraging his wife and children to be openly recusant.

Sir William and Lady Anne Ingleby had fourteen children, six sons and eight daughters. Between 1571 and 1581, Lady Anne was summoned to appear before the Council of the North on no fewer than twenty-seven occasions, each time offering feeble excuses for her nonattendance or simply failing to show up at the appointed

[4] Ibid., 21.

[5] Roland Connelly, *No Greater Love: The Martyrs of the Middlesbrough Diocese* (Great Wakering, Essex: McCrimmons, 1987), 30.

time. The fourth of Sir William and Lady Anne's sons, Francis Ingleby, joined the many young men crossing the sea to train for the priesthood, the Douai Diary recording his arrival in August 1582. By the spring of 1584, he had been ordained and had returned to England, becoming the confessor of one of the most remarkable and courageous of women, St. Margaret Clitherow.

As early as 1576, Mrs. Clitherow was imprisoned for her recusancy, the records indicating that she was pregnant at the time. For the next ten years, she would provide a safe refuge for priests in her home in the knowledge that harbouring a priest was punishable by death. Years later, awaiting her execution, she would show that resolution that was the hallmark of the English Martyrs. "I confess death is fearful and flesh is frail," she said, "yet I mind by God's assistance to spend my blood in this faith as willingly as ever I put my paps into my children's mouths."[6]

As for Bloody Bess, she seemed to take sadistic pleasure in being personally present at the arrest of her Catholic subjects. During a royal visit to Norfolk in 1578, she made a point of staying at Euston Hall, near Thetford, the home of the young and newly married Edward Rookwood. The young couple did their utmost to entertain the queen and her retinue in a decorous manner; then, on the morning of the queen's departure, when Rookwood presented himself to kiss his guest's hand, he was told to stand aside. Condemned by the queen for being a Catholic, he was placed under arrest and marched away to Norwich gaol.

Four days later, the queen stayed at the home of Thomas Townshend, who had taken the Oath of Supremacy but was related to several recusants and was on friendly terms

---

[6] Margaret T. Monro, *St. Margaret Clitherow: The Pearl of York* (Rockford, Ill.: TAN Books, 2003), 20.

with others. During a party held in her honour, hosted by Townshend, the queen took pleasure in having nine of her fellow guests arrested under her host's roof, dispatching them to the same prison in Norwich in which Edward Rookwood was now incarcerated. Commenting on the queen's cynical and sadistic treatment of her Catholic subjects during this visit to Norfolk, Evelyn Waugh encapsulated the perilous position of those families who had the courage and temerity to resist the royal tyranny. "These were the conditions of life, always vexatious, often utterly disastrous, of ... people drawn from the most responsible and honourable class, guilty of no crime except adherence to the traditional faith of their country."[7]

In the midst of the suffering and with the onset of the new wave of martyrdom which had begun with the execution of St. Cuthbert Mayne in 1577, England's beleaguered Catholics found solace in the discovery of St. Priscilla's catacombs in Rome. A contemporary source saw parallels between the persecuted Christians of the early Church "who were wont to lie hidden and secret from their enemies" and those facing persecution in contemporary England.[8]

As for the escapades of the many missionary priests who were ministering in secret to England's Catholics, they resemble the adventures of swashbuckling heroes, such as the Scarlet Pimpernel. Take, for instance, the elusive presence throughout the country of Blessed Montford Scott. His progress around England for a period of fourteen years, staying one step ahead of Elizabeth's spy network, is well-documented in contemporary government

[7] Evelyn Waugh, *Edmund Campion* (London: Longmans, Green, 1935), 113.

[8] Gaspare Loarte, *The Exercise of a Christian Life*, 1579; quoted in Robert S. Miola, ed., *Early Modern Catholicism: An Anthology of Primary Sources* (Oxford: Oxford University Press, 2007), 22.

records. Having arrived in England in 1577, two weeks after his ordination, he was arrested the following year in Cambridge and taken to London "with the books, letters, writings and other trash" which were discovered in his possession.[9] Released on bail, he promptly disappeared and would evade recapture for a further twelve years. In 1580, a spy reported him as being "about Kent". A couple of years later, another spy claimed that he was in London. In 1584, hearing reports that he was in Yorkshire, the queen herself ordered a special search of the northern part of the county. Once again, the elusive Fr. Scott slipped through the net. In April 1585, he was charged in Norwich with "distributing divers hallowed beads" and "saying of divers Masses" but the proceedings were held in the absence of the accused.[10] Charged with further crimes in London, he was officially declared an outlaw in June 1585. In spite of such notoriety, Fr. Scott continued with his priestly ministry, evading the eyes of Elizabeth's spies until his eventual arrest near Horncastle in Lincolnshire in December 1590.

Defiant to the last, we learn how he reconciled a fellow prisoner to the faith while awaiting trial in London and then made a daring escape attempt. He was recaptured and brought to trial with another priest, Blessed George Beesley, both of whom confessed their priesthood and both of whom refused any bargaining for their lives. They were hanged, drawn, and quartered on July 1, 1591, and were both beatified by St. John Paul II in 1987.

In 1579, Fr. Allen, who was now in Rome, having founded the Venerable English College, persuaded the Father-General of the new Jesuit Order that those

[9] Roland Connelly, *The Eighty-Five Martyrs* (Great Wakering, Essex: McCrimmon Publishing, 1987), 57.
[10] Ibid.

Englishmen who had become Jesuit priests should be sent to their homeland as missionaries. "Our harvest is already great in England," Fr. Allen wrote to the recently ordained Jesuit, Edmund Campion. "Ordinary labourers are not enough; more practiced men are wanted, but chiefly you and others of your order. The General [of the Jesuits] has yielded to all our prayers; the Pope, the true father of our country, has consented; and God, in whose hands are the issues, has at last granted that our own Campion, with his extraordinary gifts of wisdom and grace, should be restored to us."[11]

In April 1580, Edmund Campion and eleven others, nine priests and two laymen, set forth to make the long journey to England. Before leaving, they were received in audience by Pope Gregory XIII, receiving his blessing. They also visited Philip Neri, receiving the saint's blessing. Ten days later, Campion and his fellows were received by another saint, Charles Borromeo, who hosted them for eight days at his palace in Milan. "These young men were on their way to the English mission, which meant almost certain death and torture," wrote Borromeo's biographer. "Nothing he could do for these future martyrs was too much."[12]

After a brief sojourn in London, Campion set out to minister to Catholics in sundry parts of England, travelling through Berkshire, Oxfordshire, Northamptonshire, Warwickshire, and Lancashire. According to Richard Simpson, Campion's nineteenth-century biographer, he visited a host of families in Lancashire, "the Worthingtons, the Talbots, the Southworths, the Heskeths, Mrs. Allen

[11] Waugh, *Edmund Campion*, 82.

[12] Margaret Yeo, *Reformer: St. Charles Borromeo* (Milwaukee: Bruce Publishing, 1938), 257.

the widow of the Cardinal's brother, the Houghtons, the Westbys and the Rigmaidens".[13] At the time that Campion visited the house, it seems that the sixteen-year-old William Shakespeare might have been working as a private tutor at Hoghton Tower, the home of the Catholic recusant Alexander Hoghton, near Preston in Lancashire. The possibility that Campion and Shakespeare might have met led Shakespeare's biographer Stephen Greenblatt to conjecture what such a meeting would have meant to the young William.

> Let us imagine the two of them sitting together then, the sixteen-year-old fledgling poet and actor and the forty-year-old Jesuit. Shakespeare would have found Campion fascinating—even his mortal enemies conceded that he had charisma—and might even have recognized in him something of a kindred spirit.... Campion—a quarter century older than Will—was someone who came from a comparably modest family; who attracted attention to himself by his eloquence, intelligence, and quickness; who loved books yet at the same time was drawn to life in the world. His was a learned but not an original mind; rather he was brilliant at giving traditional ideas a new life through the clarity and grace of his language and the moving power of his presence. Witty, imaginative, and brilliantly adept at improvisation, he managed to combine meditative seriousness with a strong theatrical streak. If the adolescent knelt down before Campion, he would have been looking at a distorted image of himself.[14]

In response to the propaganda emanating from Elizabeth's Privy Council that the Jesuit mission to England

---

[13] Quoted in Stephen Greenblatt, *Will in the World* (New York: W. W. Norton & Company, 2004), 108.

[14] Ibid., 108–9.

was politically seditious and treasonous in nature, Campion wrote what is known as his *Challenge to the Privy Council*, or *Campion's Brag*. Contrary to the charges of treason being made against him, Campion insisted that his only purpose in coming to England was "to preach the Gospel, to minister the Sacraments, to instruct the simple, to reform sinners, to confute errors—in brief, to cry alarm spiritual against foul vice and proud ignorance, wherewith many of my dear Countrymen are abused". Furthermore, he explicitly rejected the claims that his mission was in any way political in nature: "I never had mind, and am strictly forbidden by our Father that sent me, to deal in any respect with matter of State or Policy of this realm, as things which appertain not to my vocation, and from which I do gladly restrain and sequester my thoughts."

The "Challenge" he set before the Privy Council was that he might be allowed to debate the religious questions that divided them, "wherein I undertake to avow the Faith of our Catholic Church by proofs innumerable, Scriptures, Councils, Fathers, History, natural and moral reasons". He also begged the queen to listen to reason so that "her zeal of truth and love of her people shall incline her noble Grace to disfavour some proceedings hurtful to the Realm, and procure towards us oppressed more equity."

Alluding to the Englishmen in exile, studying for the priesthood in the English Colleges in Rome and Rheims, Campion asserted that he and his companions were only the first wave of many future missions:

> Many innocent hands are lifted up to heaven for you daily by those English students, whose posterity shall never die, which beyond seas, gathering virtue and sufficient knowledge for the purpose, are determined never to give you

over, but either to win you heaven, or to die upon your pikes. And touching our Society, be it known to you that we have made a league—all the Jesuits in the world, whose succession and multitude must overreach all the practice of England—cheerfully to carry the cross you shall lay upon us, and never to despair your recovery, while we have a man left to enjoy your Tyburn, or to be racked with your torments, or consumed with your prisons. The expense is reckoned, the enterprise is begun; it is of God; it cannot be withstood. So the faith was planted: So it must be restored.

This was fighting talk, to be sure, but it was the rhetoric of the missionary, the soldier of Christ, not the politician.

During this time, Campion also wrote his *Decem Rationes* (Ten Reasons), a polemical pamphlet, written in Latin, in which he laid out his arguments against the validity of the Anglican church. Printed on a clandestine press at Stonor Park—near Henley in Oxfordshire, part of the emerging Catholic underground—this latest rhetorical broadside caused a sensation, especially when four hundred copies were found on the benches of St. Mary's, Oxford, at the Commencement, on June 27, 1581. Such escapades were turning Campion into a romantic hero, seen by many as a sort of latter-day Robin Hood, a noble outlaw fighting for justice in a wicked age, always staying one step ahead of his pursuivants. And yet many suspected that it was only a matter of time before Campion would be betrayed by one of Elizabeth's spies.

Four days before the distribution of Campion's pamphlet in Oxford, Fr. Allen had written to Fr. Alphonsus Agazzari, the Jesuit rector of the English College in Rome, that "the persecution still rages with the same fury, the Catholics being haled away to prison and otherwise vexed, and the Fathers of the Society being most diligently looked for."[15] His words were ominously portentous. Three weeks later, the hounds would finally run Campion to the ground. He was betrayed by a spy named George Eliot and taken to London with his arms pinioned and bearing on his hat an inscription which read "Campion, the Seditious Jesuit".[16] Over the next few months, he was tortured repeatedly in an effort to get him to betray the whereabouts of other priests. Campion's appearance at his trial on November 20 confirmed the extent of the sadistic treatment meted out to him in the four months since his arrest:

> Yet if we had not heard of their several and often rackings, master Campion, his coming to the bar with his hands folded in linen cloth, and with that feebleness, as he was neither able to pluck off his own mitten of frieze [i.e., course cloth gloves] nor lift a cup of drink to his mouth without help, may well show how he had been handled.[17]

Edmund Campion and his fellow defendants were found guilty of treason. "In condemning us," Campion responded upon hearing the verdict, "you condemn all your own ancestors, all our ancient bishops and kings, all that was once the glory of England—the island of saints, and the most devoted child of the See of Peter."[18]

Lord Chief Justice Christopher Wray read the sentence:

> "You must go to the place from whence you came, there to remain until ye shall be drawn through the open city of

---

[15] John Henry de Groot, *The Shakespeares and "The Old Faith"* (Fraser, Mich.: Real-View Books, 1995), 87–88.

[16] Hugh Chisholm, ed., *Encyclopædia Britannica*, 11th ed. (Cambridge: Cambridge University Press, 1911), s.v. "Campion, Edmund".

[17] Gerard Kilroy, *Edmund Campion: Memory and Transcription* (Aldershot: Ashgate Publishing, 2005), 18.

[18] Richard Simpson, *Edmund Campion* (London: Williams & Norgate, 1867), 307–8.

London upon hurdles to the place of execution, and there
be hanged and let down alive, and your privy parts cut off,
and your entrails taken out and burnt in your sight; then
your heads to be cut off and your bodies divided into four
parts, to be disposed of at Her Majesty's pleasure. And
God have mercy on your souls."[19]

On hearing the death sentence, Campion and his co-
defendants broke into the words of the *Te Deum*, the traditional hymn of the Church at times of special celebration,
such as a royal coronation, the election of a pope, or, most
significantly, the canonization of a saint. In condemning the
martyrs to death, the worldly judge was unwittingly opening the doors of heaven to Our Lord's faithful servants.

On December 1, 1581, Campion, along with two fellow priests—Fr. Ralph Sherwin and Fr. Alexander Briant,
the former of whom had been one of Campion's travel
companions on the long trek from Rome to England—
were dragged by hurdle to Tyburn. Then, as stipulated
in the judge's sentence, Campion was hanged but taken
down while still alive. He was then laid out flat in full view
of the crowd, stripped naked, castrated, and cut open. His
internal organs were then removed, one by one, and held
aloft for the crowd to see before being thrown into the
fire. The last organ to be removed was the heart, which
by this time had hopefully and mercifully stopped beat-
ing. The body was then decapitated and hacked into four
pieces. At some stage in this gory and gruesome process,
some of Campion's blood had spattered on a young man
in the crowd. Converted instantly and therefore miraculously, it is said, by the touch of the saint's sanctified
blood, the young man, Henry Walpole, gave up his law

[19] Ibid., 308–9.

practice and followed in the hallowed footsteps of his martyred mentor; he became a priest of the Society of Jesus before returning to England to face arrest, torture, and the same gruesome death he had witnessed at Tyburn, being hanged, drawn, and quartered on April 7, 1595, thereby following Campion to heaven. Both men were canonized in 1970 by Pope Paul VI.

It is appropriate to end this chapter as we began, with some lines from St. Henry Walpole's poem in homage to Edmund Campion, the words of one saint in praise of another.

> You thought perhaps when learned Campion dies,
> His pen must cease, his sugared tongue be still,
> But you forgot how loud his death it cries,
> How far beyond the sound of tongue and quill,
> You did not know how rare and great a good
> It was to write his precious gifts in blood. . . .
>
> His hurdle draws us with him to the Cross,
> His speeches there provoketh us to die,
> His death doth say, his life is but our loss,
> His martyred blood from heaven to us doth cry.
> His first and last, and all agree in this,
> To show the way that leadeth unto bliss.
>
> Blessed be God, who lent him so much grace,
> Thanked be Christ, that blest his martyr so,
> Happy is he that sees his master's face
> Cursed are they that thought to work his woe
> Bounden we be to give eternal praise
> To Jesus' name, who such a saint did raise.

Chapter Fifteen

England on the Rack

Rain, rain on Tyburn tree
Red rain a-falling
Dew, dew on Tyburn tree
And the swart bird a-calling.

—Francis Thompson,
from "Ode to the
English Martyrs"

Responding to the great success of the English mission- ary priests in winning many converts to the faith, Eliza- beth's government introduced a new statute in 1581 which made it a crime of treason, punishable by death, to "persuade" someone to become a Catholic. William Lampley, a layman, was sentenced to death under this law for "persuading" a member of his own family to convert. According to a near contemporary source, dating from around 1592,[1] he was convicted and was condemned to death on the evidence of only one witness, a man of con- siderable ill repute. Having passed sentence, the judge, Sir Roger Manwood, assured Lampley that he would be released if he agreed to attend the Protestant service. Lampley refused. He was hanged, drawn, and quartered

---

[1] Roland Connelly, *The Eighty-Five Martyrs* (Great Wakering, Essex: McCrimmon Publishing, 1987), 44.

in Gloucester and would be beatified by the Church as one of the Eighty-Five Martyrs.

The Elizabethan regime also made war on the underground Catholic press, mindful of the stir caused by Edmund Campion's published broadsides. In 1582, Stephen Vallenger, having been convicted of writing and publishing *A True Report* of Campion's death, had his ears cut off in punishment and was then imprisoned until his death in 1591. In the same year, Blessed William Carter was arrested for running a secret Catholic press. He was tortured and then executed for treason. Stephen Brinkley's secret press had moved from East Ham in Essex to Southwark in London to stay one step ahead of the spy network; he was finally located at Stonor House in Oxfordshire. The press was seized, and Brinkley was imprisoned for two years.

The owner of Stonor House was the indomitable Lady Cecily Stonor, whose uncle, the Carthusian monk Sebastian Newdigate, had been hanged, drawn, and quartered at Tyburn during the reign of Henry VIII. Apart from allowing her home to be used for the underground Catholic press, it was also one of the main hideouts for priests, newly arrived from the continent. It is known that Edmund Campion stayed there, he and other priests living and working in a secret hiding place high above Stonor's front porch which was known as Mount Pleasant. Should the house be searched and this hiding place discovered, there was another secret door leading to a ladder which came out under the central gable of the roof. A makeshift chapel was hidden in the rafters. Many of these secret places and hideouts, known as priest holes, were designed and built by St. Nicholas Owen, an ingenious and gifted craftsman who would be tortured repeatedly following his arrest—refusing even under the greatest torment to divulge the whereabouts of any of the secret places he had built across the country.

The increasing devotion to the growing number of English Martyrs was exemplified in 1583, when frescoes depicting sixty-three martyrs were commissioned and then publicly exhibited at the Venerable English College in Rome, from whence Campion and others had set forth on their glorious quest to nourish and nurture the faith in the land of their birth. Back in England, the places at which the martyrs were put to death became holy shrines to which Catholics, under cover of darkness, would make pilgrimages. Outside York, at the gallows known as the Knavesmire, the remains of martyred Catholics were left hanging for many days as a warning to others who might be tempted to similar acts of "treachery". This became a place of clandestine pilgrimage for Margaret Clitherow and her recusant friends, who would slip out of the city after dark, walking barefoot to the place of butchery which had become hallowed ground.

By the 1580s, there were so many priests being put to death in England that it's not possible to list or mention them all. In February 1584, fourteen priests were accused of a wholly fictitious plot to kill the queen, at least five of whom were subsequently hanged, drawn, and quartered. Another priest, John Hart, kept a prison diary from 1580 to 1585 in which he named eleven prisons in London alone where Catholics suffered seven different forms of torture. In spite of such treatment, incarcerated Catholics remained active in the faith. Contemporary records, letters, and autobiographical accounts all attest to a lively and vibrant prison culture. "Prisons are full of priests," wrote the Jesuit William Weston in the summer of 1585, shortly after his arrival in England; "but God's word is not in chains. In the midst of tribulation, sorrow and weariness our mother Jerusalem is not sterile, and ceases not to bear her children."[2]

The nobleman Sir Philip Howard, who was incarcerated in the Tower of London in 1585, remaining there until his death ten years later, carved a Latin inscription on his cell wall, which might be translated thus: "Just as to be bound because of sin is a disgrace, so, in contrast, to suffer the chains of imprisonment for Christ is the greatest glory."[3] Dying of dysentery, Sir Philip petitioned the queen to be able to see his wife, who had been pregnant at the time of his arrest and imprisonment, and the son whom he had never seen. "If he will but once attend the Protestant Service," the queen responded, "he shall not only see his wife and children, but be restored to his honors and estates with every mark of my royal favor." Howard is said to have replied: "Tell Her Majesty if my religion be the cause for which I suffer, sorry I am that I have but one life to lose."[4]

The deadly danger facing England's Catholics was the presence in their midst of Elizabeth's burgeoning spy network. These were men of no principle who would sell their own mother for the thirty pieces of silver that treachery brings. This was literally the case with the infamous lapsed Catholic Arthur Webster, who had become a professional priest catcher. To the horror and squalor of York prison, he had condemned his own mother, described as "a good and constant Catholic gentlewoman", and his own sister, the "saintly" Frances

---

[2] William Weston, *An Autobiography from the Jesuit Underground* (New York: Farrar, Straus and Cudahy, 1955), xxii–xxiii.

[3] Robert S. Miola, ed., *Early Modern Catholicism: An Anthology of Primary Sources* (Oxford: Oxford University Press, 2007), 24.

[4] Basil Cardinal Hume, Homily given on the fourth centenary of St. Philip Howard's martyrdom, Arundel Cathedral, October 25, 1995.

Webster.[5] Blessed Marmaduke Bowes, who welcomed priests to his house, was betrayed by the Catholic teacher whom he employed for his children. He was hanged in November 1585 for the heinous "crime" of harbouring priests; we can only wonder how his betrayer could assuage his conscience, having left a wife bereft of a husband and children bereft of a father. The close-knit community of Catholic prisoners in York Castle was betrayed by a non-Catholic prisoner who feigned a desire for conversion. Receiving encouragement, he then reported the prisoners for the crime of "persuading to popery", a crime punishable by death. Thus entrapped, three men—William Knight, George Errington, and William Gibson—all laymen, were hanged, drawn, and quartered. Two women prisoners who were similarly entrapped by the same spy were condemned to be burned to death, but they were temporarily reprieved by the Privy Council, acting upon the queen's orders, their executions being delayed until further notice. The two women, Ann Tesh and Bridget Maskew, were then left to rot in jail indefinitely, not being released until the queen's death and the accession to the throne of James I.

Although the missionary priests were almost invariably put to death, the queen could occasionally be more lenient with those who sheltered them. John Stonor spent only eight months in the Tower of London following his conviction for harbouring priests at Stonor House. During his incarceration, the lieutenant's daughter fell in love with him; she was converted and carried messages between the Catholic prisoners in the Tower and those in the Marshalsea prison. Upon his release, Stonor went into

<hr />

[5] Roland Connelly, *No Greater Love: The Martyrs of the Middlesbrough Diocese* (Great Wakering, Essex: McCrimmons, 1987), 53.

exile. He would never see either his home or his unhappy paramour again.

Lady Cecily Stonor was also treated with relative leniency, presumably because of her age. Convicted of harbouring priests, she was spared prison. Undeterred, she continued to shelter priests at Stonor House. Convicted a second time in 1590, when she was seventy years old, she was sent to prison, dying behind bars, unbroken in spirit until the last.

Fr. William Weston gave a firsthand account of life in the Clink, one of London's prisons in the 1580s. "Besides criminals and thieves ... there were many Catholic priests in this prison, gentlemen of quality, men of middle means, women, and some who were little more than boys."[6] Fr. Weston also met a lay Catholic who was incarcerated along with his wife and two children, offering this singular act of injustice as an example of "how iniquitous the heretics could be".[7] Astonishingly, Fr. Weston offered Mass in his cell, lowering a rope to the cell below, in which the vestments were hidden. Drawing these up to his own cell, he would offer Mass in the middle of the night. "Early in the morning, when Mass was over and before the other prisoners and the warders were awake, we would let down the rope again in the same way."[8] Even more astonishingly, Fr. Weston wrote of a convert to the faith and fellow prisoner who prior to his conversion had been a keeper of Catholic prisoners. This convert was adept at picking the locks of the cells and closing them again. In the middle of the night on the Feast of Christ's Nativity in 1586, he went from cell to cell, picking the locks, so

[6] Weston, *Autobiography from Jesuit Underground*, 116.
[7] Ibid.
[8] Ibid., 117.

that the Catholic prisoners could come to Fr. Weston's cell for the celebration of the Christmas liturgy. The priest heard the confessions of his fellow prisoners and "there was not one of them who did not receive the Body of our Saviour Christ in communion."[9]

Apart from the numerous Catholics in England's prisons, there were those who had chosen exile. Many Catholic scholars, excluded from Oxford and Cambridge, gravitated to the University of Louvain in what is now Belgium, which became a centre for English Catholic scholarship. Those with a vocation to the priesthood studied at the seminaries founded by William Allen, Robert Persons, and others in Douai, Rheims, Saint-Omer, Seville, Valladolid, and, of course, Rome. Other exiles took up service in royal courts—especially the court of King Philip of Spain, who was very generous in helping England's displaced Catholics—or attached themselves to the households of prominent European nobles, such as those of the dukes of Savoy, Parma, and Guise. Other exiles, less well connected, became mercenaries or servants. The most evocative encapsulation of the plight of English exiles is the epitaph on the tomb of one such exile in the church of San Gregorio in Rome: "Here lies Robert Peckham, Englishman and Catholic, who, after England's break with the Church, left England not being able to live without the Faith and who, coming to Rome, died not being able to live without his country."[10]

If Robert Peckham's death might be said to have been caused by an exile's broken heart, his Catholic compatriots back home were suffering excruciating deaths for the

[9] Ibid.
[10] Joseph Pearce, *Literary Converts* (San Francisco: Ignatius Press, 1999), 13–14. The poignancy of this moving epitaph would serve as the inspiration for the historical novel *Robert Peckham*, by Maurice Baring.

sake of the faith. The slow and torturously cruel death by hanging, drawing, and quartering, the fate of many of England's martyrs, was not felt appropriate as a punishment for women. Margaret Clitherow, having harboured priests in her home in York for many years, was sentenced to death by "pressing". The exact details of this "milder" form of execution were given by the judge in his sentencing of her:

> You must return from whence you came, and there, in the lowest part of the prison, be stripped naked, laid down, your back upon the ground, and as much weight laid upon you as you are able to bear, and to continue three days without meat or drink, except a little barley bread and puddle water, and the third day to be pressed to death, your hands and feet tied to posts, and a sharp stone under your back.[11]

Margaret Clitherow prepared for death as though she were preparing for a feast and a marriage. She fasted, prayed, and dressed in white linen. She sent her hat to her husband "in sign of her loving duty to him" and her hose and shoes to her daughter, Anne, "signifying that she should serve God and follow her steps of virtue".[12]

The sentence was duly carried out on March 25, which, appropriately enough, was both the date of the Feast of the Annunciation and the date, according to tradition, of Christ's Crucifixion. It has been conjectured that Margaret, the mother of three, could possibly have been pregnant at the time of her martyrdom, which would have meant the death of her unborn child, forging a mystical

[11] Margaret T. Monro, *St. Margaret Clitherow: The Pearl of York* (Rockford, Ill.: TAN Books, 2003), 62.

[12] Miola, *Early Modern Catholicism*, 138.

connection with the Annunciation. What is not open to conjecture is that she was laid on the ground and that her hands were bound to two stakes on the floor, forcing her to lay with arms outstretched in the form of a cross. A stone, the size of a man's fist, was placed under her back and a door upon her body. Ordered to ask for the queen's forgiveness for assisting priests, Margaret replied that "I have prayed for her."[13] Four hired beggars then began to place the weights upon her. As she was being crushed to death, she was heard to pray: "Jesu! Jesu! Jesu! Have mercy on me!" It is said that she took about fifteen minutes to die, a pool of blood spreading across the floor. At the time of her death, she is believed to have been around thirty-three years old. Of her three children, aged fourteen, twelve, and ten at the time of their mother's death, all would not only remain true to the faith for which their mother had died but would pursue religious vocations. Her two sons became priests, and her daughter became a nun.

Devotion to the martyred Margaret Clitherow spread rapidly. A manuscript entitled *A True Report of the Life and Martyrdom of Mrs. Margaret Clitherow* written by Fr. John Mush, her confessor whom she had sheltered many times in her home, was circulating in York within weeks of her death. A widely read and influential account of her life and death appeared in Richard Verstegan's *Theatrum crudelitatum haereticorum*, published in 1587.

Although Fr. Mush escaped the clutches of Elizabeth's spy network, another priest whom Margaret Clitherow had sheltered, Fr. Francis Ingleby, was captured only a few weeks after the saint's martyrdom. He was hanged, drawn, and quartered in York in June 1586; he was beatified by St. John Paul II a little over four hundred years later, in

[13] Monro, *St. Margaret Clitherow*, 84.

November 1987. Other Catholics, priests and laity alike, were martyred in York in the months of anti-papist fervour that followed; yet newly ordained priests were still arriving from the continent, undaunted and determined, willing to lay down their lives for England's besieged faithful. Two such priests, destined to play a major role in the recusant resistance over the following years, were the Jesuits Robert Southwell and Henry Garnet, who arrived in England in early July 1586, much to the delight of their fellow Jesuit William Weston. "Although the persecution at this time was very severe," Fr. Weston wrote, "many were executed, houses sacked, and through the length and breadth of the entire kingdom Catholics were hunted down and imprisoned—still it was a great consolation to me, in the midst of all these anxieties, to have faithful and brave companions in my perils."[14]

Little could any of these courageous confreres have known, in the heat of the perils and persecution of 1586, that the following year would prove even more perilous for those in the Jesuit underground.

---

[14] Weston, *Autobiography from Jesuit Underground*, 69.

Chapter Sixteen

God's Spice

The pounded spice both taste and scent doth please;
In fading smoke the force doth incense show;
The perished kernel springeth with increase;
The lopped tree doth best and soonest grow.
God's spice I was, and pounding was my due;
In fading breath my incense favoured best;
Death was my means my kernel to renew;
By lopping shot I up to heavenly rest.

—St. Robert Southwell,
from "Decease Release"*

Fr. Weston was arrested shortly after the arrival in England of his two Jesuit colleagues, Robert Southwell and Henry Garnet. Fr. Southwell, writing to the Jesuit Superior in Rome four days before Christmas 1586, reported that Fr. Weston was "devout and steadfast" in prison, "so much so that he makes imprisonment more pleasant to those in chains, and less fearful to them that are free".[1]

---

*The spelling has been modernized for ease of comprehension.
[1] William Weston, *An Autobiography from the Jesuit Underground* (New York: Farrar, Straus and Cudahy, 1955), 125.

Early in the New Year, a new law was passed "for the more speedy and due execution" of the anti-Catholic legislation which would make life even more difficult for England's recusants.[2] The new law increased the fines for nonattendance at the services of the state religion and allowed the Crown to seize two-thirds of the estate of any recusant who defaulted on the payment of the fines. Another law, "An Act against Jesuits, seminary priests and such other disobedient persons", extended the crime of treason to any Englishman ordained abroad as a Catholic priest who entered or remained in England. This made it unnecessary to prove that a priest was plotting against the queen; merely setting foot in the country was now an act of treason punishable by death.

On February 8, 1587, Mary Stuart, Queen of Scots, was executed. She had been a prisoner of Elizabeth for nineteen years and was put to death for allegedly plotting Elizabeth's assassination. Controversy still rages with respect to Mary's guilt or innocence, but at the very least, she was the victim of entrapment by Elizabeth's spymaster, Sir Francis Walsingham. The fact is that Elizabeth wanted Mary dead, and she employed lies, spies, and torture to get what she wanted. For England's Catholics, most of whom considered Mary to be the true queen due to Elizabeth's illegitimacy, the news of the execution aroused nothing but sympathy for the unfortunate monarch who had been a prisoner of circumstance as much as she had been a prisoner of Elizabeth. This view was encapsulated by Robert Southwell in his evocative poem, "Decease Release", written in the first person with Queen Mary as the speaker. The crushing of the

---

[2] Jessie Childs, *Terror & Faith in Elizabethan England* (Oxford: Oxford University Press, 2014), 140.

Catholic queen is seen as analogous to the pounding of incense, the fragrance of which rises to heaven:

> God's spice I was, and pounding was my due;
> In fading breath my incense favoured best;
> Death was my means my kernel to renew;
> By lopping shot I up to heavenly rest.

In this powerful metaphor, the Catholic poet transforms and transfigures the queen into a Catholic martyr who, like St. Margaret Clitherow, was crushed into "God's spice":

> Alive a Queen, now dead I am a Saint;
> Once Mary called, my name now Martyr is;
> From earthly reign debarred by restraint,
> In lieu whereof I reign in heavenly bliss.

Meanwhile the martyrdom of priests continued unabated. In March, Thomas Pilcher was hanged, drawn, and quartered in Dorchester. In the same month, Stephen Rowsham and John Hambley suffered the same fate in Gloucester and Salisbury, respectively. In Oxford, Fr. Thomas Belson, having watched two brother priests being mutilated with the butcher's knife in the customary fashion, embraced the mangled bodies of the two dead martyrs, remarking to those who had come to witness the barbarity that he was glad to appear before God in such company. He then suffered the same gruesome disemboweling at the hands of the executioner. A similar scene unfolded in Derby when three priests, known collectively as the Padley Martyrs, were hanged, drawn, and quartered. Fr. Nicholas Garlick, Fr. Robert Ludlum, and Fr. Richard Simpson were dragged through the streets on a hurdle to the place of execution. Upon their arrival at the scaffold, Fr. Simpson appeared frightened at the prospect of his imminent and slow and tortuous death. He then watched his two colleagues being butchered, one after the other. Finally, when his time came, he embraced the ladder and kissed the steps that led to the gallows. Dying bravely, he was remembered, along with his two colleagues, in the famous "Epitaph upon the Death of Three Most Blessed Martyrs", published by a secret Catholic press in 1604:

> And what though Simpson seemed to yield
> For doubt and dread to die:
> He rose again and won the field,
> And died most constantly.[3]

As was so often the case, the Padley Martyrs were betrayed by Catholic apostates working in league with the government's network of spies. In this case, Thomas Fitzherbert, having made a pact with Richard Topcliffe, Elizabeth's chief torturer and priest hunter, betrayed his own family. He informed Topcliffe of the whereabouts of the priest hole in which the Jesuits Nicholas Garlick and Robert Ludlum were hiding, thereby sending the priests to their torture and deaths.

Even as England's Catholics were suffering from new draconian laws and a new spate of executions, tensions between Spain and England were reaching a breaking point. King Philip of Spain shared the outrage of the whole of Christendom at the execution of Mary Stuart; in the summer of 1588, he raised an armada to liberate England from the Elizabethan tyranny. Since the defeat of the Spanish Armada has become part of the English national mythos—something enshrined in the patriotic psyche—it is difficult to see it objectively within the context of the times. Hilaire Belloc rises above such jingoism

---

[3] Roland Connelly, *No Greater Love: The Martyrs of the Middlesbrough Diocese* (Great Wakering, Essex: McCrimmons, 1987), 60.

in his appraisal of this crucial chapter in the histories of both England and Spain:

> The English attitude towards the Armada was confused. The official version that the whole country was enthusiastic for the cause of the Cecils[4] and Protestantism, or even for the repelling of the effort mainly because it was launched by a foreigner, is nonsense. The great quarrel of the time was still the religious quarrel, the crushing out of Catholicism in England by the Cecils; and though Protestantism had large support by 1588, it was still sincerely felt by no more than a minority. Had it been possible to land Spanish troops there would certainly have been a violent and widespread Catholic rising.[5]

In October 1588, a few short weeks after the defeat of the Armada, a young Jesuit priest who just turned twenty-four years old landed secretly on the coast of Norfolk. This was Fr. John Gerard, who was destined to become one of the most successful of all the missionary priests and therefore one of the most wanted by Elizabeth's government. He would serve the English mission in East Anglia for the next five and a half years, evading arrest and eluding the authorities. He was finally arrested in April 1594, and then, after three years in prison, was moved to the Tower of London to be tortured. In October 1597, he made a daring escape from the Tower, by means of a rope stretched from a cannon on the roof of one of the towers across the moat to a wharf on the River Thames.

Fr. Gerard remained at large for the next eight years, moving mostly between Northamptonshire and London,

---

[4] William Cecil was Elizabeth's chief adviser for most of her reign and is attributed by Belloc as being the real power behind the throne.

[5] Hilaire Belloc, *A Shorter History of England* (London: George G. Harrap, 1934), 335.

serving England's Catholics, including those high-ranking
Catholics who had access to the queen's court such as the
Earl of Southampton—a favourite of the queen who was, at
the same time, a devout Catholic and confidant of the Jesuit
priest St. Robert Southwell as well as being William Shakespeare's patron. William Byrd, composer of the Chapel
Royal, was another of the queen's favourites. Although Elizabeth knew of Byrd's recusancy, she not only chose to turn
a blind eye to it but instructed her ministers to protect him
from the anti-Catholic laws. On more than one occasion,
court records show that efforts to fine Byrd and his wife
for their refusal to attend Anglican services were abandoned
"by order of the Queen's Attorney General".[6] Not only did
Elizabeth intervene personally to rescue Byrd from persecution; she even made him a gift in 1595 of the lease of Ston-
don Place, in recognition of his faithful service as her court
composer. It seems that the queen looked upon Byrd in the
same way that she looked upon another Catholic favourite:
Edward Somerset, the fourth Earl of Worcester, whom she
described as having "reconciled what she thought inconsistent, a stiff papist, to a good subject".[7] And yet, according to
Byrd's biographer, "loyal and circumspect as Byrd undoubt-
edly was, he was more intimately involved in Catholic circles, and probably knew more about Catholic intrigues, than
is betrayed by the bare written records."[8] If this is true of
Byrd, it is equally true of William Shakespeare, who was
raised in a recusant home and who appears to have retained
his Catholic sympathies following his arrival in London.

The parallels between William Byrd and William
Shakespeare are worthy of note. There is evidence that

[6] David Mateer, "William Byrd's Middlesex Recusancy", *Music and Letters* 78, no. 1 (February 1997): 1–14.

[7] John Harley, *William Byrd: Gentleman of the Royal Chapel* (Bookfield, Vt.: Ashgate Publishing, 1997), 77.

[8] Ibid.

Byrd might have known the Jesuit martyr Edmund Campion, as there is evidence that Shakespeare probably knew the Jesuit martyr Robert Southwell; it is conjectured that Byrd might have been in the crowd who witnessed Campion's martyrdom, and that Shakespeare might have witnessed the martyrdom of Southwell. William Byrd set part of St. Henry Walpole's poem eulogizing Campion to music, risking the ire of the queen by publishing his musical setting of the poem in 1588; Shakespeare alludes to the poetry of St. Robert Southwell in several of his plays, including *Romeo and Juliet*, *The Merchant of Venice*, *Hamlet*, and *King Lear*.

If Jesuit priests, such as John Gerard and Robert Southwell, managed to evade capture for several years, other newly arrived priests were not so fortunate. Four priests who arrived on the northeast coast of England in March 1590, expecting to be met as they landed and then taken from one safe house to another, found that they were utterly alone and without any help, the underground network having been betrayed by spies. With little option but to make the long journey south without any assistance, they made the fatal mistake of travelling together and not splitting up. Betrayed by someone who pretended to be a Catholic to gain their confidence, they were tried and executed. Fr. Richard Hill, Fr. John Hogg, Fr. Richard Holiday, and Fr. Edmund Duke were hanged, drawn, and quartered on May 27, 1590, at Dryburn on the outskirts of Durham.

The way in which the homes of recusants were raided and searched by the government's priest hunters was described by Robert Southwell:

> Their manner of searching is to come with a troop of men to the house as though they come to fight a-field.

They beset the house on every side, then they rush in and ransack every corner—even women's beds and bosoms—with such insolent behavior that their villainies in this kind are half a martyrdom. The men they command to stand and to keep their places; and whatsoever of price cometh in their way, many times they pocket it up, as jewels, plate, money and such like ware, under pretense of papistry.... When they find any books, church stuff, chalices, or other like things, they take them away, not for any religion that they care for but to make a commodity.[9]

In October 1591, nine or ten Jesuits and several other priests, as well as a number of laymen who were living in hiding, were gathered for a conference at Baddesley Clinton, a large recusant house in Warwickshire. Fearing that there were not enough priest holes in which to hide such a large number of outlaws, the meeting was kept short. Several of the priests and laymen dispersed, leaving the remnant at the house. At five o'clock on the following morning, the house was raided. "I was making my meditation," wrote Fr. Gerard, "Father Southwell was beginning Mass and the rest were at prayer, when suddenly I heard a great uproar outside the main door." There was much shouting and swearing at a servant who was refusing entrance to the priest hunters. Had not this "faithful servant held them back ... we should have all been caught."

With no time to lose, Fr. Southwell slipped off his vestments and stripped the altar bare. Meanwhile, the other priests grabbed all their personal belongings so that nothing was left to betray the presence of a priest. "Even our boots and swords were hidden away," wrote Fr. Gerard; "they would have roused suspicions if none of the people they

[9] Robert S. Miola, ed., *Early Modern Catholicism: An Anthology of Primary Sources* (Oxford: Oxford University Press, 2007), 34.

belonged to were to be found."[10] The five Jesuit priests, three of whom were destined to die martyrs' deaths, two secular priests, and two or three laymen clambered into a sort of cave hidden underground, the floor of which was covered with water. Here they remained for four hours while the priest hunters delved into every corner, and every nook and cranny, seeking in vain for their prey. Although Robert Southwell escaped the clutches of Elizabeth's henchmen on this occasion, he would finally be betrayed the following year after eluding capture for six years. He would face three years of brutal torture, never once divulging information to his torturers. His astonishing resilience and courage earned him the grudging respect of one of those who witnessed his excruciating suffering. "They boast about the heroes of antiquity," wrote Robert Cecil, the son of Lord Burghley (William Cecil), Elizabeth's chief minister, "but we have a new torture which it is not possible for a man to bear. And yet I have seen Robert Southwell hanging by it, still as a tree trunk, and no one able to drag one word from his mouth."[11]

In 1593, a new anti-Catholic law, the Five Mile Act, restricted the movement of Catholics to within five miles of their homes and gave the government the power to seize the property of any Catholic who refused to return to his home. In the face of these latest affronts to religious liberty, it was often the women who were most determined in offering resistance. In the recusant rolls of 1593–1594, which list those fined for their refusal to conform to the state religion, more than half were women, 489 of a total of 895.[12] Bridget Strange, the fifty-year-old wife

[10] John Gerard, *The Autobiography of an Elizabethan* (Oxford: Family Publications, 2006), 41–42.

[11] Hugh Ross Williamson, *The Day Shakespeare Died* (London: Michael Joseph, 1962), 57.

[12] Miola, *Early Modern Catholicism*, 21.

of Thomas Strange, was languishing in London's Gatehouse prison in 1593 for her refusal to attend the services
of the state church. In the same year, another courageous
woman, Anne Thwing, was thrown into York prison,
without trial, for fearlessly professing her Catholic faith.
It is not known what happened to her. There's no record
of her facing trial or ever being released from prison. Like
so many others, she simply disappeared. Her family continued in her defiant spirit, two family members suffering
future martyrdom, Edward Thwing in 1600 and Thomas
Thwing in 1680.

Another problem faced by England's Catholics was
how to educate their children. Homeschooling was an
obvious option, of course, but the founding in 1593 of
the College of Saint-Omer in northern France offered
another solution. Founded by Fr. Robert Persons, under
the financial patronage of the king of Spain, Saint-Omer
would be the destination for generations of young English
Catholics. Returning to their ancestral homes fortified by
a Jesuit education, these young men would play a crucial
role in keeping alive the faith. It was from Saint-Omer,
in the autumn of 1593, that Fr. Henry Walpole set sail for
England. His journey was tracked by Elizabeth's spies, and
he was hunted down and arrested only three days after he
had landed at Bridlington in Yorkshire. After a brief
period of imprisonment in York Castle, he was transferred
to the Tower of London. There he was tortured on no
fewer than fourteen occasions under the supervision of the
sadistic Richard Topcliffe, suffering the same grisly fate as
his Jesuit confrere Robert Southwell. In 1595, both men
would be hanged, drawn, and quartered, the common fate
of most of the martyrs.

Standing in the cart at Tyburn, beneath the gibbet
and with the noose around his neck, Fr. Southwell made
the sign of the cross and recited a passage from Romans,

chapter nine. When the sheriff tried to interrupt him, those in the crowd, many of whom were sympathetic to the Jesuit's plight, shouted that he should be allowed to speak. He confessed that he was a Jesuit priest and prayed for the salvation of the queen and his country. As the cart was drawn away, he commended his soul to God in the same words that Christ had used from the Cross: *In manus tuas* (Into your hands, Lord, I commend my spirit). As he hung in the noose, some onlookers pushed forward and tugged at his legs to hasten his death before he could be cut down and disemboweled alive. Southwell was thirty-three years old, the same age as Christ at the time of His Crucifixion.

Elizabeth's obsession with crushing her Catholic subjects made her hostile to Christian Europe; therefore, she was an ally by default of the Muslim forces of the Ottoman Empire which were threatening to overrun Christendom. Nowhere was this more evident than her imprisonment of Sir Thomas Arundell, who had shown great heroism in the defence of Hungary from the Islamist conquest in 1595. Sir Thomas had been created a Count of the Holy Roman Empire and had been received by the pope in recognition of his heroism in battle. This outraged the queen. "As chaste wives should have no glances but for their own spouses," she is reported to have remarked, "so should faithful subjects keep their eyes at home and not gaze on foreign crowns."[13]

In spite of the grim reality of torture and execution, there was something almost swashbuckling in the romance of the Scarlet Pimpernel priests, staying one step ahead of those who hunted them. Fr. John Gerard's daring escape

---

[13] Peter Stanford and Leanda de Lisle, *The Catholics and Their Houses* (London: Harper Collins, 1995), 57.

from the Tower of London in 1597 must have heartened England's Catholics, as must Fr. Henry Garnet's ability to elude Elizabeth's clutches continually. Having arrived in England in 1586, Fr. Garnet was still serving as the Jesuit Superior to the English mission at the end of Elizabeth's reign, moving from one safe house to another and hiding in priest holes when the need arose.

In March 1600, six priests escaped from Wisbech prison. Three moved southwards towards London, the heart of the beast, and were soon recaptured; the remaining three headed north to resume their work of ministering to the resolute faithful. In the Catholic heartland of Lancashire in July 1600, an eyewitness account of the martyrdom of Fr. Robert Nutter and Fr. Edward Thwing described how the large crowd of Catholics who had gathered to witness the execution of the two priests had rushed forward to gather relics. "They ended their days by an illustrious martyrdom," the eyewitness reported, "which greatly edified the whole region."[14] There were similar scenes at the martyrdom of two other Lancashire priests, Robert Middleton and Thurston Hunt, in the following year. All four newly martyred priests were celebrated in a contemporary popular ballad, "A Song of Four Priests":

> In this our English coast much blessed blood is shed:
> Two hundred priests almost in our time martyred,
> And many lay-men die with joyful sufferance,
> Many more in prison lie, God's cause for to advance.

> Amongst this gracious troop, that follow Christ his train
> To cause the Devil stoop, four priests were lately slain:—
> Nutter's bold constancy and his sweet fellow, Thwing,
> Of whose most meek modesty angels and saints sing.

---

[14] Connelly, *No Greater Love*, 130.

Hunt's haughty courage stout, with godly zeal so true,
Mild Middleton, but oh what tongue can half thy virtue
    shew!
At Lancaster, lovingly, these martyrs took their end
In glorious victory, true faith for to defend.[15]

Meanwhile, in London, Anne Line, a convert to the Faith who, like Robert Southwell, was probably an acquaintance of Shakespeare,[16] was martyred on February 26, 1601, in the last years of Elizabeth's reign. She had been arrested when priest hunters raided her apartments during the celebration of Mass. The Jesuit priest who had been celebrating the Mass managed to remove his vestments in the nick of time and escape by mingling into the congregation; but Mrs. Line was arrested for hiding priests and went to the gallows to suffer the martyrdom for which she had prayed. Devout and defiant to the last, she remarked of her conviction for harbouring priests that "would God that where I harboured one, I had harboured a thousand."[17]

The Elizabethan reign of terror came to an end on March 24, 1603, the queen finally going to meet her reward after ruling tyrannically for forty-four blood-soaked years. The total number of those who suffered for their faith during those years is unknown. Those put to death as Catholics numbered 189, of which 126 were priests. According to the historian Gerard Culkin, this terrible death toll was "the measure not of the failure but the triumph of the Catholic cause for which these martyrs died":

[15] Ibid., 131.

[16] It has been conjectured by several critics that Shakespeare's poem "The Phoenix and the Turtle" and his "Sonnet 74" make cryptic references to Anne Line's martyrdom.

[17] Martin Dodwell, *Annie Line: Shakespeare's Tragic Muse* (Sussex, England: Book Guild Publishing, 2013), 112.

It is the measure of the strength of the Catholic faith in this England of the first Elizabeth, and of her government's failure in this, the most determined and thorough-going attempt ever made, to confirm the establishment of Protestantism by the total destruction of the ancient Church.[18]

But this terrible body count was only the tip of the iceberg. Hidden from view is the countless number of men and women, and even children, who died in the squalor of England's prisons. The Jesuit William Weston spent seventeen years in prison, and the recusants Francis Tregian and Thomas Pounde were imprisoned for twenty and thirty years, respectively. Grace Babthorpe, a neighbour of Margaret Clitherow, endured five years of imprisonment, becoming a nun following her release. Apart from the priests put to death for their faith, many others died during their incarceration. About 130 Marian priests (those ordained during the reign of Mary Tudor) were imprisoned in the reign of Elizabeth, with approximately thirty of them, aged and sick, dying in prison. In addition, there are the countless others, priests and laity alike, who simply disappeared from all historical record following their imprisonment, presumably having died in jail. Of the 471 seminary priests who came to England during Elizabeth's reign, 285 were captured and incarcerated.[19]

As for the facts surrounding the queen's final days and death, there is a contemporary account written in 1607 by Elizabeth Southwell, a royal maid of the queen who

[18] Gerard Culkin, *The English Reformation* (London: Sands, 1955), 134–35.

[19] Miola, *Early Modern Catholicism*, 22. According to Stanford and de Lisle, the number of seminary priests smuggled into England during Elizabeth's reign was much higher, numbering "some 800 ... of whom about 300 were still at large" at the time of the queen's death. Stanford and de Lisle, *Catholics and Their Houses*, xv.

was often in the queen's presence during the last weeks of her life. Terrified of the approach of death, Elizabeth had taken to the sort of superstition which was suggestive of witchcraft. She wore a gold amulet around her neck which was said to bestow longevity upon its wearer, sent to her by an old woman in Wales who had allegedly been 120 years old when she died. The occult trinket notwithstanding, the queen became sick and told Lady Scrope, one of her Ladies-in-waiting, that she had been visited by what she described as an apparition of herself "exceeding lean and fearful in a light of fire".[20] Prompted by this visitation, the queen commanded that a true looking glass be brought to her, "which in twenty years before she had not seen but only such a one which of purpose was made to deceive her sight". Horrified at the sight of her own decrepit and aging body, unperceived for two decades, she "took it so offensively that all those which had before flattered her durst not come in her sight".[21]

Elizabeth was known to daub cosmetics onto her face in ever-increasing quantities as she got older, hiding her aging (mortal) face in a mask of youth. A description of Elizabeth at the end of 1600 paints a lurid picture of her painted features: "It was commonly observed this Christmas that her Majesty when she came to be seen was continuously painted, not only all over her face, but her very neck and breast also, and that the same was in some places near half an inch thick."[22] It was around this time that Shakespeare was working on *Hamlet*, and it is hard to avoid the suspicion that the playwright had Queen Elizabeth in mind in

[20] Miola, *Early Modern Catholicism*, 466.
[21] Ibid.
[22] G. B. Harrison, ed., *Elizabethan and Jacobean Journals 1591–1610*, vol. 3 (London: Routledge, 1999), 132.

Hamlet's words to the skull of Yorick: "Now get you to my lady's chamber, and tell her, let her paint an inch thick, to this favor [i.e., death] she must come."[23]

Becoming seriously ill in March 1603 and "falling into extremity", Elizabeth sat for two days and three nights, fearful of sleeping and refusing to eat or drink. Urged by Robert Cecil that she "must go to bed", the queen responded that the word *must* was not to be used to princes. "Little man, little man," she told him, "if your father had lived, ye durst not have said so much; but thou knowest I must die and that maketh thee so presumptuous."[24] Cecil's father, Lord Burghley, had masterminded Elizabeth's persecution of the Church until his death in 1598, a role that Robert would fulfil in the final years of Elizabeth's reign and in which he would continue after the accession of King James.

Elizabeth Southwell also mentions the discovery of a playing card, the queen of hearts, which had been nailed to the bottom of the queen's chair, suggestive of witchcraft being used against her by her own treacherous courtiers. Another of her Ladies-in-waiting, Elizabeth Guilford, was shocked to see the queen walking through the palace in the middle of the night. Approaching her to apologize for having left her unattended, the queen's figure vanished before her eyes. Rushing to the royal bedchamber, she found Elizabeth asleep as she had left her.

Believing that the queen's death was near, the Privy Council summoned the Archbishop of Canterbury and other senior prelates of the state religion to her presence, "upon sight of whom she was much offended, cholerically rating, bidding them be packing, saying she was no

---

[23] Shakespeare, *Hamlet*, Act V, Scene 1.
[24] Miola, *Early Modern Catholicism*, 466.

atheist, but knew that they were [illegible word] hedge-priests, and took it for an indignity that they should speak to her".[25] Although the word preceding the reference to "hedge-priests" is illegible in the manuscript, Elizabeth's dismissive and derogatory reaction to her own bishops suggests that she considered their priesthood doubtful, a recognition perhaps that Anglican ordination was invalid and that, therefore, the priests of the state religion were illicit. It is little wonder, when racked with such doubts, that she must have feared for the destiny of her soul, which would explain her tortured and torturous last days.

After the queen's death, she was sealed in a wooden coffin, lined with lead and velvet. Elizabeth Southwell was one of six ladies in attendance at the coffin when the corpse was said to have exploded, the queen's "body and head brake with such a crack that splitted the wood, lead, and cerecloth!"[26] In consequence, as a grim postmortem and gruesome postscript to the most bloody of lives, Queen Elizabeth's body had to be stitched together again prior to burial.

As for the lingering legacy of Elizabeth's cruel reign, let's allow William Cobbett to wax indignant:

> It is hardly necessary to attempt to describe the sufferings that the Catholics had to endure during this murderous reign. No tongue, no pen is adequate to the task. To hear mass, to harbor a priest, to admit the supremacy of the Pope, to deny this horrid virago's spiritual supremacy, and many other things which an honourable Catholic could scarcely avoid, consigned him to the scaffold and to the bowel ripping knife.... The gallows and gibbets and racks were in constant use, and the gaols and dungeons choking

[25] Ibid., 467.
[26] Ibid., 468.

with the victims. See a gentleman of perhaps sixty years of age or more, see him, born and bred a Catholic, compelled to make himself and his children beggars, actual beggars, or to commit what he deemed an act of apostasy and blasphemy....

As to the poor conscientious "recusants", that is to say, keepers away from the tyrant's church, they who had no money to pay fines with were crammed into prison until the gaols could (which was very soon) hold no more, and until the counties petitioned to be relieved from the charge of keeping them. They were then discharged, being first publicly whipped, or having their ears bored with a hot iron. This not answering the purpose, an act was passed to compel all "recusants" not worth twenty marks a year to quit the country in three months after conviction, and to punish them with death in case of their return....

The other deeds and events of the reign of this ferocious woman are now of little interest.... Historians have been divided in opinion as to which was the worst man that England ever produced ... but all mankind must agree that this was the worst woman that ever existed in England.[27]

[27] William Cobbett, *A History of the Protestant Reformation* (Sevenoaks, Kent: Fisher Press, 1994), 164–70.

Chapter Seventeen

God's Spies

Come, let's away to prison:
We two alone will sing like birds i' th' cage:
When thou dost ask me blessing, I'll kneel down
And ask of thee forgiveness: so we'll live,
And pray, and sing, and tell old tales, and laugh
At gilded butterflies, and hear poor rogues
Talk of court news; and we'll talk with them too,
Who loses and who wins, who's in, who's out;
And take upon's the mystery of things,
As if we were God's spies: and we'll wear out,
In a walled prison, packs and sects of great ones
That ebb and flow by th' moon.

— William Shakespeare, from *King Lear*

Queen Elizabeth's death was seen as a deliverance by England's Catholics. Her successor, King James VI of Scotland, who became James I of England, was the son of Mary, Queen of Scots and, as such, had no great love for the deceased queen who had almost certainly personally ordered the death of his mother. Although he had been raised a Protestant and practised the Protestant religion, his wife was believed to have strong Catholic sympathies, and he had made it known that he intended to repeal many of the anti-Catholic laws.

At first, it appeared that James was as good as his word. In May 1603, the Jesuit William Weston was released from the Tower of London, having been imprisoned since his arrest in 1586 and having spent the previous four and a half years in solitary confinement. He travelled to Saint-Omer in France and would soon settle in Spain, spending the final years of his life at the English seminary in Valladolid. He would never return to England.

With the onerous pecuniary burden removed, thousands of conforming or closet Catholics stayed away from Anglican services and sought once again to practise their faith fully and openly. "It was at once apparent," wrote Heinrich Mutschmann and Karl Wentersdorf in their comprehensive study, *Shakespeare and Catholicism*, "that Elizabeth's policy of extermination had not achieved its purpose, and that Catholicism still constituted a formidable power in most parts of the country."[1]

Predictably, the Puritan-dominated Parliament, fearing a resurgent and resurrected Catholicism, immediately began to put pressure on the king to reintroduce penal measures against the "papists". In February 1604, James yielded to the intense pressure being placed on him and once more banished all Catholic priests from the country. In the following month, however, he read a proclamation to Parliament declaring his intention to examine the anti-Catholic laws of his predecessor with a view to amending them. Although he sought to placate Parliament with a promise that the reestablishment of Catholicism in England would not be tolerated, he remarked nonetheless that he would like to see an end to the persecution of the Catholic laity, especially the aged and the young. The king's

---

[1] H. Mutschmann and K. Wentersdorf, *Shakespeare and Catholicism* (New York: Sheed & Ward, 1952), 27–28.

words were greeted with great suspicion and displeasure by most Protestants. Rumours began to circulate that the king was a secret papist and that his wife was a convert to Catholicism. Even if such rumours were untrue, Catholics gained succour from the fact that the queen might be a Catholic. After all, if the king was prepared to tolerate the Catholicism of his own spouse, surely he would tolerate it amongst the rest of his subjects. Such were the hopes of the Catholics and the fears of the Protestants.

The fact that William Shakespeare shared the joy of his co-religionists is discernible not so much from what he said on the occasion of the queen's death but from what he failed to say. The playwright Henry Chettle, challenging Shakespeare to write a eulogy to the deceased Elizabeth, lamented that England's foremost poet had failed to pay her tribute. In his own eulogy to the queen, *Englande's Mourning Garment*, Chettle, calling Shakespeare by the fanciful name of "Melicert", urged him to add his voice to the chorus of praise:

> Nor doth the silver tongued *Melicert*,
> Drop from his honied muse one sable teare
> To mourne her death that graced his desert,
> And to his laies opend her Royall eare.
>   Shepherd, remember our *Elizabeth*,
>   And sing her Rape, done by that *Tarquin*, Death.

If Chettle was awaiting "Melicert's" response, he would have found the silence deafening. Shakespeare apparently had no intention of shedding a solitary tear for Elizabeth, sable or otherwise, nor had he any intention of calling upon his "honied muse" to mourn her death. The apparent allegory of his poems *Venus and Adonis* and *The Rape of Lucrece* had already testified, albeit somewhat cryptically,

to the view that Elizabeth had not been the victim of violence but the predatory perpetrator of it. It was not of her
rape by death that he desired to sing but of the rape of
England and the death of the martyrs.

Far from shedding tears for the recently deceased queen,
Shakespeare wrote the aptly titled *All's Well That Ends
Well* and the most overtly Catholic of all his plays, *Measure
for Measure*, in the months following her death. It was also
probably at this time that Shakespeare and other contemporary playwrights collaborated on a play on St. Thomas
More, hoping to get it passed by the king's censor, Sir
Edmund Tilney, something which would have been
unthinkable during the reign of Elizabeth.

Unfortunately, the religious liberty that followed the
death of Bloody Bess was doomed to be short-lived. In
July 1604, Parliament, flexing its anti-Catholic muscles
in implied defiance of the king's wishes, passed a bill that
confirmed all the Elizabethan statutes against recusants.
The king, practiced in the art of realpolitik, could see that
Parliament had more power than England's besieged and
impoverished Catholics and conformed his own wishes
to the politically dominant Puritans. With the authorities renewing their persecution with renewed vigour,
England's Catholics were plunged from a premature sense
of elation to the abyss of despondency and despair, their
hopes dashed by the knowledge that James' promises were
worthless in the face of Parliamentary defiance. Many
Catholics had held on to their faith grimly, in the knowledge that the aging queen could not live forever and in
the hope that things would be better under James. Now
they were faced with the dark and stark reality that there
would be no respite under the new king. For some, this
was the final straw. Realizing that there was no immediate
prospect of religious liberty, many succumbed at last to the

state religion, conforming reluctantly; others were tempted to violence as a last desperate effort to restore the faith of their fathers. Whereas the former group had surrendered, the latter group became the unwitting tools of the new generation of spymasters. With regard to the latter, scholars such as Antonia Fraser, Hugh Ross Williamson, and others have shown that the angry Catholics who became involved in the infamous Gunpowder Plot of 1605, such as Robert Catesby and Guy Fawkes, were the dupes of the Machiavellian machinations of Sir Robert Cecil, son of the infamous Lord Burghley, and his network of spies. The plot may not have been instigated by Cecil but there seems ample evidence to suggest that he knew about it well in advance and, through the deployment of his spies, manipulated events in order to ensure that the plot would fail in its aim of killing the king and his ministers but would result instead in increasing the persecution of England's Catholics. The failed plot certainly served as a veritable coup for the virulent anti-Catholic party in James' government, under the leadership of Cecil, who bayed for the blood of all "treacherous" Catholics.

The execution in May 1606 of Fr. Henry Garnet, the Superior of the Society of Jesus in England, caused a great deal of controversy due to the alleged miracles that accompanied his martyrdom. It was said by eyewitnesses that Fr. Garnet's head retained its natural colour, even after it had been immersed in hot water as was the custom following decapitation. "His head appeared in that lively colour as it seemed to retain the same hue and shew of life which it had before it was cut off, so as both heretics and Catholics were astonished thereat."[2] The controversy continued

---

[2] John Gerard, *The Autobiography of an Elizabethan* (Oxford: Family Publications, 2006), 282.

after the head was placed on a spike upon London Bridge. "Whereupon there was such resort of people for the space of six weeks ... the citizens flocking thither by hundreds to see so strange and wonderful a spectacle, as the head of this glorious martyr did exhibit, whose face continued without any change, retaining a graceful and lively countenance, and never waxed black, as usually all heads cut from the bodies do."[3]

Even more strange was the report that an ear of corn spattered with Fr. Garnet's blood had miraculously received an image of a human face "in glorious manner, having with all proportion most exactly beard, mouth, eyes, forehead, and upon his head a crown, a cross in the forehead and a star".[4] News of the miracle spread, and the miraculous image was put on public show at the Spanish ambassador's house. "For many days there was such public resort of nobility and gentlemen, not only Catholics, but also schismatics and heretics to view it ... and having seen it departed so confounded, edified, and comforted therewith, as with one accord they acknowledged it to be supernatural."[5]

As for Shakespeare's reaction to King James' betrayal of his Catholic subjects, it is discernible in the darkness of *Othello*, *King Lear*, and *Macbeth*, the plays that he wrote following the renewal of the persecution. In *Othello*, it is surely no coincidence that the evil Machiavellian figure is given the name Iago, the Spanish name for James, nor that Shakespeare should write about a cynical and malevolent Scottish king whose name, "Macbeth", translates coincidentally as "the son of Beth", that is, Elizabeth. As for *King*

[3] Ibid.
[4] Ibid., 283.
[5] Ibid.

Lear, the choice by the play's saintly heroine, Cordelia, to "love, and be silent"[6] was the very same choice faced by England's courageous recusant remnant. There was also a clear allusion to St. Robert Southwell's depiction of Mary Stuart as "God's spice" in Lear's punning reference that he and Cordelia would be "God's spies":

> Come, let's away to prison:
> We two alone will sing like birds i' th' cage:
> When thou dost ask me blessing, I'll kneel down
> And ask of thee forgiveness: so we'll live,
> And pray, and sing, and tell old tales, and laugh
> At gilded butterflies, and hear poor rogues
> Talk of court news; and we'll talk with them too,
> Who loses and who wins, who's in, who's out;
> And take upon's the mystery of things,
> As if we were God's spies: and we'll wear out,
> In a walled prison, packs and sects of great ones
> That ebb and flow by th' moon.[7]

When King Lear and Cordelia are taken to prison, Lear responds with words of joy evocative of Southwell's allusion to incense as "God's spice". "Upon such sacrifices, my Cordelia, / The gods themselves throw incense."[8] It is difficult to read these lines without the ghostly presence of martyred Catholics coming to mind. The Jesuits were "traitors" and "spies" in the eyes of Elizabethan and Jacobean law but were "God's spies" in the eyes of England's Catholics. If caught they were imprisoned and tortured, crushed as "God's spice", being publicly executed and then rising to heaven like incense.

---

[6] Act I, Scene 1, line 64.
[7] Act V, Scene 3, lines 8–19.
[8] Act V, Scene 3, lines 20–21.

Lear and Cordelia, from the sanity and sanctity of their prison cell, will "laugh / At gilded butterflies", those elaborately attired courtiers fluttering over nothing but fads and fashions, and will "hear poor rogues / Talk of court news". Aloof from such worldliness, as "God's spies", they will outlast, even in "a walled prison", the "packs and sects of great ones" which "ebb and flow by th' moon". Fashions come and go, Lear seems to be saying, but the truth remains. He also seems to be implying, through his reference to the moon, that it is the "gilded butterflies" and "poor rogues" who are the real lunatics, trading the promise of virtue's eternal reward for life's transient pleasures, trading sanity for the madness of Machiavelli. And surely Shakespeare is speaking for his fellow Catholics in the play's closing lines:

> The weight of this sad time we must obey,
> Speak what we feel, not what we ought to say.
> The oldest hath borne most: we that are young
> Shall never see so much, nor live so long.[9]

As for William Cobbett, he was unequivocal in his condemnation of King James' duplicity and general character. James had "abandoned his mother ... and amongst his first acts in England took by the hand, confided in, and promoted that Cecil who was the son of the old Cecil, who ... had also been, as all the world knew, the deadly enemy of this new king's unfortunate mother". James, Cobbett continued, "was at once prodigal and mean, conceited and foolish, tyrannical and weak; but the staring feature of his character was insincerity."[10]

---

[9] Act V, Scene 3, lines 325–28.

[10] William Cobbett, *A History of the Protestant Reformation* (Sevenoaks, Kent: Fisher Press, 1994), 170–71.

Even in the midst of the renewed persecution and the increased apostasy, there were still courageous souls who took the dangerous step of conversion. One of the most noble and notable of these Jacobean converts to the faith was Toby Matthew. Son of the viciously anti-Catholic archbishop of York, Matthew outraged his father by travelling to Rome in 1604. He was welcomed by Cardinal Pinelli, who told him that, as an Englishman, he "might expect and should receive a double welcome, both because that country had been formerly one of the dearest children of God's Church, as also for that it had not forsaken the Catholic faith out of heresy and election, but only by the imposition and power of temporal princes who had misguided themselves".[11] The cardinal hosted Matthew in his own residence and made his private coach available for his guest's use. In his memoir, *A True Historical Relation of the Conversion of Sir Toby Matthew*, Matthew recounts that Cardinal Pinelli told him that "he would oblige me to nothing, yet he would make one request of me for mine own sake—namely, that ... I would be careful not only to view the antiquities of the old, decayed Roman Empire but also of the not-decayed Catholic Roman Church." The cardinal then added that "the very stones might serve for preachers, and not only the buildings above ground but even the very vaults and caves under it."[12] As the cardinal had no doubt hoped and prayed, the experience of visiting these sights would have a profound impact on the English visitor:

> I must confess in the presence of God that the sight of those most ancient crosses, altars, sepulchers, and other

---

[11] Quoted in Robert S. Miola, ed., *Early Modern Catholicism: An Anthology of Primary Sources* (Oxford: Oxford University Press, 2007), 155.
[12] Ibid.

marks of Catholic religion, having been planted there in the persecution of the primitive Church (which might be more than fifteen hundred years ago and could not be less than thirteen hundred), did strike me with a kind of reverent awe and made me absolutely resolve to repress my insolent discourse against Catholic religion ever after.[13]

Proving Chesterton's maxim that one is drawn towards the Church as soon as one stops resisting her, Toby Matthew underwent instruction while in Rome and was received before returning to England. Arriving home during the period of intense persecution following the Gunpowder Plot, he was imprisoned in 1607. Having very powerful connections, which included Francis Bacon and Robert Cecil, he secured release from prison and went into exile. In 1614, he was ordained to the priesthood in Rome by St. Robert Bellarmine. Having retained his friendship with Francis Bacon, who had become Lord High Chancellor in 1617, Matthew was allowed to return to England. Thereafter, except for a further period of exile from 1619 to 1622, he prospered during the reigns of both James and his son Charles I, translating Bacon's essays into Italian and many religious works into English, including Augustine's *Confessions*. Knighted by King James, he worked diligently for the Catholic cause in the court of Charles I until the onset of the Civil War, at which point he was once again forced into exile.

If Toby Matthew enjoyed a degree of protection and favour, due to his powerful friends, the main body of England's Catholics were not so fortunate. In 1606, an Act for Better Repressing of Popish Recusants made communion at the services of the state religion compulsory, as well as empowering the government to seize two-thirds

[13] Ibid.

of the property of recusants and requiring all office holders to swear a new Oath of Allegiance. In February 1607, Fr. Robert Drury, who had served London's Catholics since 1595, was arrested and found guilty of treason for being a priest. He was offered the king's mercy if he agreed to take the Oath of Allegiance. The alternative was death by the usual barbaric means of hanging, drawing, and quartering. Fr. Drury chose martyrdom and was duly taken to Tyburn for execution in the company of thirty-two thieves and murderers. The common criminals rode in a cart; Fr. Drury was dragged through the streets on a hurdle. On the scaffold, he was offered one last opportunity to take the Oath of Allegiance but chose to accept death as a loyal son of the Church.

In August 1607, three priests were together at Upsall Castle, a recusant home in Yorkshire, when the castle was surrounded by priest hunters. One of the priests managed to escape, but the other two were arrested along with "the gentlewoman who was caring for them".[14] The priests were accused of their priesthood and the lady of harbouring them. All were found guilty and sentenced to death, and all refused to take the Oath of Allegiance which would have saved them from the gallows. One of the priests managed to escape from prison, and the lady was reprieved but sent to prison indefinitely. The one remaining priest, Fr. Matthew Flathers, was hanged, drawn, and quartered on March 21, 1608.

As the Puritans tightened their grip on the reins of power, they sought to control those aspects of culture which they considered papist, not least of which was the theatre. The fact that the Puritans considered the theatre to be a dangerous

[14] Roland Connelly, *The Eighty-Five Martyrs* (Great Wakering, Essex: McCrimmon Publishing, 1987), 89.

disseminator of papist ideas can be gleaned from a sermon by the Puritan preacher William Crashaw, delivered at St. Paul's Cross in London in 1608: "The ungodly plays and interludes so rife in this nation: what are they but a bastard of Babylon [a euphemism for Rome in puritanical Bible-speak], a daughter of error and confusion; a hellish device— the devil's own recreation to mock at holy things—by him delivered to the heathen and by them to the Papists, and from them to us?"[15] Apart from its attack on "papist plays", Crashaw's puritanical sermon is noteworthy as being one of the pithiest putdowns of Western civilization ever made. In one terse, bombastic sentence, the entire legacy of the West is dismissed as being a contagious disease, passed from the devil to the Greeks, and then to the Romans and the Catholics until finally, via Shakespeare and his fellow play-wrights, it had contaminated modern England.

Two years later, in February 1610, Crashaw was again equating Shakespeare and his ilk to the devil in a sermon he preached to the Lord Governor of Virginia. On this occasion he fulminated that the greatest threat to the newly founded colony was to be found in Catholicism and its culturally satanic manifestations: "We confess this action hath three great enemies: but who be they? even the Devil, Papists, and Players."[16] Considering William Crashaw's shrill attack on Catholic poets, such as Shakespeare, it is ironic that his own son, Richard, one of the greatest of the metaphysical poets, would convert to Catholicism, dying in lonely exile in Italy in 1649.

Responding to these puritanical attacks upon plays and players, Phillip Rosseter, a Catholic actor and lessee of the Whitefriars Theatre, retorted in December 1610 "that a

[15] Mutschmann and Wentersdorf, *Shakespeare and Catholicism*, 102.
[16] Ibid.

man might learn more good at one of their plays or interludes than at twenty of our roguish sermons".[17]

In addition to these general attacks on the theatre,
Shakespeare's own plays came under scrutiny in 1610 following the conviction of a Catholic recusant gentleman
for hosting a group of players who performed "papist"
plays at his own and at other recusant houses. Intriguingly,
King Lear and *Pericles* were among the plays performed at
these secret gatherings, indicating that recusant audiences
readily deduced the Catholic meaning of the plays, and
suggesting also that Shakespeare's faith, however discreetly
practised, was known to his fellow Catholics.

Further evidence of the disdain with which the Puritans
held the theatre in general, and Shakespeare in particular, emerged in the *History of Great Britain* by John Speed,
which was published in 1611. Discussing the Lollard leader,
Sir John Oldcastle, Speed was at pains to discredit attacks
upon his reputation by papists and playwrights. Complaining that the Jesuit Robert Persons had described Oldcastle as "a ruffian, a robber and a rebel", Speed riposted by
suggesting that Persons was a liar, along with "his poet"
Shakespeare:

> And his [Persons'] authority, taken from the stage-players,
> is more befitting the pen of his slanderous report than the
> credit of the judicious, being only grounded from this
> Papist [Persons] and his poet [Shakespeare], of like con-
> science for lies, the one ever feigning and the other ever
> falsifying the truth.[18]

This astonishing attack upon Shakespeare, calling
him a falsifier of the truth and a sidekick of the Jesuits,

[17] Ibid.
[18] Ian Wilson, *Shakespeare: The Evidence* (New York: St. Martin's Griffin,
1999), 228.

demonstrates the general suspicion with which he was held by the Puritans. The specific connection between Persons and Shakespeare, upon which Speed was grounding his attack, is to be found in Persons' account *Of Three Conversions of England*, published in 1603, and its connection with Shakespeare's *Henry IV Part I*. Persons' work was effectively a piece of revisionist history in which he refutes John Foxe's version of England's history. In his discussion of Oldcastle, Persons dismisses him as "a ruffian knight, as all England knoweth, and commonly brought in by comedians on their stages".[19] This is seen by most scholars as an allusion to Shakespeare's depiction of Oldcastle, under the tactful alias of Sir John Falstaff, whom Prince Hal addresses as "that father ruffian, that vanity in years". The fact that Falstaff is Shakespeare's alias for Oldcastle has been generally accepted by scholars ever since the connection between Oldcastle and Falstaff was made by James O. Halliwell-Phillips in 1841. The connection is not only deduced from Oldcastle's appearance in *The Famous Victories of Henry the Fifth*, which is generally thought to be Shakespeare's source play, but also from Shakespeare's punning reference to Falstaff, by Prince Hal, as "my old lad of the castle" in the play's second scene.

Persons' "ruffian knight" is clearly a reference to the "father ruffian" in Shakespeare's play, and shows, equally clearly, that Shakespeare shared the Jesuit's view of Oldcastle as a heretic and a rogue, not Foxe's and Speed's view that he was a hero and a martyr. It is, therefore, of little wonder that Speed attacks Persons and Shakespeare as feigners and falsifiers of the truth, the former "feigning" the truth in his history of England and the latter "falsifying" it in his history plays. Nor is it any wonder that he should seek to

---

[19] Ibid.

shackle them together as "this Papist and his poet", endeavouring to tar Shakespeare with the Jesuit brush.

In the same year of 1610, a Royal Proclamation "for the
due execution of all former laws against recusants" ushered
in a new wave of persecution against Catholics, tempting
many recusants to conform to the state religion as the only
way of avoiding the payment of increasingly crippling fines.
Amongst those who did so was Shakespeare's friend Ben
Jonson, who formally rejoined the Anglican church after
the years of recusancy that had followed his earlier conversion to Catholicism, perhaps under Shakespeare's influence.

But what of Shakespeare himself? Did he succumb to
this new trend of capitulation? Did he follow Jonson's
example, surrendering the faith of his fathers and accepting, however reluctantly, the new religion? Was he, like
so many of his co-religionists, tiring of the tempest of religious persecution? Was he willing to surrender his principles and beliefs in order to gain the worldly peace that
could only come with conformity to the dictates of the
Jacobean state? These questions would be answered in
March 1613, when Shakespeare purchased the Blackfri-
ars Gatehouse, a major hub of Catholic recusant activity
in London, ensuring that it would remain a safe haven
for "God's spies". Although this solitary act illustrates that
Shakespeare remained a Catholic, it is likely that he had
tired of the unwelcome and potentially dangerous attention he was receiving from the increasingly powerful and
vituperative Puritans. Perhaps he perceived the writing on
the wall. Perhaps he could see that the Puritans, who were
gaining ever-increasing power in Parliament, would eventually succeed in shutting down the theatres.

Desiring a peaceful life, Shakespeare returned to his
home and family in Warwickshire, disappearing into the
sunset of his own life. As he bid farewell to London and

the stage, taking his final bow, his last words to posterity were spoken in the last words of his last play, *The Tempest*. Fittingly, they were a request for prayers.

> And my ending is despair,
> Unless I be reliev'd by prayer,
> Which pierces so, that it assaults
> Mercy itself, and frees all faults.
>> As you from crimes would pardon'd be,
>> Let your indulgence set me free.

Chapter Eighteen

Prelude to War

And the face of the King's Servants grew greater than the King:
He tricked them, and they trapped him, and stood round him in
*   a ring.*
The new grave lords closed round him, that had eaten the abbey's
*   fruits,*
And the men of the new religion, with their bibles in their boots.

— G. K. Chesterton, from "The Secret People"

Although most of the martyrs were Jesuits or secular clergy, there were some who belonged to older religious orders. One such was the Benedictine monk John Roberts, a Welshman by birth who ministered to the Catholics of London. Having been banished from England on several occasions, always returning and having escaped from prison in 1608, he was finally executed at Tyburn in December 1610. The report of his final speech from the gallows is memorable for its powerful evocation of the original Benedictine mission to England by St. Augustine of Canterbury more than a thousand years earlier:

And to the objection that he came into England without due authority he replied, that he was sent into England by the same authority by which Augustine the Apostle of England was sent, whose disciple he was; being of the same order, and living under the same rule in which he lived; and thus for the profession and teaching of that religion, which St. Augustine planted in England, he was now condemned to die.[1]

Apart from the continual smuggling of priests into England, there was also the ongoing smuggling of books. From 1608 until the commencement of the Civil War in 1642, the Jesuit press at Saint-Omer in northern France published over three hundred titles in English. In addition, other foreign presses and the twenty-one secret presses operating at one time or another in England itself ensured a continual supply of Catholic devotional and apologetic works for the besieged Catholic recusant community. In 1609, a raid on the Venetian ambassador's residence in London uncovered thousands of Catholic books, hidden away in the cellar. A bookseller, in a memoir published in 1652, recalled his time as an apprentice in Staffordshire during the reign of King James and the illegal trade his master conducted in "popish books, pictures, beads, and such trash".[2] According to Robert Miola, "devout readers and risk-taking profiteers created a thriving black-market business in Catholic publication, sustained by a local network of agents and merchants."[3]

This thriving market in secretly published and smuggled books suggests a considerable Catholic presence in Jacobean England. According to the Spanish ambassador, in a report to King Philip III in 1614, a twelfth of the population of England were still committed Catholics (i.e.,

---

[1] Benedictines of Stanbrook, *In a Great Tradition: Tribute to Dame Laurentia McLachlan, Abbess of Stanbrook* (London: John Murray, 1956), 71.

[2] Robert S. Miola, ed., *Early Modern Catholicism: An Anthology of Primary Sources* (Oxford: Oxford University Press, 2007), 33.

[3] Ibid.

recusants), two-twelfths were committed Catholics "but outwardly conforming to the law" and a further three-twelfths were "favourably inclined to Catholicism".[4] If this is so, it indicates that half the population were still sympathetic to Catholicism, even after almost eighty years of incessant persecution.

The fact that Catholicism was still a lively part of the cultural life of England, or at least the northern parts of England, is suggested by the groups of strolling players who lampooned Protestantism in their frolicking and impromptu performances. One such group, based in the relative seclusion of the Yorkshire moors, were known as the Egton Interlude Players or the Simpson Players. This group of latter-day troubadours was popular for their mocking allusions to the Jacobean state and its established church. One "interlude" consisted of a dialogue between a priest and a Protestant parson which ended with the parson being carried off to hell by the devil. It is said that these rambunctious entertainments were popular at Douai, the seminary in northern France at which young Catholic men went to be educated and to study for the priesthood; they had been introduced to England upon the return of the Douai alumni to their native shore. In January 1616, a thirteen-year-old boy by the name of Nicholas Postgate was fined ten shillings for taking part in one of these "interludes", along with seven other strolling players. It seems very likely that this was the same Nicholas Postgate who would enter the English College at Douai three years later and who would be martyred in 1679, as an old man, having served secretly as a priest for more than half a century in those same Yorkshire moors in which he had been raised and had spent his childhood.

[4] Ibid., 27.

In 1618, when King James was in the midst of delicate negotiations with the king of Spain concerning the possible marriage of his son Prince Charles to the Infanta Maria, he had promised the Spanish king that the persecution of Catholics would cease. It was, therefore, an embarrassment when news arrived of the hanging, drawing, and quartering of the priest William Southerne in the northern city of Newcastle-upon-Tyne. Assuring King Philip that he had known nothing of the arrest or trial of Fr. Southerne, James promised that whoever was responsible would be punished. Lord Sheffield, who had overseen the legal proceedings against the priest, was removed from his position as president of the Council of the North. Thereafter, as relations between England and Spain improved, England's Catholics enjoyed a temporary respite, no priests being put to death for the next ten years.

With the shadow of the hangman no longer looming ominously, there were signs that Catholics were once again emerging from their hidden lives to practice their faith more publicly. One such manifestation of Catholic piety was the increasing numbers going on pilgrimage to holy shrines. A government informer, John Gee, writing in 1624, reported on the number of people visiting the holy well of St. Winefride in Wales:

> Every year about midsummer many superstitious Papists of Lancashire, Staffordshire and other more remote places go in pilgrimage, especially those of the feminine and softer sex, who keep there their rendezvous, meeting with divers priests, their acquaintance, who make it their chief synod or convention for consultation and promoting the Catholic cause, as they call it.... Let me add that they were so bold, about midsummer last year that they intruded themselves divers times into the church or public chapel

at Holywell and there said Mass without contradiction. It is not unlike they will easily presume to the same liberty here in England.[5]

Possibly as a direct consequence of this informer's report, efforts were made to deter pilgrims to Holywell by the reporting of the names of pilgrims to the Justices of the Peace. Although a government report indicated that this had curtailed the number of pilgrims visiting the shrine in 1626, it was evident from subsequent reports that the pilgrimages continued. In 1629, many significant pilgrims visited the shrine, their names being reported to the Privy Council. These included Lord William Howard, Lord Shrewsbury, Sir Thomas Gerard, Sir John Talbot, and Lady Falkland, "with divers other knights, ladies, gentlemen and gentlewomen of divers counties to the number of fourteen or fifteen hundred; and the general estimation about a hundred and fifty or more priests, the most of them well known what they were".[6]

The easing of the persecution was also reflected in the number of Catholic books being sold and read. According to an informer's "catalogue" of 156 "popish books" being sold in London in 1624, the works being read included "controversial works, histories, translations of the Bible, catechisms, devotional works, prayer-books including primers and offices, and saints' lives".[7] Among the bestsellers were ancient works by Bede and Augustine, as well as the more modern writings of Thomas More and Robert Bellarmine.

[5] John Gerard, *The Autobiography of an Elizabethan* (Oxford: Family Publications, 2006), 275.

[6] Ibid., 275–76.

[7] Robert S. Miola, ed., *Early Modern Catholicism: An Anthology of Primary Sources* (Oxford: Oxford University Press, 2007), 35.

In March 1625, upon the death of James I, his son acceded to the throne as Charles I. Tensions were running high between king and Parliament in the final years of James' reign, and relations would continue to worsen under Charles. The Puritans in Parliament were relieved when negotiations for Charles' marriage to the Infanta Maria had failed, averting the prospect of the king having a Spanish Catholic wife, but their relief would be short-lived. A few weeks after his coronation, Charles married Henrietta Maria, youngest daughter of the king of France, an avowed Catholic whose first act upon her arrival in England was to make a pilgrimage to Tyburn, the place of execution of so many of the English martyrs. Such an ostentatious show of reverence for those who had died for the faith and such an act of solidarity with England's Catholics could only serve to heighten tensions still further between king and Parliament. In the following years, this unabashedly Catholic queen greatly increased the number of Catholics in court and used whatever power she had to urge religious toleration. The extent to which such power was limited was made abundantly clear with the martyrdom of St. Edmund Arrowsmith in August 1628. Convicted of being a Catholic priest, he was hanged, drawn, and quartered in Lancaster, his last confession having been heard in prison by fellow prisoner and future martyr St. John Southworth. It is noteworthy that the faith was still so strong in Lancashire that, according to a contemporary account of Arrowsmith's martyrdom,[8] nobody could be found to serve as his executioner. In the end, a prisoner serving a sentence for desertion from the army agreed to do the deed.

---

[8] Anonymous, *A True Account of the Life and Death of Saint Edmund Arrowsmith* (London: Office of the Vice-Postulation, 1960), 11–12.

In 1633, William Laud was appointed Archbishop of Canterbury, an appointment that would hasten England's descent towards civil war. Laud despised the Catholic Church and shared with Parliament a disapproval of the lax enforcement of anti-Catholic laws during the relatively tolerant reign of King Charles. He ordered the destruction of devotional articles placed at St. Winefrid's Well by pilgrims and burned copies of St. Francis de Sales' *Introduction to the Devout Life*. Yet he was also critical of Protestantism, affirming the efficacy of good works, refuting the Protestant dogma of *sola fide*, and questioning the Calvinist doctrine of predestination. He also upheld the place of sacrament and ritual in church services. Such a prelate reflected the king's "high church" preferences but was utterly anathema to Parliament's Puritans who attacked Archbishop Laud for his "popish" tendencies.

The stand-off between the king and his archbishop and the Puritans and Parliament set the country on course for war. As Hilaire Belloc wrote, the "economic revolution" which had begun with the dissolution of the monasteries had resulted in "a powerful oligarchy of large owners overshadowing an impoverished and dwindled monarchy".[9] The Catholics, for all their mistreatment at the hands of the king and Archbishop Laud, rallied to the Royalist cause in the knowledge that the victory of the Puritan Roundheads would be much worse than victory for the monarchy. After war broke out in 1642, recusant homes were occupied, looted, and set on fire by Roundhead troops. Lady Blanche Arundell, whose husband had died of wounds received while fighting for the king at the Battle of Reading in May 1643, defended Wardour Castle against the Roundheads in an epic siege. Wardour was bombarded for five days. Lady Arundell had twenty-five

[9] Hilaire Belloc, *The Servile State* (Indianapolis: Liberty Classics, 1977), 94.

men to defend the castle; the Parliamentarian army besieging it numbered thirteen hundred men. Lady Arundell's daughter-in-law Cecily, "along with the maidservants, reloaded the weapons after each round of fire, while Lady Blanche rallied her forces each morning after Mass with an exhortation to return every shot with a volley".[10] After she was eventually forced to surrender, with sixty of the attacking force dead, the castle came under siege by the Royalists, under the command of Lady Arundell's son. By the end of the war, the castle was in ruins.

Another recusant stronghold, Warblington Castle in Hampshire, former home of the sixteenth-century martyr Margaret Pole, was captured by the Roundheads from its Royalist defenders in January 1644 and destroyed. Coughton Court, home of the recusant Throckmorton family, was attacked and subsequently occupied by Roundhead forces who set fire to the house when they left. The Royalist general Sir Marmaduke Langdale, a Yorkshire Catholic, lost the then enormous sum of £160,000 in the service of the king, "for which his only recompense, apart from the honour and glory, was to be made Lord Langdale by the exiled Charles II".[11]

Even in the midst of war, the martyrdoms continued. Alban Roe, a Benedictine, was martyred at Tyburn in 1642, declaring from the scaffold that he wished that he had "a thousand lives to sacrifice for a cause so worthy".[12] In the same year, John Lockwood was executed in York for being a priest. He was eighty-one years old. Another priest, Edward Catherick, was executed with him. In September 1642, Thomas Bullaker was saying Mass at the

[10] Peter Stanford and Leanda de Lisle, *The Catholics and Their Houses* (London: Harper Collins, 1995), 56.

[11] Mark Bence-Jones, *The Catholic Families* (London: Constable, 1992), 29.

[12] Elizabeth Hamilton, *The Priest of the Moors: Reflections on Nicholas Postgate* (London: Darton, Longman and Todd, 1980), 18.

London home of Margaret Powell when priest hunters burst in, dragging the priest from the altar to prison. He was hanged, drawn, and quartered a month later. And so it continued. Henry Heath, a Franciscan, was hanged, drawn, and quartered at Tyburn in April 1643; Arthur Bell, another Franciscan, suffered the same fate on the same infamous gibbet later the same year.

The war also led to a renewal of iconoclasm. William Dowsing was appointed by Cromwell's Puritan army as Commissioner for the Destruction of Monuments of Idolatry and Superstition, empowered to carry out a Parliamentary Ordinance of August 28, 1643, which stated that "all Monuments of Superstition and Idolatry should be removed and abolished", specifying "fixed altars, altar rails, chancel steps, crucifixes, crosses, images of the Virgin Mary and pictures of saints or superstitious inscriptions". In May 1644, the scope of the ordinance was widened to include representations of angels, rood lofts, holy water stoups, and images in stone, wood, and glass and on plate. Dowsing boasted that, in 1644, he had "purged" no fewer than 150 churches in Suffolk alone of stained glass, brasses, paintings, and other "relics of popery".[13]

The Roundhead victory at the Battle of Naseby in June 1645 would prove ultimately decisive, bringing the Civil War to an end and plunging the country into a period of turmoil in which religious fanatics would endeavour to impose a Puritan theocracy on England and its people. As for England's Catholics, who had rallied nobly to the king's cause, the triumph of Puritanism boded ill. All, it seemed, was lost.

---

[13] H. M. Gillett, *Shrines of Our Lady in England and Wales* (London: Samuel Walker, 1957), 289.

Chapter Nineteen

Regicide, Restoration, and Revolution

We saw their shoulders moving, to menace or discuss,
And some were pure and some were vile; but none took heed of us.
We saw the King as they killed him, and his face was proud
and pale;
And a few men talked of freedom, while England talked of ale.

— G. K. Chesterton, from "The Secret People"

The period following the Civil War was anything but peaceful. Efforts to secure a just settlement proved elusive and were thrown into turmoil by a Royalist uprising in Wales and by an invasion of northern England by a Scottish army in support of the king. Order was finally imposed by the defeat of the Scots at the Battle of Preston in 1648 and by the subsequent trial and execution of the king in the following year.

Although the act of regicide sent shockwaves through Europe, William Cobbett considered it the natural culmination of the previous century of tyranny:

If it was right to put More, Fisher, and thousands of others to death, not forgetting the grandmother of Charles, on a charge of treason, why was Charles's head so very sacred? If it were right to confiscate the estates of the monasteries and to turn adrift or put to death the abbots, priors, monks, friars and nuns ... could it be so very wrong to take away merely the titles of those who possessed the plundered property?[1]

As for the religious settlement, it was marked by what might be called a purityrannical intolerance, epitomized by the execution in 1645 of William Laud, the Archbishop of Canterbury, who, in spite of his robust anti-Catholicism, was still too much of a "papist" for England's new Puritan rulers. Laud was beheaded on Tower Hill, suffering the same fate at the same place of execution as had been suffered by Thomas More and John Fisher over a century earlier.

Given free rein to impose their extreme form of Calvinism on England and its people, the Puritan-controlled English government passed legislation to abolish Christmas, considering, reasonably enough, that the celebration of "Christ-Mass" was papist. Since the celebration of the Mass had been outlawed, it was natural that the celebration of "Christ-Mass" should be outlawed also. Traditional Christmas customs were banned, and it was decreed, in the spirit of Ebenezer Scrooge and in league with a certain White Witch of Narnia, that it would be always winter but never Christmas. It was from this time that the figure of "Father Christmas", who had his roots in the Merrie England of mediaeval times, emerged as a spirit of resistance. Old Father Christmas became the symbol of "the good old days", a personification of Merrie England, with its feasting and good cheer, and its celebration of the liturgical year.

[1] William Cobbett, *A History of the Protestant Reformation* (Sevenoaks, Kent: Fisher Press, 1994), 177.

In such a climate of anti-papist fundamentalism, England's Catholics could expect little mercy. Blessed Philip Powell, a Benedictine who was arrested in 1646, had served as the chaplain to Catholic soldiers fighting for the Royalists in the Civil War. Sentenced to death for his priesthood, he invoked his Benedictine forebears who had brought the faith to England a thousand years earlier:

> I glory that I am a monk of this holy order, which first converted this kingdom from being heathens and infidels to Christianity and the knowledge of God; St. Augustine being their leader, sent by St. Gregory the Great, Pope of Rome, with forty monks.[2]

In 1651, the son of the executed king, the future Charles II, led an army from Scotland in a bid to regain the kingdom. He was defeated at the Battle of Worcester and fled the battlefield pursued by Cromwell's men. He evaded his pursuers by hiding in an oak tree in the grounds of Boscobel House in Shropshire, which had been built by the recusant Catholic John Gifford in 1630. Ostensibly a hunting lodge, it had been used to conceal missionary priests and would now prove an ideal place of refuge for the exiled king.

After the pursuing Roundheads had left, bereft of their prey, King Charles found shelter in the house itself. Containing several priest holes, two of which still exist, it was an ideal place to hide. Acknowledging that those who hosted him at Boscobel were Catholics, the king told Samuel Pepys in 1680 that "I chose to trust them because I knew they had hiding holes for priests that I thought

[2] Benedictines of Stanbrook, *In a Great Tradition: Tribute to Dame Laurentia McLachlan, Abbess of Stanbrook* (London: John Murray, 1956), 71.

I might make use of in case of need."[3] Other Catholic houses in which the king hid included White Ladies' Priory, a former nunnery which was now owned by recusants, about half a mile from Boscobel, and a house in nearby Madeley, also owned by Catholics and which also had a priest hole. This particular hiding place had been discovered by the authorities, however, necessitating the king's sleeping in the barn.

At Boscobel the king discovered that Major William Careless, a recusant who had fought with him at Worcester, had also sought refuge in the house. He also learnt that his diplomatic envoy, Lord Wilmot, was being hidden by a neighbouring Catholic family. During his stay, King Charles slept in the priest hole in the attic. Known as "the Cheese Room", it measured only four foot by four foot by three foot four inches, hardly a chamber fit for a king! The Cheese Room was so called, as legend has it, because cheese was stored in and around it to put bloodhounds off the scent of priests hidden within.

The next day, disguised in "a pair of ordinary greycloth breeches, a leather doublet and a green jerkin",[4] the king was taken to Moseley Old Hall, the house of another recusant Catholic, at which he was introduced to the resident priest, Fr. John Huddlestone. After two days, Charles set off for Bristol, from whence he departed to exile in France. During his time in hiding, a reward of £1,000 was offered to anyone giving information leading to his capture, and it was an act punishable by death to aid and abet his escape. As such, his Catholic subjects were putting themselves at great risk to help him. "It is ironic," wrote

[3] Peter Stanford and Leanda de Lisle, *The Catholics and Their Houses* (London: Harper Collins, 1995), 61–62.
[4] Ibid., 63.

Peter Stanford and Leanda de Lisle, "that Charles, later a persecutor of Catholics as his father and grandfather before him, should not only have been rescued by Catholics and sheltered alongside a missionary priest but that he was concealed in a hide designed to protect Catholic clergymen from agents of the Crown."[5]

In 1653, Oliver Cromwell dissolved Parliament and was named Lord Protector of England, Scotland, and Ireland, effectively making the entire British Isles a political dictatorship until his death in 1658. The Restoration of the monarchy in 1660 came as a great relief, not necessarily because the people had any great love for Charles II but because they had no love whatever for the puritanical tyranny of the previous fifteen years. As for the king himself, his power had been circumscribed to such a degree that he had much less power, in real terms, than had his predecessors. "When a final settlement was arrived at in 1660," wrote Hilaire Belloc, "you have all the realities of power in the hands of a small powerful class of wealthy men, the king still surrounded by the forms and traditions of his old power, but in practice a salaried puppet."[6]

The Restoration brought a brief respite for Catholics. One of the families who helped Charles escape after the ill-fated Battle of Worcester was granted a pension in perpetuity, which is still paid to this day. The Bedingfield family of Oxburgh Hall in Norfolk were given a baronetcy by Charles II in 1661 in lieu of the £47,000 they had spent to support his father during the Civil War. Queen Henrietta Maria, the king's mother and widow of the executed Charles I, returned from exile and reopened the Catholic chapel at Somerset House, which was served by French

[5] Ibid.
[6] Hilaire Belloc, *The Servile State* (Indianapolis: Liberty Classics, 1977), 95.

Capuchins. Like his father, Charles II also married a Catholic, Catherine of Braganza, who had the English Dominican Philip Howard as her chaplain.

Far from the splendours of court, the missionary priests continued their stealthy work as "God's spies" with the humility and understated diligence of Chaucer's "poor Parson". Fr. Nicholas Postgate, in a letter written to the president of the English College at Douai in 1664, spoke of the thirty-four years he had served his flock in the Yorkshire moors. He had joined in marriage 226 couples, baptized 593 infants, buried 719 dead, and received 2,400 converts into the Church. At the time of writing, he had at least "600 penitents" whom he served.[7]

In September 1666, the Great Fire of London destroyed a great portion of the city, the conflagration being ascribed as being yet another "papist plot". Although few gave credence to this bigoted scapegoating of Catholics, and although historians have since shown conclusively that Catholics had nothing to do with the fire, the black legend was inscribed and enshrined on the monument erected to commemorate the fire. The inscription reads thus: "This monument is erected in memory of the burning of this Protestant city by the Popish faction, in September A.D. 1666, for the destruction of the Protestant religion and of old English liberty, and for the introduction of Popery and slavery. But the fury of the Papists is not yet satisfied." This and other plots were dismissed by William Cobbett as nothing but lies and propaganda. "These were plots ascribed to the Catholics," he wrote, "but really plots against them."[8]

---

[7] Elizabeth Hamilton, *The Priest of the Moors: Reflections on Nicholas Postgate* (London: Darton, Longman and Todd, 1980), 40.

[8] Cobbett, *History of Protestant Reformation*, 182.

Cobbett was especially incensed by the fact that Charles II had allowed the lie to be disseminated and had acceded to the scandalous inscription:

> Nobody knew better than the King the monstrousness of this lie ... and this king, who had twice owed his life to Catholic priests, and who had in fifty-two instances held his life at the mercy of Catholics (some of them very poor) while he was a wandering fugitive, with immense rewards held out for taking him, and dreadful punishments for concealing him, this profligate king ... had the meanness and injustice to suffer this lying inscription to stand.[9]

Although the inscription was erased during the brief reign of Charles II's successor, James II, it was reinstated following the revolution that brought William III to the throne and was still in place as an affront to truth at the time that Cobbett was writing in the 1820s. "What an infamy to put the lying inscription on the pillar," Cobbett continued, "what an act of justice in James II to efface it; what a shame to William to suffer it to be restored; and what is it to us, then, who now suffer it to remain without petitioning its erasure!"[10] The inscription was finally removed in 1830, a year after Catholic emancipation. Considering the impact and influence of Cobbett's *History of the Protestant Reformation*, from which the above-quoted lines are taken, it's possible that Cobbett was himself partially responsible for the belated removal of the bigoted lines. As for the view of England's Catholics,

[9] Ibid., 183.
[10] Ibid., 213.

it was encapsulated by the eighteenth-century poet Alexander Pope in the following couplet:

> Where London's column, pointing at the skies,
> Like a tall bully, lifts the head and lies.[11]

In 1671, John Caryll, the sixth of that name in a long line of recusants, gave an endowment of £600 to establish a presbytery for three priests at a cottage in West Grinstead in Sussex, the endowment being made in penitential reparation for his having taken the oath of conformity against his conscience. This presbytery would remain in continual use thereafter but had already been used as a safe house for missionary priests since at least 1580. Known today, appropriately, as the Priest's House, it contains two priest holes and is adjacent to the church and shrine of Our Lady of Consolation in this small Sussex village, the churchyard of which is the final resting place of the indomitable Hilaire Belloc, the convert novelist Antonia White, and the convert artist Sir James Gunn, the last of whom is best known for his portrait of Queen Elizabeth II, as well as his group portrait of the three Catholic writers Hilaire Belloc, G. K. Chesterton, and Maurice Baring.

Life was certainly easier for Catholics under Charles II than it had been under the rule of Cromwell, but the Protestant Ascendancy was wary of the growth of Catholic influence at court and was determined not to relinquish any of its power to a resurgent "popery". Such wariness was heightened by rumours that James, Duke of York, the heir to the throne, had secretly become a Catholic, and rumours were also rife that the king himself was contemplating conversion. In what might be seen as a preemptive strike, the first of a series of Test Acts,

---

[11] From *Moral Essays*, Epistle iii.

passed in 1672, began a process whereby Catholics were excluded by law from holding office under the Crown or from becoming members of Parliament, effectively removing them and debarring them from any positions of political power or influence.

One of the first victims of this renewed attack upon the Church was Fr. Philip Howard, the Dominican chaplain to the queen. It was claimed that his book, *The Method of Saying the Rosary ... as It Is Said in Her Majesty's Chapple at St James*, which had been published in 1669, contained illegal copies of papal bulls. Forced into exile, he would be named a cardinal by Pope Clement X in 1675.

In October 1678, a new fabricated "plot" would prove to be much more deadly to England's long-suffering Catholics than the mythical "plot" twelve years earlier that had alleged "popish" involvement in the Great Fire of London. This was the so-called "Popish Plot" invented by the notorious liar Titus Oates, probably in collaboration with senior members of Charles II's court.

The instigator and inventor of the "plot", a convicted perjurer, was described by the historian Elizabeth Hamilton as "a dishonourable, disreputable, despicable creature, a turncoat, guided by self-interest, who changed his allegiance and his religion (now a Protestant, now a Catholic, now a Protestant) as the fad took him".[12] Oates had enrolled at St. Alban's College, the Catholic seminary in the Spanish city of Valladolid, presumably as a spy. The rector of the college, Fr. Manuel de Calatuyad, expelled him in October 1677 *ob pessimos mores* (for bad behavior). "Little more than a month went by," wrote Fr. Calatuyad, "and he was in such a hurry to begin his mischief that I was obliged to expel him from the College. He was a curse. What I went through and suffered for that man,

---

[12] Hamilton, *Priest of the Moors*, 56.

God alone knows."[13] Having been expelled, Oates visited the Catholic seminary in Saint-Omer in France on his way back to England, feigning an air of piety, before returning to England weaving a web of lies that would send many people to their deaths. Accusations from such a man, wrote E. I. Watkin in *Roman Catholicism in England from the Reformation to 1950*, were as ill-founded as those of the emperor Nero when he accused the Christians of having set fire to Rome.[14]

A resolution in Parliament revealed the discovery of this "damnable and hellish plot, contrived and carried on by the popish recusants for the assassinating and murdering of the King, and for subverting the Government and rooting out and destroying the Protestant religion". As with the allegations surrounding the cause of the Great Fire, it is clear from the facts that there was no such plot. And yet, in spite of the lack of any tangible evidence against any of the accused and in spite of the thoroughly disreputable character of the accuser, innocent men were imprisoned and put to death for their alleged involvement in the nonexistent "plot".

"Two thousand Catholics were soon in prison," wrote Hilaire Belloc, "and of the whole Catholic population in the capital 30,000—one-eighth of the city—who had held out and refused to deny their religion during the terror were driven out of London."[15] The trials of the falsely accused were held over a period of two and a half years and resulted in many completely innocent men being executed for treason. Echoing William Cobbett's disdain for

[13] Michael E. Williams, *St. Alban's College Valladolid: Four Centuries of English Catholic Presence in Spain* (London: C. Hurst, 1986), 49.

[14] Cited in Hamilton, *Priest of the Moors*, 56.

[15] Hilaire Belloc, *A Shorter History of England* (London: George G. Harrap, 1934), 421.

the duplicitous cowardice of the king, Belloc wrote that Charles "knew the innocence of the accused and despised the lunacy of the day [but] had the weakness to prefer his constant policy of saving the Throne to pure justice".[16] Ignoring whatever conscience he still possessed, "reluctantly, and sometimes after long delay",[17] he signed the death warrants, sending innocent men to the gallows.

The father of two of Titus Oates' classmates in Valladolid, Richard Langhorne, was executed at Tyburn while both his sons were still students in Spain. Two former students of the college were martyred and other alumni, such as Thomas Downes and Thomas Molyneux, would die in prison. Fr. Nicholas Postgate, who had served the Catholics of the Yorkshire moors so discretely and faithfully for almost fifty years, was executed in August 1679. He was certainly in his late seventies and perhaps in his early eighties when he suffered the usual gruesome execution by hanging, disemboweling, and quartering. Two weeks later, the elderly Fr. John Wall was executed in Worcester. He was so popular and well-known locally that it is said that the Protestants wept, side by side with the Catholics, as they witnessed the old man being put to death in the usual barbaric fashion.

As had so often been the case over the past century, the Jesuits bore the brunt of the persecution. Between 1678 and 1681, as the "plot" ran its wicked course, nine Jesuits were executed and a further twelve died in prison. Among the Catholic aristocracy, the most prominent of those put to death was William Howard, the Duke of Norfolk's uncle. Lord Petre was imprisoned in the Tower of London, dying there in 1683 after more than four years of confinement; Lord Arundell was imprisoned in the Tower

---

[16] Ibid., 422.
[17] Ibid.

for five years, writing these faith-filled lines of holy resig-
nation during the first months of his incarceration:

> How vainly should that beggar chide his fate
> Who quits his dunghill for a chair of state:
> So fare it with us, when God doth displace
> The gifts of fortune for the gifts of grace.[18]

Writing of the "plot" almost two hundred years later, St.
John Henry Newman spoke of its "remarkable frenzy ...
its deeds of blood ... the hangings, and embowellings [sic],
and the other horrors of which innocent Catholics were in
the course the victims", adding that Titus Oates, who was
awarded a pension of £1,200 a year for his treachery, has
gone down in history as a dealer in lies. "Well had it been
had the pretended plot ended with the worldly promotion
of its wretched fabricators, whom at this day all the world
gives up to reprobation and infamy."[19]

It is said that Fr. Nicholas Postgate and other martyrs
had prayed from the scaffold for the conversion of the
king. These prayers were apparently answered because
Charles II was reconciled to the Church on his deathbed
by Fr. John Huddlestone, the very same priest whom the
king had met when hiding in the homes of Catholics after
his defeat at the Battle of Worcester.

The accession of James II to the throne in February 1685,
upon the death of Charles II, his brother, brought new but
tragically short-lived hope for England's Catholics. A practising Catholic himself, James was at pains to placate the
Protestants, no doubt fearful that a failure to do so would
put his position on the throne in peril. He made a speech,
which was printed and widely distributed, in which he

---

[18] Quoted in Stanford and de Lisle, *Catholics and Their Houses*, 55.
[19] John Henry Newman, *The Present Position of Catholics in England* (New York: America Press, 1942), 206.

stated that he would support the state religion, as presently established in law. As a further sign that he had no intention of making major changes, he appointed his brother-in-law, Lord Rochester, a strong Protestant and supporter of the Anglican church, as the head of the government. Privately, James attended Mass in the queen's chapel, but he did so as a private individual and not in his capacity as monarch. Whether such an accommodation would have worked as a modus vivendi, it was thrown into turmoil by James' insistence on religious toleration. He released the thousands of Catholics who were in prison for their faith, as well as the smaller number of Protestant Nonconformists who had also incurred the wrath of the ministers of the state religion. He also made it clear that further prosecutions on grounds of religion were strongly discouraged. In such a climate of religious tolerance, Catholics once again began to practice their faith openly. To give but one example, in September 1687, a Catholic bishop confirmed no fewer than 1,099 people at Ladywell Chapel, a Marian shrine at Fernyhalgh, near Preston in Lancashire, "in accordance to the Catholic ritual".[20]

The trial of Titus Oates, the fabricator of the "Popish Plot", which had been postponed by the death of Charles II, was finally held. His guilt was established beyond any doubt; the judges, imposing a heavy fine, flogging, and the pillory, expressed regret that they could not hang him. His public disgrace had served to exonerate the many Catholics who had been falsely accused and put to death or otherwise punished as a result of his calumnious "evidence", but it could not bring back the deceased nor the time spent unjustly incarcerated.

In the year in which James became king, one of the great giants of English literature, John Dryden, England's

---

[20] H. M. Gillett, *Shrines of Our Lady in England and Wales* (London: Samuel Walker, 1957), 133.

first poet laureate, converted to the faith. Two years later, he published his greatest work, *The Hind and the Panther*, a monumental apologia for the Catholic faith and an equally monumental rebuttal of the claims of Anglicanism.

Like so many of his contemporaries, Dryden was buffeted by the religious conflicts that plagued the seventeenth century. His family had been staunch Parliamentarians during the English Civil War, and his cousin, Sir Gilbert Pickering, was Cromwell's chamberlain, a fact which worked to the young Dryden's advantage when he came to London in 1657. His *Heroic Stanzas* on Cromwell's death in 1658 marked the beginning of his literary career.

Having begun with Puritan sympathies, Dryden modified his religious position over the years. His didactic poem, *Religio Laici*, published in 1682, had argued the case for Anglicanism, a view which *The Hind and the Panther* unabashedly recants. Although the latter poem was attacked venomously and vociferously for its Catholicism by contemporary critics, which is not surprising considering the very anti-Catholic times in which it was written, later generations of critics, including some truly great writers, lavished praise upon it. Among its admirers were Alexander Pope, Samuel Johnson, Sir Walter Scott, and William Hazlitt.

As King James continued to promote religious tolerance, the political oligarchy and the bishops of the state religion increasingly showed their intolerance towards any acceptance of Catholics into the mainstream of political life. These anti-Catholic forces joined in a conspiracy with the Dutch prince William of Orange, which would lead to the so-called "Glorious" Revolution of 1688. It was certainly a revolution, in the sense that the legitimate king was overthrown by a usurper, but there was little about it that could be called "glorious". William's victory at the head of an army of Dutch mercenaries was an invasion of England by a foreign army made possible by the collusion and treason of the new plutocracy and its parliamentary servants, coupled with James' ineptitude in defending his realm from the military threat. James was forced into exile with his wife and newborn son, the legitimate heir to the throne, whose birth had been the cause of the Revolution, a Catholic heir being unacceptable to England's protestant plutocracy.

"James II ... wished for general toleration," wrote William Cobbett. "He issued a proclamation suspending all penal laws relating to religion, and granting a general liberty of conscience to all his subjects. This was his offence. For this he and his family were set aside for ever!"[21] As for England's Catholics, the hope of freedom had once again been snatched away, departing with the deposed king.

---

[21] Cobbett, *History of Protestant Reformation*, 214.

Chapter Twenty

The Recusant Remnant

I tell you naught for your comfort,
Yea, naught for your desire,
Save that the sky grows darker yet
And the sea rises higher.

Night shall be thrice night over you,
And heaven an iron cope.
Do you have joy without a cause,
Yea, faith without a hope?

— G. K. Chesterton,
from *The Ballad of the White Horse*

We few, we happy few, we band of brothers.

— William Shakespeare,
from *Henry V*

The renewal of the anti-Catholic spirit reigning in
England following the Glorious Revolution was evident
in attacks upon recusant homes in the immediate wake of
the Revolution itself. The newly built chapel at Coughton Court in Warwickshire was wrecked and desecrated
by a Protestant mob, and the newly renovated mediaeval
chapel at Hendred House in Berkshire was desecrated and
damaged by stragglers from William's revolutionary army

who celebrated a blasphemous parody of the Mass in the sacked chapel. The priest's vestments, having been used in the mockery of the Mass, were then stolen and taken to Oxford, where they were placed on a dummy and publicly burnt.

Other recusants were forced into exile with the deposed king. John Caryll, of West Grinstead Park in Sussex, followed King James to France. Becoming secretary to James' queen, Mary, he was given the title of the first Lord Caryll by the exiled king. Like the king himself, he would never be able to return to his native land. Others joined the king as he fought to regain his throne in Ireland. Thomas Arundell, grandson of Lord Arundell, who had served as Keeper of the Privy Seal in King James' court until the Revolution, was killed fighting for the king at the Battle of the Boyne in 1690.

John Dryden, having refused to swear an oath to the usurping William, was stripped of his position as poet laureate. Remaining undaunted in his faith, he translated a "Life of St. Francis Xavier" and was also the translator of many Latin hymns. It is generally believed that all or nearly all the translations of the 120 hymns published in the Primer of 1706 were the work of Dryden, undertaken in the fifteen years from his conversion in 1685 to his death in 1700.

In 1692, a double land tax was imposed on Catholics, further impoverishing the recusant remnant, and, in addition, many Catholics were forbidden to travel more than five miles from their homes. Two years later, William's government authorized the founding of the Bank of England, which would revolutionize the economy through the growth of the national debt and the tax burden that it imposed on the general population. The first action of the new central bank was to loan William £1.2 million to finance the usurper's foreign wars. The debt-financing snowball having been established, it grew exponentially. Within four years, the national debt had risen from a little over £1 million to £20 million, and by 1714, only twenty years after the Bank of England's founding, the debt had burgeoned to over £50 million. "In this fashion," wrote Hilaire Belloc, "Governments were enabled, for their immediate purposes, to saddle posterity with the duty of financing their wars, while, what was worse, wealthy men found an opportunity for levying a permanent tax upon the community."[1]

As for England's Catholics, the new century brought new challenges. "The position of the Catholic families for most of the eighteenth century was both better and worse than it had been in earlier times since the Reformation," wrote the historian Mark Bence-Jones.[2] It was better in the sense that Catholics were no longer put to death for the practice of their faith, nor were the draconian penal laws very strictly enforced, the authorities, for the most part, choosing to turn a blind eye to the discreet practice of the faith in recusant homes. The old Catholic families could now maintain chaplains to say Mass for them and for local Catholics in the knowledge that they were unlikely to be molested for doing so. Discretion was, however, still necessary. The Mass, being still theoretically illegal, was advertised euphemistically as "Prayers" and was always celebrated behind locked doors and by invitation only. And yet the new Test Acts excluded Catholics from any position of power or

---

[1] Hilaire Belloc, *A Shorter History of England* (London: George G. Harrap, 1934), 457.

[2] Mark Bence-Jones, *The Catholic Families* (London: Constable, 1992), 31.

influence. They could not hold public office, nor could they hold commissions in the navy or the army. They were banned from any participation in politics and from the practice of law.

"In earlier times," wrote Mark Bence-Jones, "they might have been accused of treason, but they could also enjoy royal favour; they were given peerages and baronetcies and had political influence. In the eighteenth century the whole great world of politics and patronage, with all its attractions and rewards, was closed to them."[3] Faced with such exclusion, it was little wonder that the more worldly minded began to conform to the demands of the state through apostasy and the acceptance of the state religion. This caused a steady decline in the number of prominent Catholic families throughout the century, alongside a general decline in the Catholic population as a whole.

Even in the midst of this general ebb, there were still notable conversions to the faith, none more significant than that of a thirteen-year-old boy, Richard Challoner, in around 1704. A year later, the boy would depart for the English College at Douai, becoming a priest and eventually a bishop, and thereafter probably the most prominent Catholic presence in eighteenth-century England.

In 1715, followers of England's legitimate king, James III, son of the deposed James II, made an audacious but ultimately futile effort to regain the throne. Known as Jacobites, they were defeated at Preston in Lancashire. Many of those who surrendered were killed in spite of promises that their lives would be spared. Other Jacobites chose exile, rather than imprisonment or death, their fate being

[3] Ibid.

captured evocatively by Lord Macaulay, in his poem "A Jacobite's Epitaph":

> O thou, whom chance leads to this nameless stone,
> From that proud country which was once mine own,
> By those white cliffs I never more must see,
> By that dear language which I spoke like thee,
> Forget all feuds, and shed one English tear.
> O'er English dust. A broken heart lies here.

In the wake of the uprising, which became known as "The Fifteen", there was a renewal of persecution of England's Catholics. The secluded Marian shrine of Fernyhalgh in Lancashire, which had been the site of the confirmation of over a thousand people during the reign of James II, was destroyed. Efforts were made to capture the missionary priest Fr. Christopher Tuttell, who had served at the shrine since 1699. In early January 1716, on the eve of the Epiphany, Fr. Tuttell hid in a barn while government agents searched a nearby home in which they'd hoped to surprise him while he slept. "The fear of being found out," Fr. Tuttell recorded, "the severe coldness of the weather, the bustling and squeaking of the mice within, and ye screeching of owls without, disturbed my rest and kept me waking all the time.... Playing at Bo Peep was all that winter's pastime."[4]

The destruction of the shrine itself was overseen by a Mr. Hitchmough, who was described as "a renegade priest".[5]

After the memory of "The Fifteen" began to fade and the Jacobite threat appeared to have dissipated, the authorities once again began to turn a blind eye to Catholic

---

[4] H. M. Gillett, *Shrines of Our Lady in England and Wales* (London: Samuel Walker, 1957), 135.

[5] Ibid.

worship. From 1723, public worship recommenced at the Lady Well Chapel at Fernyhalgh, presided over by the same Fr. Tuttell who was thereafter left unmolested until his death in 1727, after which another priest, Fr. Melling, continued to minister to pilgrims to the shrine until his own passing in 1733.

As the continuance of the pilgrimages to the Marian shrine at Fernyhalgh illustrated, the faith was still resiliently alive in Lancashire, which had always been the seat of the most spirited resistance to the imposition of the state religion. "Catholicity survived in Lancashire not only because of the staunchness of its people, the tenacity with which they cling to old traditions," wrote Dom F. O. Blundell in *Old Catholic Lancashire*, "but because the Faith itself is the very marrow of their being."[6] Typical of the Catholic gentry of Lancashire who clung doggedly and dogmatically to the faith was the Blundell family. The Blundells had inhabited the manor of Ince since the thirteenth century and were still refusing to compromise their adherence to the faith in the 1720s, after almost two centuries of almost persistent persecution. Such was the family's confidence in happier times ahead that Robert Blundell built Ince Blundell Hall in 1720, a new and grandiose home one hundred yards from the manor house. He was, however, careful to avoid any ostentatious show of religion in the design of the house, wary of the dangers of appearing to seek to evangelize. There was, therefore, no chapel. Instead, at the end of the servants' block was a staircase leading to a small oratory, secluded coyly under the gables. Throughout the eighteenth century, the newly constructed hall became one of the hubs of the Jesuit mission in Lancashire.

[6] Quoted in Peter Stanford and Leanda de Lisle, *The Catholics and Their Houses* (London: Harper Collins, 1995), 75.

In contrast to the defiant Catholic heartland in the north, London had long since succumbed to the increasing secularism of the age. Although a Jacobite, writing from London to the Jacobite court of James III at Rome, had claimed that "the whole kingdom is running mad for popery", claiming "great convulsions in the city",[7] the reality was that Protestantism and post-Protestant scepticism was now the dominant force in England's capital city. The historian Simon Jenkins spoke of the cultural climate of London as a "clash of opposites": "It was seen politically in the rivalry between Tories and Whigs, between the old 'patriotic' Stuarts and new 'European' Hanoverians, as well as between a latent Catholicism and a dominant Protestantism."[8]

It was into the midst of these culture wars, that Fr. Richard Challoner returned to England. Having left in 1705 as a fourteen-year-old recent convert to the faith and having been ordained in 1716, he arrived back on his native shore in 1730 afire with evangelical zeal. At the time of his return, Catholicism was at a very low ebb with the number of Catholics continuing to dwindle. Three years earlier, Sir William Gage, the youngest son of the Catholic recusant who had been Challoner's patron, had apostatized, being awarded a seat in parliament for his conformity. Undeterred by such outward signs of decline and decay, Fr. Challoner began ministering to the poorest of the poor in London's notorious slums and to the most wretched of the wretched in London's prisons. Within a few years, he was causing great controversy through his engagement with the Protestant anti-Catholic polemic of

[7] Jeremy Black, *Culloden and the '45* (New York: St. Martin's Press, 1993), 30–31.

[8] Simon Jenkins, *A Short History of London* (London: Viking, 2019), 105.

the day, having such a flare for apologetics that he has been compared with Monsignor Ronald Knox and G. K. Chesterton.[9] He was, however, living in far more dangerous times than those in which Knox and Chesterton wrote and needed to leave England to avoid arrest. By 1740, he had returned to London and was consecrated a bishop in January of the following year.

In 1742, in a letter to Henry Roper, tenth Baron Teynham, Bishop Challoner sought to dissuade the Catholic nobleman from apostasy, urging him "(whom divine providence seems to have designed for the chief support of religion in Kent) to follow with the constancy of a Christian nobleman the happy and glorious path of virtue, in spite of all opposition of the world, the flesh, and the devil".[10] At this time the number of Catholics in Kent had dwindled to fewer than three hundred, eighty of whom were in Baron Teynham's congregation. Considering that Kent had been the first of the Anglo-Saxon kingdoms to convert to Catholicism following the arrival of St. Augustine in 597, and considering that the shrine to St. Thomas Becket at Canterbury had been one of the major shrines of the whole of Christendom, the shrinking and shriveling of the faith in this corner of England was both tragic and portentous.

Although the situation in Kent was particularly bad, it was hardly much better in many other parts of the country. It is estimated that there were fewer than one hundred thousand practising Catholics in the whole of the country, with some estimates placing the figure at only half that number. They had no hierarchy, no colleges,

---

[9] Maisie Ward, ed., *The English Way: Studies in English Sanctity from Bede to Newman* (Tacoma, Wash.: Cluny Media, 2016), 313.

[10] Ibid., 320.

convents, or monasteries, and no public places of worship, all Masses being said in private chaplaincies. In addition, the German king George II and his German wife were staunchly anti-Catholic as was the Court and Parliament. To all intents and purposes, Catholics in England were now effectively powerless and could be safely ignored by the powers-that-be. It is, therefore, indicative of Bishop Challoner's indomitable spirit that he always retained hope of a future revival. "There will be a new people," he proclaimed fearlessly.[11]

This spiritually impoverished England, bereft of the faith of its fathers, was shaken into life, albeit only temporarily, by the arrival of Charles Edward Stuart, better known to history as Bonnie Prince Charlie, a descendent of James II and legitimate heir to the throne, who made a truly courageous effort to regain the Crown. Crossing into England from Scotland, he and his Jacobite army got as far south as Derby before the fateful and fatal decision was taken to withdraw, rather than continue the march south to London. According to Hilaire Belloc, the position of the Jacobites "was impossible unless there should be a rising in his favour, and of this there was no sign":

> It is often said that a bold march on London by Prince Charles would have succeeded. It is doubtful. The people were apathetic. The Hanoverian dynasty was not popular, but it had behind it all the organized forces of the country, and was identified with the money power of the City, especially the Bank of England, and the security of most of the landowners.[12]

---

[11] Anonymous [no editor listed], *Catholic Emancipation, 1829 to 1929* (London: Longmans, Green, 1929), 3.

[12] Belloc, *Short History of England*, 483.

The final decisive defeat of the Jacobite army at the Battle of Culloden in the north of Scotland in April 1746 represented the heroic last stand of the House of Stuart. It also struck another blow against English Catholics, as Belloc explains:

> The effects of this rising and its defeat were considerable. Till that moment there had lingered a strong Stuart tradition even in England, and, of course, a much stronger one in Scotland; further, that tradition had been vaguely associated, especially in England, with lingering memories of Catholicism. In numbers those Englishmen who still openly called themselves Catholic were reduced to a very small number, though in many families vague traditions of Catholicism remained. After the Forty-five [the name given to the second Jacobite uprising to distinguish it from the first, which was called "the Fifteen"] all that disappeared.[13]

Seen in this decidedly gloomy light, the few English Catholics who sided actively with Bonnie Prince Charlie can be considered quixotic followers of an impossible dream, though they are nonetheless heroic for that. Some of the Catholic gentry in the Catholic heartland of Lancashire answered the Jacobite call to arms, amongst them Francis Towneley, who was executed following the defeat at Culloden for raising and commanding the Manchester Regiment in support of Prince Charles. Other English and Welsh Catholics fought and fell at Culloden, alongside English exiles who hoped that a Jacobite victory would enable them to return home. Charles Radcliffe, an English Catholic nobleman who had spent most of his life in exile, was captured at sea on his way to

[13] Ibid., 483–84.

join Prince Charles. He was executed, as had been his brother, the Earl of Derwentwater, after the earlier Jacobite uprising in 1715.

If the defeat at Culloden could be seen as the climax of the final chapter of the history of the Jacobite cause, there was a less than climactic postscript which is worth noting, albeit only in passing. James III, nicknamed the Old Pretender by his English enemies as his son Charles had been nicknamed the Young Pretender, retained papal recognition as the rightful king of Great Britain, of which de jure there could be little doubt considering that his removal was indubitably a Revolution, "glorious" or otherwise. From a Jacobite perspective, it was the present Hanoverian incumbents on the throne who were the true "pretenders". Nonetheless, the defeat at Culloden had represented the final nail in the coffin of any realistic hopes of a Stuart restoration, rendering the Church's de jure position increasingly anomalous in terms of realpolitik. Furthermore, Prince Charles had descended into habitual drunkenness following the failure of "the Forty-five" and had become an apostate, embracing Anglicanism, a move which had alienated him from his friends and which had failed to win him any friends amongst his enemies. He also had no legitimate heir. His brother Henry had become a priest and cardinal of the Church and would also, therefore, have no legitimate heir. Faced with this scenario, Pope Clement XIII ceased to support the claims of the exiled House of Stuart upon the death in 1766 of James III and gave de facto, if not de jure, recognition to George III as the king. Such considerations of realpolitik aside, it is intriguing to note that the final de jure king of England, who acceded to the throne upon the death of Charles III in 1788, was Henry Stuart, a cardinal of the Catholic Church and Henry IX of England!

Away from the macrocosmic politics of the papacy and the rival royal courts, the lives of the faithful in England continued in the face of relentless persecution. In 1745, after a Protestant mob had sacked and burned the Lady Well Chapel at Fernyhalgh in "revenge" for the Jacobite rising, the local Catholics, undaunted, rebuilt it once again. Pilgrimages continued and the numbers of pilgrims increased over the next couple of decades. This pattern of persecution and resistance continued. In 1765, an anti-Catholic mob stormed through the town of Preston, only a few short miles from Fernyhalgh, burning and looting Catholic chapels and Mass centres. Two years later, a priest, Fr. John Baptist Maloney, was sentenced to perpetual imprisonment for the sole crime of being a priest, a reminder that such laws were still on the statute and still enforceable. As late as 1771, Bishop James Talbot, a brother of the Earl of Shrewsbury, had been brought to trial at the Old Bailey in London for "exercising the functions of a Popish bishop".[14] Speaking of this slow, grinding war of attrition on England's Catholics, Samuel Johnson expressed his outrage at the persecution and his sympathies for the persecuted. "Better to hang or drown people at once," he wrote, "than by an unrelenting persecution to beggar and starve them."[15]

In the lingering and seemingly interminable shadow of such injustice, a dispassionate observer or a disconsolate Catholic could be forgiven for believing that it was only a matter of time before the Catholic presence in England would be completely obliterated and vanquished. In spite of Bishop Challoner's irrepressible optimism, there seemed

[14] Bence-Jones, *Catholic Families*, 24.

[15] George Birkbeck Hill, ed., *Wit and Wisdom of Samuel Johnson* (Oxford: Clarendon Press, 1888), 145.

little reason to hope. But then, as Chesterton quipped, "Christendom has had a series of revolutions and in each one of them Christianity has died. Christianity has died many times and risen again; for it had a God who knew the way out of the grave."[16]

In 1778, just as cynics and those of little faith were predicting the demise of the Catholic Church in England, the hints of a new dawn were stirring suggestively on the horizon. And as for the heroic recusant remnant, the thin true line of fidelity which had held fast to the faith for almost 250 years, there were signs that the incessant siege was about to be lifted and that relief was finally on the way.

[16] G. K. Chesterton, *The Everlasting Man* (London: Hodder and Stoughton, 1947), 290.

Chapter Twenty-One

The Tide Turns

"The high tide!" King Alfred cried.
"The high tide and the turn!"

—G. K. Chesterton,
from *The Ballad of the White Horse*

In June 1778, the passing of the Catholic Relief Act brought respite for England's Catholics from some aspects of the systemic persecution that had been put in place following the "Glorious" Revolution ninety years earlier, though it would be a further fifty years before full emancipation would be granted. The Act of 1778 was a consequence of a softening of attitudes towards the Church, especially as voiced in the writings of leading intellectual figures of the day, such as Edmund Burke and Samuel Johnson. It ended the ban on Catholics buying and inheriting land, as well as abolishing the statutory life sentence for priests and the life sentence that had previously been applied to anyone convicted of running a Catholic school. Although the abolition of such heinous laws was a sign of real progress, it made little practical difference to the day-to-day life of Catholics. There had always been ways of getting around the laws prohibiting the inheritance of land and, with few notable exceptions, the laws against priests were seldom enforced. Nonetheless, the passing of the Act was itself heartening, suggesting a turn of the tide, giving grounds for confidence about the future and the promise of further relief in the years ahead. Such confidence was buttressed by the fact that King George III and Queen Charlotte had chosen to stay with the Catholics Lord and Lady Petre, in October 1778, signalling royal approval of the recent Relief Act and a thawing of the king's relationship with his Catholic subjects.

In spite of these developments, many Catholics remained frustrated by the many laws that still existed which discriminated against them on the grounds of their religion. Thomas Sheldon, who had been deprived of the right to serve as an officer in the British army because of his faith, wrote in anger to his mother that "being born a Catholic was something he would not wish on his worst enemy."[1] It was little wonder, therefore, that the more worldly minded sought escape. In 1780, the Earl of Surrey—thirty-four-year-old son of the tenth Duke of Norfolk, England's most senior Catholic family in the aristocratic hierarchy—apostatized, defecting to the state religion. He did so as quietly as possible, "that I might give as little mortification as possible to a set of men who are laboring under persecution".[2] On another occasion, he offered a reason for his apostasy, the levity of which belied the gravity of the decision. "I cannot be a good Catholic," he is alleged to have quipped, "I cannot go to Heaven, and if a man is to go to the devil he may as well go thither from the House of Lords as from any other place on Earth."[3]

Such was the anti-Catholic prejudice of the bulk of the English population by the end of the eighteenth century

---

[1] Mark Bence-Jones, *The Catholic Families* (London: Constable, 1992), 45.
[2] Ibid.
[3] Ibid.

that it was inevitable that the Catholic Relief Act would cause a great deal of anger. There were anti-Catholic riots in Edinburgh, north of the border. Then, in June 1780, there were the notorious Gordon Riots in London, so-named after Lord George Gordon, president of the newly formed Protestant Association. Gordon led a march on Parliament of between sixty thousand and one hundred thousand "anti-papists" to deliver a petition demanding the repeal of the Catholic Relief Act. The demonstration turned violent as the mob began burning Catholic chapels and the homes of Catholics and those deemed to be sympathetic to Catholicism. A witness to the riots, Ignatius Sancho, described the rioters as "the maddest people that the maddest times were ever plagued with . . . a poor, miserable, ragged rabble . . . ready for any and every mischief".[4]

The riots spread to other cities. In Hull, the Catholic chapel was burned, as was the house of the mathematician Bishop Walmesley, who lost his library and his manuscripts in the ensuing blaze. In Bath, Catholics hid for their lives as the mob burned the chapel and attacked their homes. The terror of the night was remembered by Henry Stonor, who had been six years old when his family was caught in the riots in Bath: "In the dead of night I was obliged to get up hastily and was led by my father to York House, where we all passed the remainder of the night, and early next morning we set off for Stonor, leaving the Catholic chapel in flames."[5]

The Gordon Riots lasted a week and could only be quelled by military intervention. Estimates of the number of people killed or injured ranged from 500 to 850. Some were killed in the fires themselves; some were lynched;

[4] Simon Jenkins, *A Short History of London* (London: Viking, 2019), 117–18.
[5] Bence-Jones, *Catholic Families*, 46.

some were killed as the military intervened; others were subsequently executed. On the one hand, the riots served as a grim reminder of the perilous situation in which Catholics still found themselves; on the other hand, it was heartening that the government had shown the necessary resilience to put down the riots and to resist the demands for a repeal of the Relief Act.

As the riots raged in London, the frail seventy-eight-year-old Bishop Challoner was evacuated from his home in central London to shelter at the home of a Catholic friend, William Mawhood, in Finchley, just north of the burning city. The chapels in which he had offered Mass and the homes of his friends were in flames. It would have been easy in such circumstances to have believed that his own apostolate, stretching back half a century, was also going up in flames, leaving nothing but ashes. Bishop Challoner, however, was not the sort of man to let setbacks deflate his innate irrepressibility. He it was who had responded to a wave of apostasies with the hopeful insistence that "there will be a new people." In January of the following year, he died. His legacy is inestimable. He had served the shriveled remnant of England's Catholics for fifty years, the last forty of which as bishop. He was a devoted servant of London's poor, visiting the slums and preaching in public houses, and was also a prodigious author, producing over thirty books and pamphlets, ranging from a translation of the Vulgate to the earliest form of what would become known as the penny catechism. Significantly, his first major publishing endeavour was a collection of "memoirs" of martyrs who had suffered death for the faith between 1577 and 1684, thereby laying the scholarly foundation for which subsequent studies of this gruesome chapter in English history have been heavily indebted. Commenting on Bishop Challoner's work as an historian within the wider context of his leadership of England's Catholics, Michael Trappes-Lomax remarked that "he was making one page of history and writing another."[6]

The decade following Bishop Challoner's death was troubled by the prevalence of a spirit of capitulation on the part of many of the most prominent Catholic families, which was nothing less than a betrayal of the uncompromising spirit of their ancestors. These lukewarm noblemen formed a Catholic Committee in 1782 to work towards more acceptance of England's Catholics by the government, a committee which the historian David Mathew described as "a closed corporation of the polite unenthusiastic Catholicism of the Thames Valley".[7] The leading light of the committee was the same Lord Petre who had hosted the king and queen four years earlier. His indifference to the faith that he was purportedly promoting was exemplified by his scornful attitude towards the piety of William Mawhood, who had hosted Bishop Challoner during the Gordon Riots. Upon being told that Mr. Mawhood had attended Mass to pray for the success of the committee's work, "His Lordship made much ridicule."[8] Lord Petre was a Freemason in spite of the fact that Freemasonry had been condemned by the pope; he was perhaps more at home with masonic ritual than with the rites of the Church.

The attitude of worldly Catholics, such as Lord Petre and his colleagues, became known as Cisalpine, a term meaning "on this side of the Alps" to denote a northern spirit distinct from the spirit of Rome. Cisalpine Catholics in England emphasized their moral obligation to the state

---

[6] Maisie Ward, ed., *The English Way: Studies in English Sanctity from Bede to Newman* (Tacoma, Wash.: Cluny Media, 2016), 323.

[7] Bence-Jones, *Catholic Families*, 66.

[8] Ibid.

and opposed all papal influence except in the matter of doctrine. They advocated the election of English Catholic bishops in England, rather than their being appointed by Rome; they even acknowledged the right of the secular government to veto the appointment of bishops. One can imagine the recusants and martyrs turning in their graves at the very suggestion of such a surrender of religious liberty to the state. The Cisalpines on the committee were opposed by other recusant noblemen, such as Lord Clifford of Chudleigh and Lord Arundell of Wardour, to whom the spirit of a national church bereft of papal influence was repugnant. The battle lines were being drawn for a very uncivil war between the opposing parties.

Matters came to a head when the government required Catholics to swear an oath in order to gain the benefits of a proposed Second Catholic Relief Act. Although the wording of the oath appeared to require Catholics to deny even the spiritual authority of the pope, the committee regarded it as acceptable. The bishops, on the other hand, objected to the oath, and Bishop Douglass denounced it openly in an encyclical. Lord Petre and his colleagues protested, denouncing the bishop's encyclical as "imprudent, arbitrary and unjust".[9] In response, those who supported the bishop published "A Refutation of the Principles, Charges and Arguments advanced by the Catholic Committee against their Bishops". This increasingly acrimonious standoff came to an end when the government agreed to amend the wording of the oath in a manner that satisfied Bishop Douglass. With all objections now removed, the Second Catholic Relief Act became law in June 1791. Thereafter, the Mass was no longer illegal and could be celebrated openly; Catholic churches could be

[9] Ibid., 70.

built; Catholic schools were permitted; and Catholic barristers could plead in court.

Although the Catholic Committee was dissolved following the passing of the Relief Act, it metamorphosed into a new entity which called itself, provocatively, the Cisalpine Club, ensuring that the spirit of Cisalpine modernism would continue as a disruptive force within the Church in England. Amongst its negative influences were efforts to minimize Catholic devotion to the Virgin and to thwart the reestablishment of monastic life. With respect to the former, an issue of *Catholic Magazine* condemned the praying of the Litany of Loreto as being "unsuited to the age".[10]

Ironically, the new spirit of relative toleration of Catholicism in England was inspired by a horror of the new spirit of absolute intolerance in France following that country's Revolution of 1789. "When I went to France," wrote William Cobbett, who visited the country in 1792, "I was full of all the prejudices that Englishmen suck in with their mother's milk against the French and against their religion: a few weeks convinced me that I had been deceived in respect to both."[11] The English people in general and the aristocracy in particular were shocked by the barbarism of the French Revolution and the infamous Reign of Terror that followed in its wake. As stories of aristocrats, priests, and nuns being guillotined came to the attention of the people of England, there was a spontaneous outpouring of sympathy for the Revolution's victims. England opened its doors to Catholic refugees from France, leading to an influx of new Catholics, adding to the waves of Irish immigrants who had begun arriving in England's cities during

[10] H. M. Gillett, *Shrines of Our Lady in England and Wales* (London: Samuel Walker, 1957), 260.

[11] William Cobbett, *A History of the Protestant Reformation* (Sevenoaks, Kent: Fisher Press, 1994), quoted in the introduction.

the previous decades. Along with the Relief Acts, these were all signs that the tide had now turned. Among the refugees were some eight thousand *emigré* priests, admitted by the government and permitted not only to practice their faith but to minister to English Catholics. Such was the unforeseeable blessing that the French Revolution bestowed upon England, albeit contrary to the designs of the revolutionaries. Such are the ways in which the hand of Providence writes with crooked lines, bringing ineffable good from unutterable evil.

Chapter Twenty-Two

Rome and Romanticism

Mother! whose virgin bosom was uncrost
With the least shade of thought to sin allied.
Woman! above all women glorified,
Our tainted nature's solitary boast.

— William Wordsworth,
from "The Virgin"

In May 1795, a small group of English Benedictine nuns whose abbey in France had been turned into a prison after the French Revolution arrived at Dover after spending over a year in a French prison. "They must have presented a sorry sight," wrote an anonymous Benedictine chronicler. "Sixteen women, starved and prematurely aged, without roof or means of support, clad in the cast-off clothing of French peasants."[1] Arriving in London, the nuns were taken under the wing of the Marchioness of Buckingham, and, two weeks later, they took over the running of a new Catholic girls school near Liverpool.

The Weld family, based at Lulworth Castle in Dorset, was especially active in supporting priests and religious who had fled from France. This staunch Catholic

[1] Benedictines of Stanbrook, *In a Great Tradition: Tribute to Dame Laurentia McLachlan, Abbess of Stanbrook* (London: John Murray, 1956), 41.

family provided a house for the exiled English Jesuits at Stonyhurst in Lancashire and established a community of Trappists at Lulworth. They also provided support for the exiled Poor Clares of Graveline, who had found a safe haven at Plymouth in Devon, and established a community of Visitation nuns at Shepton Mallet in Somerset. Many other stories could be told of the experiences of those English religious congregations based in France, especially communities of nuns and sisters, comprising the daughters of old recusant families who made their way back to England—in the presence of considerable peril as the anti-Catholic fervor reached its cataclysmic crescendo after the Revolution.

Michael Blount, whose ancestor of the same name had known the martyrs Robert Southwell and Philip Howard, built a chapel in the Gothic style at Strawberry Hill in Middlesex to provide a place of worship for Catholic emigrés who had fled the Revolution. To the west of Strawberry Hill, in Reading in Berkshire, a significant community of French refugees had settled, each of whom had its own story of terror to tell. More surprising perhaps is the terror experienced in France by the English priest Fr. John Lingard, later to receive fame as the author of a multivolume history of England. He had been a seminarian at Douai in northern France at the time of the Revolution and had witnessed a French acquaintance being dragged by the mob, presumably to his death. When Fr. Lingard sought to intervene, a cry went up from the mob of "le calotin à la lanterne!" (the priest to the lamppost), which was the revolutionary cry calling for priests to be lynched. Faced with the anger of the mob, Fr. Lingard took to his heels and ran for his very life.

In the light, or more correctly the shadow, of the French Revolution, coupled with a general disgust of the extreme bigotry that had animated the Gordon Riots, the popular view of many English people had been moderated with respect to the Catholic Church. The sort of knee-jerk anti-Catholicism that had characterized Oliver Goldsmith's "anti-papist" four-volume "history" of England, published in 1771, was decidedly out of favour by 1791, when a fifteen-year-old Jane Austen, the daughter of a minister of the state religion, wrote her own "History of England", which lampooned and satirized the anti-Catholic stance of conventional history books. In stark and remarkable contrast to the bias of conventional Protestant history which overlooked the tyranny of Tudor England, except for the reign of Mary Tudor, the teenage Miss Austen depicted Elizabeth I as an unmitigated tyrant and considered Mary Stuart, Queen of Scots, to be the martyred victim of Tudor tyranny, echoing St. Robert Southwell's own poetic depiction of the martyred queen as "God's spice". In supporting Mary Stuart against the anti-Catholic Tudors, the young Miss Austen was countering the pride and prejudice of her times and was exhibiting the sense and sensibility that would make her one of the finest and most perceptive novelists of the following century.

This aesthetic sensibility was also present in the poetry of William Wordsworth and Samuel Taylor Coleridge, whose jointly authored volume of verse, *Lyrical Ballads*, published in 1798, would herald the birth of a distinctly English Romanticism—very different from its counterparts in France and Germany, and as counter-revolutionary in spirit as French and German Romanticism had been revolutionary. Although Wordsworth and Coleridge had initially been attracted by the French Revolutionary cause, the full horrors of its butchery and totalitarianism, carried out in the name of "reason" against religion, caused them to recoil in the direction of Christianity. Both poets rejected their youthful agnosticism and pantheism and embraced Anglican Christianity, expressing their rediscovery of beauty in the poetry of praise.

One of the fruits of English Romanticism was the rise of neo-mediaevalism, heralding a rediscovery of the beauty of the Catholic Middle Ages by a new generation of English poets, artists, and thinkers. At the forefront of this neo-mediaevalist revival was Kenelm Digby, whose defence of chivalry, *The Broadstone of Honour*, published in 1822, remained enduringly popular and influential for the remainder of the century. It struck a chord with a new generation of Englishmen who were seeking something more noble and edifying than the spirit of self-serving cynicism that had characterized the Regency period. This neo-mediaeval spirit would inspire the Gothic Revival in architecture, the Pre-Raphaelites in art, and the Oxford Movement within the Church of England, the last of which was a movement within the Anglican church seeking to embrace a "catholic" understanding of the liturgy and a "catholic" interpretation of ecclesiology. These three neo-mediaeval movements would sow the seeds of what would become a Catholic cultural revival in the English-speaking world.

Even as these aesthetic undercurrents were beginning to make themselves felt, there was also an inevitable backlash against the increased Catholic presence throughout the land in the wake of the arrival of so many refugees from France. The General Election of 1807 was dominated by fear of a resurgent Catholicism, the cry of "No Popery" becoming a popular battle cry. The anti-Catholic party triumphed in the election, ending any immediate hopes of Catholic emancipation.

In spite of such temporary setbacks, the Church was once more increasingly seen as being in the ascendant. "It is really become fashionable to be a Catholic," the recusant Frances Jerningham had remarked in 1819,[2] a fact borne out by the fact that she was now counting members of the royal family among her associates. The Duke of Sussex, younger brother of the future king William IV, had visited the stately home of Sir George and Frances Jerningham in August 1819, admiring the portrait of Mary Tudor in the library and being "delighted" with the Catholic chapel in which the organist played *God Save the King* as he entered.[3] In the following year, the new king, George IV, had written a note in Latin to Pope Pius VII, the first time a reigning English monarch had corresponded with the pope since England's Revolution in 1688. Pope Pius was understandably "pleased" to receive such a courteous overture from England's new king, answering it in the same cordial spirit.[4]

This new spirit of acceptance of Catholicism was praised by William Cobbett, in the opening chapter of his *History of the Protestant Reformation*. Writing in 1824, Cobbett rejoiced that "truth has ... made great progress in the public mind in England within the last dozen years":

> Men are not now to be carried away by the cry of "No-Popery" ... and it is now, by no means rare to hear Protestants allow that, as to faith, as to morals, as to salvation, the Catholic religion is quite good enough; and a very large part of the people of England are forward to declare that the Catholics have been most barbarously treated, and that it is time that they had justice done them.[5]

[2] Mark Bence-Jones, *The Catholic Families* (London: Constable, 1992), 127.

[3] Ibid., 124.

[4] Cardinal Wiseman, *Recollections of Four Popes* (London: Burns and Oates, 1858), 92.

[5] William Cobbett, *A History of the Protestant Reformation* (Sevenoaks, Kent: Fisher Press, 1994), 7.

Even the dastardly Lord Byron seemed to have been attracted by this ascendant and fashionable Catholicism, being inspired to write some of his finest lines by the allure of a mysterious Catholic lady, possibly one of the three daughters of Cosmas and Maria Nevill of the ancient Catholic family residing at Nevill Holt in Leicestershire. In his poem *Don Juan*, composed between 1819 and 1824, Byron writes of a beautiful Catholic girl to whom he gives the elusive name of "Aurora Raby":

> Aurora Raby, a young star who shone
> O'er life, too sweet an image for such glass,
> A lovely being, scarcely form'd or moulded,
> A rose with all its sweetest leaves yet folded....
>
> She was a Catholic, too, sincere, austere,
> As far as her own gentle heart allow'd,
> And deem'd that fallen worship far more dear
> Perhaps because 'twas fall'n: her sires were proud
> Of deeds and days when they had fill'd the ear
> Of nations, and had never bent or bow'd
> To novel power; and as she was the last,
> She held their old faith and old feelings fast.[6]

Ironically, even as the quintessential anti-hero Lord Byron was waxing lyrical about Catholic sanctity, a future Catholic saint, John Henry Newman, was coauthoring an anti-Catholic verse romance, *St. Bartholomew's Eve*, which belied his own future conversion.

In 1819, the first three volumes of Fr. John Lingard's multivolume *History of England* were published, a monumental work which built upon the foundations that had been laid by Bishop Challoner's groundbreaking scholarship. A fourth volume was published in 1823 with further

---

[6] Lord Byron, *Don Juan*, Canto XV.

volumes published subsequently. Having read the first four
volumes, William Cobbett began his own very popular
History of the Protestant Reformation in 1824, using Lingard's
work as his principal source. Although Cobbett "acknowledged Lingard as his master",[7] the two men had very little
in common. Lingard was a Catholic priest who lived an
outwardly uneventful life of quiet and diligent scholarship;
Cobbett was a firebrand political radical and globetrotting
adventurer who rejoiced in polemic:

> Cobbett, a politician, aflame with indignation at the suf-
> ferings of the poor of his own day ... had, he tells us,
> up till then accepted the conventional Whig history....
> It was Lingard who opened his eyes, through whom he
> first learnt that there had been an England very differ-
> ent from that of the early nineteenth century.... Cobbett
> eagerly seized his Lingard, translated it into his own tre-
> mendous prose, used what suited him, omitted what did
> not suit him, blurred out all qualifications and set it out as
> a trumpet-call to bid the people rise for liberty.[8]

One example of Cobbett's strident rhetoric will suffice
to illustrate the impact his fiery polemic would have had
on his contemporaries:

> If, however, we still insist that the Pope's supremacy and its
> accompanying circumstances produced ignorance, supersti-
> tion and slavery, let us act the part of sincere, consistent and
> honest men. Let us knock down, or blow up, the cathedrals
> and colleges and old churches: let us sweep away the three
> courts, the twelve judges, the circuits and the jury boxes; let
> us demolish all that we inherit from those whose religion

[7] Claude Williamson, ed., *Great Catholics* (London: Nicholson and Watson,
1938), 335.
[8] Ibid.

we denounce, and whose memory we affect to heartily despise; let us demolish all this, and we shall have left—all our own—the capacious jails and penitentiaries, the stock-exchange, the hot, ankle and knee-swelling and lung-destroying cotton-factories; the whiskered standing army and its splendid barracks . . . ; the poor-rates and the pauper-houses; and, by no means forgetting that blessing which is peculiarly and doubly and "gloriously" Protestant,— the National Debt. Ah! people of England, how you have been deceived![9]

The consequence of William Cobbett's populism was that Lingard's scholarship became much more widely known and his Catholic view of English history much more widely accepted. It helped indeed that Cobbett was not a Catholic and could therefore claim impartiality with respect to the religious question, denouncing the Reformers as avaricious plutocrats irrespective of the creed they theoretically espoused. According to Christopher Hollis, Cobbett's *History* was a significant influence on some of the major political and cultural movements of the following century, including the Gothic Revival, led by Augustus Pugin; the Young England movement, led by Benjamin Disraeli; the "back-to-the-land" wing of the Chartists, led by Feargus O'Connor; the Pre-Raphaelite Brotherhood, led by John Ruskin and William Morris; and the Distributist movement, led by Chesterton and Belloc. "They all, to a large extent derived, whether they were conscious of it or not, from Cobbett and, through Cobbett, from Lingard."[10]

Following the accession to the throne of King George IV in January 1820, a petition for full Catholic emancipation,

[9] Cobbett, *History of the Protestant Reformation*, 34–35.
[10] Williamson, *Great Catholics*, 336.

with twenty thousand signatures, was presented to the new king by England's senior lay Catholic, the Duke of Norfolk. At the king's coronation, Catholic peers were permitted to attend the ceremony in Westminster Abbey, a significant step on the path to full political acceptance. In 1822, a Bill to allow Catholic peers to sit and vote in the House of Lords was defeated, a rejection of religious liberty which would mark the beginning of a last desperate rearguard action by England's "no popery" party in their efforts to block Catholic emancipation. In 1824, a private members Bill was passed by the House of Lords, in spite of the furious opposition of the Duke of York, the king's brother, which enabled the Duke of Norfolk to exercise his hereditary office of Earl Marshall, irrespective of his religious allegiance. In the following year, another Bill for Catholic emancipation was introduced in the Lords and defeated.

In 1825, Kenelm Digby was received into the Church, a bold step in the days before emancipation, as was a young man, Ambrose Lisle March Phillips, whom Digby had befriended at Cambridge and who would later be immortalized as Eustace Lyle in Benjamin Disraeli's novel *Coningsby*. Digby was already well-known, due to the popularity of *The Broadstone of Honour*, published three years earlier, whereas March Phillips, the son of landed gentry whose father was a Member of Parliament, was destined to exert a considerable influence on nineteenth-century England—through his tireless efforts to reestablish the ancient religious communities on English soil and through his patronage of the Catholic architect Augustus Pugin.

At long last, in April 1829, the Tory government, led by the Duke of Wellington, passed the Catholic Emancipation Act, which finally granted religious liberty to the Catholics of England, ending almost three hundred years of persecution. The Duke of Norfolk was finally able to reclaim his hereditary seat in the House of Lords, being joined by a handful of other Catholic peers: the Lords Clifford, Dormer, Stourton, Stafford, and Petre. An eyewitness, seeing these Catholic peers walking together in the House of Lords a few months after emancipation, was moved to remark that it was "a pity we have so long excluded from our deliberations such a fine-looking set of men".[11] Such was the ascendency in which England's long-suffering Catholic nobility now found themselves that the Duke of Norfolk officiated at the coronation of Queen Victoria in 1838 as Earl Marshall; and such were the Catholic sympathies of the new teenage queen that she raised three more Catholics to the peerage during the first four years of her reign and visited the Duke and Duchess of Norfolk at their home, Arundel Castle, in 1846. Such would be the upturn in the fortunes of England's leading Catholics in the twenty or so years following their emancipation.

As well as enabling Catholics to take their seats in both Houses of Parliament, the Lords and the Commons, the Catholic Emancipation Act also enabled them to vote in elections. Although a few anti-Catholic laws remained,[12] the Act of 1829 was the decisive moment in terms of bringing Catholics onto an equal footing with their countrymen. *The Times* described Catholic emancipation as "in truth what may be called a thundering event [which] will sound from one end of the Kingdom to the other and the echo will be heard in foreign parts".[13] Such was

---

[11] Bence-Jones, *Catholic Families*, 132.

[12] It was, for instance, not until an Act of Parliament of 1837 that Catholics were released from the onerous requirement to be married in a Protestant church.

[13] Anonymous [no editor listed], *Catholic Emancipation, 1829 to 1929* (London: Longmans, Green, 1929), 215.

the importance to England's Catholics of the Emancipation Act, and such the sense of relief that accompanied
it, that Cardinal Wiseman, speaking thirty-four years later,
remarked that the Act "was to us what the egress from the
Catacombs was to the early Christians".[14]

In 1830, Charlotte Bedingfeld, wife of Sir Richard, was
named a Lady-in-waiting to Queen Adelaide, spouse of
England's new king, William IV—an early sign that the
Catholic Emancipation Act of the previous year was leading to the acceptance of Catholics at court. More important, the number of Catholics and the number of churches
in which they worshipped had increased dramatically in
the wake of emancipation. By 1835, there were 510 Catholic chapels in England, whereas sixty years earlier there
had been only thirty. More than forty new churches were
under construction, and Protestant chapels at Kiddermin-
ster and Dover had been consecrated as Catholic churches.
In addition, nine Catholic colleges and seminaries had
been recently opened.[15] This dramatic rise in the number
of Catholics was greeted with horror by the no-popery
faction. In October 1838, an article entitled "The Progress of Popery" in *Blackwood's Magazine* was reprinted in
pamphlet form, causing a great stir. Two articles in *Fraser's
Magazine* in the spring of the following year berated the
"vaunting" spirit of Catholicism and called on Protestants
to oppose it vigourously. According to the writer of the
articles, "the number of Roman Catholics in England and
Wales is estimated at two millions," a figure which, if true,
indicated an exponential increase in the number of Catholics: "If the number is about 2,000,000, then they are
nearly twenty-nine times more numerous now than they

[14] Ibid.
[15] Ibid., 245.

were in 1780."[16] Although this figure is likely to be much higher than the real number of Catholics, its being a lurid reflection of the author's fear-driven alarmist ignorance, even the most conservative estimates put the number of Catholics in England and Wales at about half a million[17]— which still constituted a considerable increase, heralding a new dawn for the faith or what John Henry Newman would call a "second spring".

[16] Ibid., 255.
[17] Ibid., 253.

Chapter Twenty-Three

A Second Spring

The past has returned, the dead lives. The English Church was, and the English Church was not, and the English Church is once again. This is the portent worthy of a cry. It is the coming of a Second Spring.

—St. John Henry Newman,
from *Catholic Emancipation, 1829 to 1929*

In 1834, a twenty-two-year-old architect by the name of Augustus Pugin was received into the Catholic Church. His father, also an architect, was born in Paris and had come to England in the aftermath of the French Revolution. The young man explained that he had "learned the truths of the Catholic Church in the crypts of the old cathedrals of Europe". By contrast, England's state religion had little to offer: "I sought for the truths in the modern Church of England, and found that since her separation from the centre of Catholic unity, she had little truth, and no life; so without being acquainted with a single priest, through God's mercy, I resolved to enter His Church."[1]

Pugin's aesthetic approach to architecture was elucidated in the book he published in 1836, which boasts one

---

[1] Claude Williamson, ed., *Great Catholics* (London: Nicholson and Watson, 1938), 399.

of the most grandiloquent of titles: *Contrasts, or a Parallel between the Noble Edifices of the Fourteenth and Fifteenth Centuries, and Similar buildings of the Present Day; Showing the Present Decay of Taste.* In this volume, the young architect and recent convert proclaimed the neo-gothic creed which was destined to sweep all before it during the nineteenth century, transforming the architectural face of England and challenging the neo-classical façade erected by the self-proclaimed age of "Enlightenment" in the previous century. Pugin's passion for the purity of the mediaeval vision of the gothic sometimes got the better of him, in the sense that he showed scant regard for the Romanesque or any rival to his gothic perpendicular perfectionism. Of the cupola of St. Peter's in Rome, he remarked dismissively that it was "a humbug, a failure, an abortion, a mass of imposition, and a sham constructed even more vilely than it was designed".[2] Such a view, indicative of an almost monomaniacal approach to aesthetics, would find few sympathizers, even among those who shared Pugin's love for the gothic.

Although Pugin is best known to posterity for his design of the new Houses of Parliament in the neo-gothic style that he championed, including the famous clock tower which houses the famous bell, Big Ben, he was also responsible for the design of new Catholic churches, such as St. Mary's in Derby and St. Alban's in Macclesfield. Bishop Wiseman, speaking at the grand opening of the former church in 1839, described it as "without exception the most magnificent thing that Catholics have yet done in modern times in this country, and quite worthy of ancient days".[3]

[2] Calvert Alexander, S.J., *The Catholic Literary Revival* (Milwaukee: Bruce Publishing, 1935), 20.

[3] Williamson, *Great Catholics*, 401.

Over the following decade, Pugin designed many of the new Catholic churches being built across the country, from Cumberland, near the Scottish border, to London and Ramsgate in the south. One of his greatest patrons was Ambrose Lisle March Phillips, the friend of Kenelm Digby, who had been received into the Church in 1825. March Philips owned vast estates in Leicestershire, and in 1835 had built himself a manor house in the gothic style at Grace-Dieu, one of his estates. When Pugin had first set eyes on the perpendicular gothic chapel at Grace-Dieu, complete with rood screen, he threw his arms round the neck of March Philips, exclaiming that "now at last I have found a Christian after my own heart."[4] Another Christian after his own heart was the Catholic Lord Shrewsbury, who became another of his great patrons. With Pugin's guidance, Lord Shrewsbury transformed Alton Towers, his estate in Staffordshire, into a manor house on a truly palatial scale. It had long galleries filled with works of art and an armoury in which figures in armour were ranged around an equestrian statue of one of the Lord's mediaeval ancestors. A vaulted octagon with stained glass windows resembled a mediaeval chapterhouse, and the vast and resplendent chapel evoked the glories of England's Catholic past. In the midst of such ostentatious pomp, Lord Shrewsbury's own private room was "bare and austere as a monastic cell".[5]

In his novel *Coningsby*, first published in 1844, Benjamin Disraeli, the future Prime Minister, waxed lyrical about Alton Towers, which he calls St. Geneviève:

In a valley, not far from the margin of a beautiful river, raised on a lofty and artificial terrace at the base of a range

[4] Ibid., 402.
[5] Mark Bence-Jones, *The Catholic Families* (London: Constable, 1992), 160.

of wooded heights, was a pile of modern building in the finest style of Christian architecture ... a gathering as it seemed of galleries, halls and chapels, mullioned windows, portals of clustered columns, and groups of airy pinnacles and fretwork spires.[6]

When the novel's eponymous hero arrives at St. Geneviève in the company of friends, "what interested them more than the gallery, or the rich saloons, or even the baronial hall, was the chapel, in which art had exhausted all its invention, and wealth offered all its resources."[7] It is perhaps appropriate that this vision of perfection should serve as our final word on Augustus Pugin, who would die in September 1851, tragically young, a few months before his fortieth birthday, depriving the new Catholic cultural revival of one of its brightest lights.

Even as the indomitable youthful vigour of Pugin and March Phillips was making its presence felt in what became known as the gothic revival, another cultural phenomenon was emerging within the Anglican church which would have a seismic impact on the state religion, precipitating numerous conversions to the Catholic Church. This was the Oxford Movement, of which a young Anglican clergyman by the name of John Henry Newman was a leading light. Between 1833 and 1841, Newman and others wrote the *Tracts for the Times*, a series of theological publications which argued from an "anglo-catholic" perspective within the Anglican church. Newman's controversial attempt to marry the Thirty-Nine Articles, which form the foundations of Anglicanism, with the Counter-Reformation teachings of the Council of Trent proved too much for the Anglican authorities, who forbade the

---

[6] Ibid., 161.
[7] Ibid.

publication of any further *Tracts* by Newman and his colleagues. Responding to this effort to silence the "anglo-catholic" voice within the Anglican church, Newman prophesied its consequences:

> Whatever be the influence of the Tracts, great or small, they may become just as powerful for Rome, if our Church refuses them, as they would be for our Church if she accepted them. If our rulers speak either against the Tracts, or not at all, if any number of them, not only do not favour, but even do not suffer the principles contained in them, it is plain that our members may easily be persuaded either to give up those principles, or to give up the Church. If this state of things goes on, I mournfully prophesy, not one or two, but many secessions to the Church of Rome.[8]

After the Bishop of Oxford suppressed the Tractarian Movement, Newman resigned from public ministry and retreated into a near-monastic life, centred on prayer and study. It was at this time that he wrote his monumental *Essay on the Development of Christian Doctrine*, which would be published in 1845, the year in which Newman was received into the Catholic Church.

As for the Oxford Movement itself, Newman insisted that "it was absurd to refer it to the act of two or three individuals." Insisting on the role of many different currents, including the influence of the Romantic poets Coleridge, Wordsworth, and Southey, he wrote that "it was not so much a movement as a 'spirit afloat'; it was within us, rising up in hearts where it was least suspected ... something one and entire ... as being the result of causes far deeper

[8]John Henry Newman, *Apologia pro Vita Sua* (London: Longmans, Green, 1889), 140.

than political or other visible agencies, the spiritual awakening of spiritual wants."[9]

As Newman had predicted, the suppression of the Oxford Movement led to a new wave of converts, both before and after Newman's own conversion. In 1842, Kenelm Digby hosted one such convert, Richard Sibthorpe, who was a fellow of Magdalen College, at his home near Southampton. Learning that the new convert was residing at the "papist" home of the Digby family, a local Protestant minister, fulminating from the pulpit during the Sunday service, exclaimed to his congregation that Mr. Sibthorpe "deserved to be burned". In the early hours of Tuesday morning, Mr. Sibthorpe having left the previous afternoon, the Digby family home was set on fire, the family being fortunate to escape with their lives from the burning building, though everything within the house was destroyed.

A sure sign of the growing confidence of England's Catholics, in spite of the fulminations of vociferous antipapists, was evident in the first public Marian procession to be held in England since the Reformation. This was held in 1845 in Coventry, which had been home to the most famous cycle of mystery plays in the days of Merrie England. The procession, following a statue of the Blessed Virgin, was held in protest at the indecency of the Lady Godiva processions held in the city.

Tensions were raised in the autumn of 1850, when Pope Pius IX restored the English Catholic hierarchy under the leadership of Cardinal Wiseman, who was appointed the first Archbishop of Westminster. The Prime Minister, Lord John Russell, condemned the pope's decision, describing the restoration of the hierarchy "as insolent and

[9] Ibid., 98.

insidious [and] inconsistent with the Queen's supremacy".[10] With knee-jerk predictability, the Anglican bishops denounced the new Catholic bishops as "foreign
intruders" seeking to deliver the people of England into
"foreign bondage".[11] The anti-papist reaction of the press
was epitomized by *The Times*, which dubbed the restoration of the hierarchy as "one of the grossest acts of folly
and impertinence which the Court of Rome has ventured
to commit since the Crown and people of England threw
off its yoke".[12] Anti-Catholic demonstrations were held
across the country, and Guy Fawkes' Day, commemorated
annually as an anti-papist celebration of the "discovery"
of the Gunpowder Plot of 1605, was observed with fre-
netic zeal, effigies of Cardinal Wiseman and Pius IX being
burned on every bonfire.

As for the response of England's Catholics, it was lamentable that those Catholic nobles who had recently gained
favour with the queen and her ministers should abandon
their faith in favour of their newfound respectability. The
Duke of Norfolk ceased practicing as a Catholic, receiving Anglican communion, and another Catholic aristocrat,
Lord Beaumont, condemned the pope in an open letter,
publicly renouncing the Catholic faith. Lord Camoys, a
member of the Stonor family which had been so heroic
during the penal times, was now a Lord-in-waiting to the
queen, informing her that he thought the restoration of
the hierarchy to be "inopportune" and that it made him
feel distinctly uncomfortable.

In contrast to this spirit of capitulation was the response
of Lord Stourton, who wrote to *The Times* expressing his

[10] Bence-Jones, *Catholic Families*, 171.
[11] Ibid.
[12] Ibid.

support for the pope and the new Cardinal Archbishop of Westminster. He affirmed "those same principles, for the support of which my ancestors have suffered for so many generations" and promised that those principles "will be held sacred and inviolate by me to my dying breath".[13] Ambrose Lisle March Phillips, exhibiting the courage and zeal of the convert, published two pamphlets in support of Cardinal Wiseman and the pope which received the public support of Lord Shrewsbury. One of the most courageous responses came not from English Catholics but from the Catholics of Wales. At a public meeting at Usk in Monmouthshire, John Vaughan, speaking on behalf of himself and another Catholic, John Herbert, told a largely hostile crowd that "we belong to two of the few Roman Catholic families in the neighbourhood who have survived three hundred years of persecution."[14] Impressed by the candid way in which Vaughan exhibited the courage of his convictions, the hecklers in the crowd were finally shamed into silence.

Divisions in the Catholic community came to the fore during the following year when Lord John Russell, the Prime Minister, introduced his Ecclesiastical Titles Bill to forbid the assumption in England of "ecclesiastical titles conferred by a foreign power". The Duke of Norfolk voted for the Bill in the House of Lords, while his son voted against it in the Commons, having returned in haste from the continent in order to do so. The duke had tried desperately to prevent his son from taking part in the parliamentary debate on the Bill and had even endeavoured to get the queen to send his son on a mission to Rome as "honourable banishment".[15] Such was the duke's rage

[13] Ibid., 173.
[14] Ibid.
[15] Ibid.

at his son, prompted perhaps by a sense of shame at his own compromised conscience, that his doctors feared that his son's arrival at Westminster could cause him to have a stroke. In the event, the Bill was passed but was never enforced, being repealed some twenty years later.

The true historical importance of the restoration of the hierarchy, irrespective of how it was perceived in the midst of the fray, was best expressed by John Henry Newman in his celebrated sermon to Cardinal Wiseman and the other bishops of the restored hierarchy, in the splendour of the Pugin-designed chapel of St. Mary's College at Oscott in July 1852. "The past has returned," he said, "the dead lives. The English Church was, and the English Church was not, and the English Church is once again. This is the portent worthy of a cry. It is the coming in of a Second Spring."[16] Newman's words were much more than mere polemic; they were prophetic. The decades following his own conversion and the subsequent restoration of the hierarchy could truly be seen as a new springtime of the faith in England, a golden age of Catholic revival.

The early signs of the Second Spring were discernible in the rising number of converts, one of whom, received into the Church in 1851, would rival Newman himself in terms of the enormity of the influence he would exert on the Catholic revival in Victorian England. This was Henry Edward Manning, who, in 1865, would succeed Cardinal Wiseman as Archbishop of Westminster.

One intriguing aspect of the Second Spring was its cultural dimension. Whereas Augustus Pugin had championed the gothic revival in architecture, other converts would express their newfound faith in terms of a flourishing and flowering of great literature, to such an extent

---

[16] Anonymous [no editor listed], *Catholic Emancipation, 1829 to 1929* (London: Longmans, Green, 1929), 3.

that the Second Spring has also been called the Catholic Cultural Revival and, more specifically, the Catholic Literary Revival.

The Irish Romantic poet Aubrey de Vere was received into the Church in 1851, having visited the graves of his mentors, Coleridge and Wordsworth, the latter of whom had died the previous year. Although neither of the great Romantic poets had felt the need to convert, their works had led many of their disciples, de Vere included, to the very threshold of the Church. Returning from Rome in 1852, de Vere visited Robert Browning in Florence, endeavouring unsuccessfully to persuade Browning to join him in the crossing of the Tiber. A few years later, Pius IX asked de Vere to compose hymns to the Virgin whose Immaculate Conception would soon be defined dogmatically. The result was the poet's collection of "May Carols", published in 1857.

In 1854, the historian Richard Simpson published his groundbreaking research into the Catholicism of William Shakespeare in three articles in *The Rambler*, rekindling interest in the faith of England's greatest poet. In the following year, Newman published an historical novel, *Callista*, set in the age of the catacombs, which had been written at the behest of Cardinal Wiseman as a sort of prequel to the cardinal's own novel of the catacombs, *Fabiola*, which had been published the previous year. *Callista* was Newman's second foray into fiction, his having already published *Loss and Gain* in 1848, a quasi-autobiographical story of religious conversion. Newman's influence also extended to the Pre-Raphaelite Brotherhood, that other neo-mediaevalist movement of the Victorian age, which dovetailed aesthetically with the gothic revival and the Oxford Movement. Specifically, Newman befriended John Hungerford Pollen, a former Anglican clergyman

who had been received into the Church in 1852. Two
years earlier, Pollen had painted the ceiling of Merton
College Chapel, surreptitiously incorporating a pope into
the composition; between 1857 and 1859, he worked with
leading Pre-Raphaelites, such as Dante Gabriel Rossetti,
William Morris, and Edward Burne-Jones on the Arthurian murals at the Oxford Union. At Newman's prompt-
ing, he worked on the design of the Catholic University
Church in Dublin and on Brompton Oratory in London.

Newman's much-publicized dispute with Charles
Kingsley in 1863 prompted the writing of his celebrated
Apologia, arguably the greatest work of conversion literature ever written, apart from Augustine's incomparable
Confessions. In the following year, Coventry Patmore, one
of the most popular poets of the time, was received into
the Church, after years of procrastination, having travelled
to Rome with Aubrey de Vere.

In October 1866, Newman received a young man into
the Church who would remain unknown in his own day
but who was destined, after the posthumous publication
of his poems in 1918, to become one of the most influential poets of the following century. This was Gerard
Manley Hopkins, whose masterpiece, "The Wreck of the
Deutschland", written in 1875, is one of the most penetrat-
ing meditations on the mystery of suffering ever written.

In the midst of such a restoration of the faith and such
a revival of Catholic culture, few would deny that Newman's prophecy of a Second Spring had become a reality.
The English Church which was, and which (almost) was
not, was once again at the heart of English life, restoring
the dead to life with a living faith resplendent with living
culture.

Chapter Twenty-Four

Manning and Newman

Oh! who of all thy toils and cares
  Can tell the tale complete,
To place me under Mary's smile,
  And Peter's royal feet!

— St. John Henry Newman,
   from "Guardian Angel"

For Christ plays in ten thousand places,
Lovely in limbs, and lovely in eyes not his
To the Father through the features of men's faces.

— Gerard Manley Hopkins,
   from "As Kingfishers Catch Fire"

Following the death of Cardinal Wiseman in 1865, Henry Edward Manning, one of the most prominent of the recent influx of converts from the Anglican church, became Archbishop of Westminster. Until his own death in 1892, Archbishop (later Cardinal) Manning would prove to be a formidable figure in the political and public life of his country, campaigning for social reform and gaining great popularity among the poor. One of his first priorities was to protect the education of Catholic children from British government plans to institute a national education system, which would be nonreligious and secular in character. In a pastoral letter written in 1868, Archbishop Manning insisted that it was a "duty laid upon parents ... to form their children in the knowledge of the faith, and in the moral and religious obligations of a Christian life".[1] In the following year, in another pastoral letter, he insisted that a secularized education system would be a betrayal of education itself:

> Education without Christianity is impossible; or, to use a modern phrase ... the secular and the religious elements of education are inseparable; or, more simply ... education is essentially religious; or ... where religion is excluded there is no education.... When we say that education without Christianity is impossible, we do not say that instruction without Christianity is impossible: we say only that instruction is not education, and that those who are only taught in secular instruction are not educated; and that a system of "national education" not based on Christianity is an imposture.[2]

Following the passing of the 1870 Education Act, the Catholic hierarchy of England and Wales issued a joint pastoral letter, echoing in even more forthright terms the concerns that Manning had expressed:

> In whatsoever school ... religion is not taught, morality is not taught: and where morality is not taught, the heart, the conscience, and the will of children, are not educated for the duties and conflicts of life. What can be more false, what more fatal, to men, to families, and to States,

[1] V. Alland McClelland and Michael Hodgetts, eds., *From Without the Flaminian Gate: 150 Years of Roman Catholicism in England and Wales 1850–2000* (London: Darton, Longman and Todd, 1999), 230.

[2] Ibid.

than to call this Education? It is not even instruction; for the deeper and more necessary parts of knowledge are excluded.[3]

In his first decade as archbishop, Manning opened forty churches, including the Pro-Cathedral of Our Lady of Victories in Kensington; but his most pressing concern was always education. "Could I leave twenty thousand children without education," he asked, "and drain my friends and my flock to pile up stones and bricks?"[4] In similar vein, he wrote that "the care of children is the first duty after, and even with, the salvation of our own soul."[5]

On the global stage, Manning was one of the most prominent proponents of the doctrine of papal infallibility during the Vatican Council of 1869 and 1870, delivering a rousing two-hour speech in support of the formal promulgation of the doctrine. Such was Manning's influence at the Council that Fr. Herbert Vaughan, who was destined to succeed Manning as Archbishop of Westminster, reported from Rome in a letter to Lady Herbert of Lea that Manning was "the most looked-up-to man in Rome after the Pope".[6] In the event, the dogma of papal infallibility was duly defined ex cathedra in July 1870.

In November 1875, Manning preached in Oxford on the university motto, *Dominus Illuminatio Mea* (the Lord is my Enlightenment), denouncing the university for its secularizing betrayal of its own Christian principles. Among those in the audience was a twenty-one-year-old undergraduate by the name of Oscar Wilde who was so taken

---

[3] Ibid.

[4] Nicholas Schofield and Gerard Skinner, *The English Cardinals* (Oxford: Family Publications, 2007), 154.

[5] Ibid.

[6] Mark Bence-Jones, *The Catholic Families* (London: Constable, 1992), 207.

by Manning's presence and his rhetoric, and by the role he had played at the recent Vatican Council, that he had filled his rooms at Magdalen College with photographs of both Manning and Pope Pius IX. Wilde's sympathy for the aging pope was prompted in part by the fact that Pius was now a prisoner within the Vatican following the taking of Rome by the soldiers of Victor Emmanuel in 1870. Wilde had written plaintively in verse, in 1875, how "far away at Rome / in evil bonds a second Peter lay"; in another poem, written at around the same time, he had referred to Pius IX as "the prisoned shepherd of the Church of God".[7]

The young Oscar Wilde, contemplating conversion, was as enchanted by the figure of John Henry Newman as he was by that of Manning. "I have dreams of a visit to Newman," he confessed to a friend in 1877, "of the holy sacrament in a new Church, and of a quiet and peace afterwards in my soul."[8] Caught between a desire for reception into the Church and the temptation to a life of decadence, Wilde would pursue the latter path before finally being received into the Church on his deathbed.

John Henry Newman was made a cardinal by the new pope, Leo XIII, in 1879, four years after Leo's predecessor, Pius IX, had bestowed the same honour on Manning. With Edward Henry Howard being made a cardinal by Pius IX in 1877, there were now three Englishmen in the Sacred College, further evidence that the Second Spring was bearing tangible fruit.

Ambrose Lisle March Phillips, who died in March 1878, had been indefatigable and indomitable, following his conversion, in preparing the way for the budding forth

[7] Oscar Wilde, *The Complete Works of Oscar Wilde*, 2nd ed. (London: Collins, 1966), 725, 730.

[8] Rupert Hart-Davis, ed., *The Letters of Oscar Wilde* (London: Rupert Hart-Davis, 1962), 31.

of the Second Spring. "No-one can forget him or his great virtues," Newman wrote, "or his claims on the gratitude of English Catholics.... He has in our history a place altogether special."[9]

Kenelm Digby, another of the pioneers and founding fathers of the Catholic Revival, died in March 1880. "All my friends are gone," he had lamented a few days before his death. "They are all in Kensal Green [a Catholic cemetery in London], and the best thing I can do is to follow them."[10] He was buried in Kensal Green, as he had desired, and there would seem to be no better epitaph to this pivotal figure and giant of the Second Spring than the final stanza of Chesterton's poem "The Rolling English Road":

> My friends, we will not go again or ape an ancient rage,
> Or stretch the folly of our youth to be the shame of age,
> But walk with clearer eyes and ears this path that wandereth,
> And see undrugged in evening light the decent inn of death;
> For there is good news yet to hear and fine things to be seen,
> Before we go to Paradise by way of Kensal Green.

Writing to Digby's daughter, Cardinal Manning paid tribute to the man who had done more than almost anyone in the previous half century to spread the faith in England:

---

[9] Peter Stanford and Leanda de Lisle, *The Catholics and Their Houses* (London: Harper Collins, 1995), 95.

[10] Bernard Holland, *Memoir of Kenelm Digby* (Sevenoaks, Kent: Fisher Press, 1992), 235.

What would you wish for your dear Father better or more beyond this, to fall asleep without pain after a life of preparation? As your husband said, he who has converted so many to God, and has led so many up the hill of a holy life is surely with his Master. May God bless and console you and all dear to you.[11]

Cardinal Manning's hopes for the immortal soul of Kenelm Digby resonated with those of Newman's poem "The Dream of Gerontius", which narrates the journey of a soul from deathbed to purgatory, assisted by its guardian angel. The theme was one which Newman had rehearsed in two earlier poems, "Guardian Angel" and "Golden Prison", the latter of which described purgatory as "the holy house of toll", the "frontier penance-place" and the "golden palace bright":

> Where souls elect abide,
> Waiting their certain call to Heaven,
> With Angels at their side.

"The Dream of Gerontius" would be set to music in 1900, ten years after Newman's death, by Edward Elgar, the marrying of the saint's words to the composer's Muse resulting in what A. N. Wilson has acclaimed as "possibly the most magnificent piece of English choral music in the repertoire".[12]

In 1883, Coventry Patmore met Gerard Manley Hopkins for the first time. It was during a visit by Patmore to Stonyhurst College, where Hopkins, now ordained as a Jesuit, was teaching Greek and Latin. The two convert poets became friends, even though Patmore failed to

---

[11] Ibid., 236.
[12] A. N. Wilson, *Eminent Victorians* (New York: W. W. Norton, 1990), 159.

understand the innovations of the younger man's poetry, nor its beauty and brilliance. Hopkins' poetry was as "hard as the darkest parts of Browning", Patmore remarked, adding that the innovations made Hopkins' verse inaccessible: "To the already sufficiently arduous character of such poetry you seem to me to have added the difficulty of following several *entirely* novel and simultaneous experiments in versification and construction—any of which novelties would be startling and productive of distraction from the poetic matter to be expressed."[13] This lack of sympathy for Hopkins' experimental approach was reiterated by Patmore in his correspondence with their mutual friend, Robert Bridges: "To me his poetry has the effect of veins of pure gold imbedded in masses of impracticable quartz."[14] It would not be until Robert Bridges finally published an edition of Hopkins' poetry, in 1918, that Hopkins' verse would find the readership it merited, almost thirty years after the poet's untimely death, at only forty-four years of age, in 1889.

In 1886, Pope Leo XIII pronounced on the merits of 361 English Catholics who had been killed during the period of Tudor and Stuart tyranny, declaring that 318 were true martyrs for the faith; of these, 255 were declared to be Venerable and the remaining sixty-three were declared to be Blessed, including the most famous, John Fisher and Thomas More. Many of these martyrs would subsequently be canonized.

Although the anti-papist bigotry that had characterized the period of martyrdom had not disappeared entirely, the relationship between the Vatican and the British government had improved significantly during the long reign of

[13] Calvert Alexander, S.J., *The Catholic Literary Revival* (Milwaukee: Bruce Publishing, 1935), 79.

[14] Bernard Bergonzi, *Gerard Manley Hopkins* (London: Macmillan, 1977), 139.

Queen Victoria, to such a degree that the heightened tension that had followed the reestablishment of the Catholic hierarchy by Pius IX in 1850 had long since dissipated. This improvement in relations was exemplified by the sending of a special envoy by Pope Leo XIII to congratulate Queen Victoria on her Golden Jubilee in 1887. The queen responded by sending the Duke of Norfolk to convey her thanks to the pope, the first time that a British monarch had sent an official envoy to the Vatican since the reign of James II two hundred years earlier.

By 1890, twenty years after the passing of the 1870 Education Act, which had raised the ire of Cardinal Manning and the rest of the Catholic hierarchy, the number of Catholic schools in England had increased from 350 at the time of the Act to 946 twenty years later. Whereas there had been 83,000 students enrolled in Catholic schools in 1870, this had increased to 224,000 by 1890. Such a success in Catholic education was a reflection of the growth of the Catholic population. In 1840, there had been 469 churches and chapels in England; fifty years later, this had increased to 1,335. Such success was a fitting testimony to the presence and leadership of Cardinals Manning and Newman, the dynamic duo who had presided over the Church in England, always allies in a common struggle, if not always the best of friends.

Cardinal Newman died in August 1890, a few months short of his ninetieth birthday, and Cardinal Manning died in January 1892 at the age of eighty-three. Both men had converted in the middle of their lives, and in the middle of the century, and thereafter had spent the remainder of the time left to them in devoted service of the faith that they had embraced. They straddled the Victorian age like a twin colossus, their towering presence serving as an indomitable witness to the resurrection of the Mystical Body of Christ in England's afflicted and conflicted culture.

One of the most poignant memories of Manning was given by G. K. Chesterton, who recalled seeing him in around 1880, when Chesterton, as a six-year-old, was walking with his father on Kensington High Street in London. Recalling the childhood vision, more than fifty years afterwards, Chesterton's child's eye view of the cardinal casts him as "a ghost clad in flames":

> In a flash a sort of ripple ran along the line and all these eccentrics went down on their knees on the public pavement.... Then I realized that a sort of little dark cab or carriage had drawn up ... and out of it came a ghost clad in flames ... lifting long frail fingers over the crowd in blessing. And then I looked at his face and was startled with a contrast; for his face was dead pale like ivory and very wrinkled and old ... having in every line the ruin of great beauty.[15]

In Chesterton's memory of his childhood encounter with the cardinal, Manning is not merely clothed in the scarlet of his ecclesial office but is also clad in the clouds of romantic legend. He is a prince of the Church enshrined as an ageing Prince Charming in the memory of an ageing G. K. Chesterton, writing half a century after the event.

At the other extreme, Lytton Strachey, in his notorious book, *Eminent Victorians*, robed Manning in a cloak of hypocrisy under which the ambitious cardinal concealed the treacherous dagger of intrigue. To the charitable Chesterton, Manning was a hero, perhaps even a saint; to the cynical Strachey, the same man was a villain worthy of vilification. It could be argued that these judgements reveal

[15] G. K. Chesterton, *Autobiography* (New York: Sheed & Ward, 1936), 49–50.

more about the men doing the judging than the man being judged. Chesterton perceived the truth in broad sweeping strokes of fanciful colour in which history was, above all, a good story, in which inimitable heroes fought iniquitous dragons; Strachey, on the other hand, subjugated the broader truth to a narrow-minded understanding of the facts, seeing Manning as an icon to be smashed in an iconoclastic debauch of cynical revisionism.

As for Manning himself, he made many enemies but was heralded at his death as "the people's cardinal". Even Strachey was forced to acknowledge Manning's huge popularity at the time of his death, though he was evidently perplexed as to the reason for it:

> The route of the procession was lined by vast crowds of working people, whose imaginations, in some instinctive manner, had been touched. Many who had hardly seen him declared that in Cardinal Manning they had lost their best friend. Was it the magnetic vigour of the dead man's spirit that moved them? Or was it his valiant disregard of common custom and those conventional reserves and poor punctilios, which are wont to hem about the great? Or was it something untameable in his glances and in his gestures? Or was it, perhaps, the mysterious glamour lingering about him of the antique organisation of Rome? For whatever cause, the mind of the people had been impressed.[16]

It is intriguing that Strachey glosses over the most obvious reason for Manning's popularity, which was his tireless work for the poor and the downtrodden. In September 1889, he had played a crucial role in the ending of the Dock Strike when, after weeks of delicate negotiation,

---

[16] Lytton Strachey, *Eminent Victorians* (London: Chatto & Windus, 1918), 114.

the eighty-one-year-old cardinal had finally obtained for the dockworkers the bare justice for which they had asked. On September 14, "the Cardinal's Peace" was signed, ending the strike and confirming Manning as a champion of the working man. A few years earlier, in 1885, he had been a member of the royal commission on the housing of the poor, and a year later, he was appointed to the royal commission on education. His social vision was gaining international recognition, and it is widely believed that Manning's social teaching, and his practical example, were influential upon Pope Leo XIII's writing of the famous social encyclical, *Rerum Novarum*, which was published in 1891, shortly before Manning's death.

As for Newman, his conversion in 1845 can be considered a defining moment in the Catholic Revival, heralding a wave of high-profile conversions, of which Manning's in 1851 was but one of many. Newman's brilliance was universally acknowledged, even by his enemies, and works such as his *Essay on the Development of Christian Doctrine* (1845), the quasi-autobiographical novel, *Loss and Gain* (1848), and his autobiographical *Apologia pro Vita Sua* (1864) have established his reputation as one of the finest prose stylists of the Victorian period, a truly rare accomplishment considering how many great writers that particular period produced. He was also a poet of considerable merit as is seen in the quality of the poetry published in his *Verses on Various Occasions* (1874). The publication of his sermons and lectures established Newman's reputation as a theologian and philosopher, a reputation that was fortified still further in 1870 with the publication of the *Grammar of Assent*, on the philosophy of faith.

Considering the sheer depth and breadth of Newman's brilliance, it is not surprising that he has outshone Manning's own considerable achievement. To the eyes of posterity, if not necessarily in the eyes of their own age, Manning is seen as walking in Newman's more illustrious shadow. This being so, and as a means of enabling Manning to emerge from Newman's shadow, we will end with Hilaire Belloc's memories of Manning and his appraisal of his historical importance and stature:

> It was my custom during my first days in London, as a very young man ... to call upon the Cardinal as regularly as he would receive me; and during those brief interviews I heard from him many things which I have had later occasion to test by the experience of human life ... and Manning did seem to me (and still seems to me) much the greatest Englishman of his time. He was certainly the greatest of all that band, small but intensely significant, who, in the Victorian period, so rose above their fellows, pre-eminent in will and in intellect, as not only to perceive, but even to accept the Faith.[17]

---

[17] Hilaire Belloc, *The Cruise of the Nona* (London: Constable, 1925), 54–55.

Chapter Twenty-Five

Literary Converts

Ah! happy they whose hearts can break
And peace of pardon win!
How else may man make straight his plan
And cleanse his soul from Sin?
How else but through a broken heart
May Lord Christ enter in?

—Oscar Wilde,
from *The Ballad of Reading Gaol*

The decade of the 1890s is popularly perceived as a time of cynicism and decadence, variously dubbed the "naughty nineties" or the fin de siècle. "A New Spirit of Pleasure is abroad amongst us," the poet Richard Le Gallienne wrote, "and one that blows from no mere coteries of hedonistic philosophies, but comes on the four winds." Le Gallienne saw such hedonism as the consequence of a deeply ingrained pessimism, adding that "an age that had lost its old faiths [was] finding expression in a widespread application of the philosophy of *carpe diem*".[1] Years later, in the 1920s, Le Gallienne lamented that "the '90s were generally sowing that wind of which we may be said to be now reaping the whirlwind."[2]

---

[1] Richard Le Gallienne, *The Romantic '90s* (London: Robin Clark, 1993), 131.
[2] Ibid.

Le Gallienne's depiction and description of the final decade of the nineteenth century, for all its evocation of the spirit of pessimism and hedonism, does not do the decade of "decadence" justice. As the writer and critic Holbrook Jackson insisted, the true aesthetic of the 1890s could be seen as a Catholic literary response to the spirit of decadence and a healthy reaction and recoil from the cynical spirit of ennui and disenchantment which pervaded the culture:

> In England the artists who represented the renaissance of the nineties were either Catholic like Francis Thompson and Henry Harland or prospective converts to Rome like Oscar Wilde, Aubrey Beardsley, Lionel Johnson, and Ernest Dowson. If Catholicism did not claim them some other form of mysticism did, and W. B. Yeats and George Russell became Theosophists. The one who persistently hardened himself against the mystical influences of the period, John Davidson, committed suicide.[3]

A major hub of the literary revival in the 1880s and 1890s was the home of Wilfrid and Alice Meynell, both devout Catholics, whose presence was not merely influential on the new generation of writers and artists but was positively catalytic. Wilfrid Meynell was the editor of two journals, the *Weekly Register*, which he had begun editing in 1881 at the invitation of Cardinal Manning, and *Merry England*, a cultural journal which supported "the social revolution of the Young England Movement, the revival of the peasantry, the abolition of the wrongs of the poor, and the spread of arts and letters".[4] The art critic and

---

[3] Calvert Alexander, S.J., *The Catholic Literary Revival* (Milwaukee: Bruce Publishing, 1935), 87.

[4] Matthew Hoehn, ed., *Catholic Authors: Contemporary Biographical Sketches 1930–1947* (Newark, N.J.: St. Mary's Abbey, 1947), 536.

historian Charles Lewis Hind wrote that "calling at that house meant arriving at half-past three, staying until midnight, and meeting in the course of the year most of the literary folk worth knowing."[5] Among the older generation of writers, those who visited the Meynells included Robert Browning, Coventry Patmore, Dante Gabriel Rossetti, Aubrey de Vere, and George Meredith; but it was the influence of the Meynells on the younger generation of writers which proved most telling to the cultural renewal that would blossom into the fully fledged Catholic literary revival of the following century. Amongst the young artists and writers who frequented the social gatherings chez Meynell were Aubrey Beardsley, Oscar Wilde, Francis Thompson, Lionel Johnson, Richard Le Gallienne, W. B. Yeats, and Katharine Tynan. Of these, Francis Thompson, a cradle Catholic, had been rescued by the Meynells from a life of destitution and drug addiction on the streets of post-Dickensian London, whereas Beardsley, Wilde, and Lionel Johnson would all soon be received into the Catholic Church as refugees from the decadent lifestyle.

Francis Thompson would be described by G. K. Chesterton as "a great poet"[6] and as "the greatest poetic energy since Robert Browning".[7] He is best known to posterity for "The Hound of Heaven", a poem which depicts Christ as a hunter, relentlessly pursuing the fleeing sinner:

> I fled Him, down the nights and down the days;
>   I fled Him, down the arches of the years;
> I fled Him, down the labyrinthine ways
>   Of my own mind.

---

[5] Alexander, *Catholic Literary Revival*, 114.
[6] G. K. Chesterton, *All Things Considered* (London: Methuen, 1926), 206.
[7] Ibid., 204.

Aubrey Beardsley's influence as the enfant terrible of the fin de siècle was so considerable that his reception into the Church in March 1897 caused shock and astonishment. "Of the piquant personalities of the 90's," wrote Fr. Calvert Alexander in his groundbreaking book, *The Catholic Literary Revival*, "none more strikingly epitomizes the spirit that gave celebrity and significance to the period than that of Aubrey Beardsley."[8] The writer Max Beerbohm declared that "I belong to the Beardsley Period,"[9] a declaration that inspired Osbert Burdett to entitle his study of the 1890s *The Beardsley Period*. Expressing similar deference to Beardsley's impact, Holbrook Jackson refers to him as "the unique expression of the most unique mood of the 'nineties".[10] No lesser figure than James McNeill Whistler was among Beardsley's admirers, telling him that he was "a very great artist", an unexpected compliment that reduced Beardsley to tears.[11]

Unlike Beardsley, Lionel Johnson, who was received into the Church in June 1891, was never very well-known, even to his contemporaries, although his best-known poem "The Dark Angel" would influence the poetic vision of T. S. Eliot. This particular poem, along with one or two others, is still regularly included in popular and reputable anthologies, ensuring that Johnson's verse has not been entirely erased from the canon. Writing of Beardsley's reception into the Church and its positive impact on Beardsley's life, Johnson could equally have been describing the healthy impact of his own conversion:

He withdrew himself from certain valued intimacies, which he felt incompatible with his faith.... There was

[8] Alexander, *Catholic Literary Revival*, 100.
[9] Ibid.
[10] Ibid.
[11] Le Gallienne, *Romantic '90s*, 136.

always in him a vein of mental or imaginative unhealthiness and nervousness, probably due to his extreme physical fragility: this he was setting himself to conquer, to transform into a spiritual and artistic source of energy.[12]

Oscar Wilde is obviously the most famous of the group of literary converts from the fin de siècle, his own reception into the Church on his deathbed representing the consummation of a lifelong love affair with the faith. Wilde's own penitential spirit was best encapsulated in *The Ballad of Reading Gaol*, which he wrote after his release from prison in 1897:

> Ah! happy they whose hearts can break
> And peace of pardon win!
> How else may man make straight his plan
> And cleanse his soul from Sin?
> How else but through a broken heart
> May Lord Christ enter in?

Another poet who should not be overlooked in this brief survey of the literary converts of the 1890s is Ernest Dowson, best known for his decadent anthem, "Non Sum Qualis eram Bonae Sub Regno Cynarae", with its famous refrain: "I have been faithful to thee, Cynara! In my fashion." This delicate acknowledgment of reckless and feckless infidelity would inspire a Hollywood film about infidelity, *Faithful in My Fashion* (1946), starring Donna Reed, and would also inspire Cole Porter's song "Always True to You in My Fashion" from *Kiss Me, Kate*. A line from Dowson's poem ("I have forgot much, Cynara! gone with the wind") would provide the title for Margaret Mitchell's

[12] Richard Whittington-Egan, *Lionel Johnson: Victorian Dark Angel* (Great Malvern, Worcestershire: Cappella Archive, 2012), xii.

bestselling novel. Such trivia aside, Dowson should also be remembered for those wistful poems inspired by his Catholic faith, "Nuns of the Perpetual Adoration", "Carthusians", and "Extreme Unction", each expressing the painful longing of the heart in exile for the peace that only comes through union with Christ. After Dowson was received into the Church in 1892, Lionel Johnson wrote joyfully to Richard Le Gallienne that "my dearest friend Dowson ... is now, *Laus Deo*, a Catholic."[13]

As the curtain fell on the nineteenth century, it also fell on this generation of literary converts, whose delicacy and dissolute lifestyle led to their tragically early deaths. Aubrey Beardsley died in March 1898, at the age of twenty-five; Ernest Dowson died in February 1900, aged thirty-two; Wilde died nine months later, aged forty-six; and Lionel Johnson died in September 1902, aged thirty-five.

Few will venture to suggest that these prodigal sons were saints or that they are ever likely to be canonized. On the other hand, few except the most judgmental and hard-hearted will fail to rejoice that these miserable sinners were received into the Church. "The Roman Catholic Church is for saints and sinners alone," Oscar Wilde is said to have quipped, "for respectable people, the Anglican Church will do."

The turn of the twentieth century also saw the end of the long reign of Queen Victoria, who died on January 22, 1901. Her death marked the end of an era and the beginning of the end of the British Empire, which had been in the ascendant during her reign. Writing to his fiancée on the day of the queen's burial, G. K. Chesterton wrote that "this is a great and serious hour and it is felt so completely by all England." He also added some words of patriotism

---

[13] Le Gallienne, *Romantic '90s*, 110.

that would be prophetic of his own role as a writer in the following decades: "It is sometimes easy to give one's country blood and easier to give her money. Sometimes the hardest thing of all is to give her truth."[14]

Queen Victoria's funeral was organized by England's leading lay Catholic, the Duke of Norfolk, in his capacity as Earl Marshall; it was in this same capacity that he was responsible for the coronation of the queen's successor, King Edward VII. One of the few remaining anti-Catholic laws required that the new sovereign make a ceremonial declaration against the Catholic doctrine of transubstantiation upon his accession to the throne, accompanied by a condemnation of the Mass as being idolatrous and superstitious. Although the new king found such a requirement distasteful, and in spite of efforts to relieve him of the onerous necessity of obeying such a draconian law, he was forced reluctantly to comply. He would be the last monarch to do so, the declaration being abolished by an Act of Parliament in 1910, prior to the accession of George V. In 1902, the new king made history as the first reigning English sovereign since mediaeval times to visit the pope. It was indicative of his well-known sympathy for Catholicism that he had initiated the visit himself.

In September 1903, Robert Hugh Benson was received into the Church, his conversion being the most seismic in terms of its impact on the Anglican establishment and the general culture since Newman's conversion almost sixty years earlier. As the son of E. W. Benson, who had been Archbishop of Canterbury from 1883 until his death in 1896, Benson's conversion and subsequent ordination as a Catholic priest struck at the very heart of the state religion. It also struck at the heart of Archbishop Benson's own

---

[14] Maisie Ward, *Gilbert Keith Chesterton* (London: Sheed & Ward, 1944), 127.

dismissive attitude to the rise of Catholicism, expressed in a pastoral letter in 1890, in which he asserted that the English people were in no danger of being led to the Catholic Church. "It has been shown," he wrote, "that in all these years she [the Catholic Church] has effected here a multiplication of edifices and institutions, but not of souls; that she makes no statistical progress. No, the ancient [*sic*] Church of England is with us. I do not fear that the new Italian Mission will make anything of our clergy or people."[15] Although Archbishop Benson had died prior to his son's reception into the Church, it is tempting to see that Benson's conversion was a case of the living haunting the dead. R. H. Benson was an Anglican priest, belying his father's claim that the "Italian Mission", so-called, "will make anything of our clergy or people". Furthermore, the rise of the Catholic Church in England throughout the twentieth century, coupled with the capitulation of Anglicanism to the spirit of modernism, would lead to the shrinking and shrivelling of the state religion and its being eclipsed by the very Church which it had usurped four centuries earlier.

As for R. H. Benson himself, he would have a considerable impact on English culture as yet another literary convert, most especially in the many bestselling novels he wrote prior to his untimely and early death in 1914. Most of his historical fiction is inspired by the heroism and martyrdom of Catholics during the reigns of Henry VIII and Elizabeth I. One notable exception is *Richard Raynal, Solitary*, which is set in late mediaeval times, showing the culture of Merrie England through the life of a holy hermit. He also wrote novels set in contemporary England,

[15] Anonymous [no editor listed], *Catholic Emancipation, 1829 to 1929* (London: Longmans, Green, 1929), 252.

as well as futuristic dystopian fiction, most notably *Lord of the World*, which depicts a world in which creeping and seditious secularism seeks to destroy religion in the name of "peace".

The most prominent Anglican priest to be received into the Church in Benson's wake was Ronald Knox, who was received in 1917. Like Benson, Knox was the son of an Anglican bishop, his father being the Bishop of Manchester, and, like Benson, he would be ordained as a Catholic priest. Knox was hugely influenced by Benson. In the last few days before his reception into the Church, Knox read several Catholic novels but especially enjoyed Benson's *Come Rack! Come Rope!*, writing that "Hugh Benson, who had set my feet on the way towards the Church, watched over my footsteps to the last." Knox would go on to be a well-known Catholic writer, of satire, detective stories, and apologetics.

Shortly before his conversion, Knox's anti-modernist satire, *Reunion All Round*, was published. It caused quite a stir. It was read aloud to the Prime Minister, Herbert Asquith, and in the refectory of the English College in Rome to those training for the priesthood, as well as receiving the approval of many of the more conservative Anglican bishops. Most satisfying to Knox was the enthusiasm with which it was reviewed by one of his heroes, G. K. Chesterton, whom Knox described as "my earliest master and model".[16] Although Chesterton was still not a Catholic himself, his pro-Catholic perspective was ushering many people into the Church, Knox being but one of many. It would be Chesterton, more than anyone else, who would inspire the Catholic literary revival of the twentieth century.

---

[16] Ward, *Gilbert Keith Chesterton*, 149.

Chapter Twenty-Six

The Catholic Literary Revival

"Oh," said Syme with a beaming smile, "we are all Catholics now."

—G. K. Chesterton,
from *The Man Who Was Thursday*

In the first decade of the twentieth century, the Church was beset by the threat of modernism from within and secularism from without. With respect to the former, the Irish priest George Tyrrell was expelled from the Society of Jesus in 1906 for preaching modernist ideas that were contrary to Catholic teaching. In the following year, Fr. Tyrrell was excommunicated for criticizing Pope Pius X's encyclical *Pascendi Dominici Gregis*, which had explicitly condemned modernism. When G. K. Chesterton was asked for his opinions on Fr. Tyrrell's excommunication, he replied that membership of any society required acknowledgment of its rules and principles and that anyone who made public statements inconsistent with those principles could have no objection to his being asked to resign his membership. He then made an impassioned defence of Pius X: "I can assure you, and I would prove it to you if I had time, that the Popes have done a hundred times more for Liberty than any of the Protestant Churches ever have."[1]

If the modernist threat from within had been subdued by the robust response of the Society of Jesus and the definitive teaching of St. Pius X, the secularist threat from without was most apparent in England by new government attempts to standardize and secularize education. This new threat to the independence of Catholic schools was met with stern opposition by England's Catholics, led by the courageous example of Archbishop (later Cardinal) Vaughan, with the support of the Duke of Norfolk and other Catholic peers. Protest demonstrations were held across the country under the slogan "Catholic religious teaching by Catholic teachers in Catholic schools under Catholic control".[2] In the Catholic heartland of Lancashire, large meetings were held in Liverpool, Manchester, Preston, and other towns; in Yorkshire and the Midlands, demonstrations were held in Leeds, Halifax, Birmingham, Nottingham, Leicester, and in many smaller towns. Meetings were held all over London, with an open-air meeting on Clapham Common being attended by fifteen thousand people. The climax of this campaign for religious liberty in education was a huge meeting at the Albert Hall in London, over which Archbishop Bourne presided, which was held on May 5, 1906, the eve of the debate on the Education Bill in the House of Commons. According to Sir John Gilbert, who had addressed the huge crowd at the earlier meeting on Clapham Common, the sheer scale of this demonstration of Catholic resistance and resilience "created an extraordinary impression in London and

---

[1] Joseph Pearce, *Wisdom and Innocence: A Life of G. K. Chesterton* (London: Hodder & Stoughton, 1996), 169.

[2] Anonymous [no editor listed], *Catholic Emancipation, 1829 to 1929* (London: Longmans, Green, 1929), 63.

the country".[3] The Albert Hall was filled to capacity with an audience of ten thousand. Outside the hall, an overflow meeting was held at which between thirty thousand and forty thousand people were present. In the face of such opposition, the government eventually abandoned the Bill, signalling a momentous political victory for a revitalized Catholic Church.

As with the controversy with modernism, the Church found a powerful ally in G. K. Chesterton, whose defence of religious liberty was coupled with a disdain for the secular vision of education. "It is typical of our time," he wrote in January 1907, "that the more doubtful we are about the value of philosophy, the more certain we are about the value of education. That is to say, the more doubtful we are about whether we have any truth, the more certain we are (apparently) that we can teach it to children. The smaller our faith in doctrine, the larger our faith in doctors."[4]

In 1908, the apostolic constitution *Sapienti Consilio* removed England and Wales from the jurisdiction of Propaganda Fide, thereby ending England's designation as "mission territory" and placing the country and its hierarchy on the same ecclesial footing as the hierarchies of the rest of Europe. In the same year, as further vindication of the status of the resurrected English Church, London was selected as the venue for the International Eucharistic Congress. For the first time since 1554, during the reign of Mary Tudor, a papal legate was sent to England, his arrival still being technically illegal according to the letter of the law.

If the legate's arrival for the congress had passed without any undue diplomatic incident, the proposed eucharistic procession through the streets of London excited a

---

[3] Ibid.
[4] *Illustrated London News*, January 12, 1907.

great deal of opposition. The king had voiced his concerns to Lord Crewe, with whom he was staying; Lord Crewe, in turn, referred these concerns to Prime Minister Herbert Asquith:

> The King has taken this d-----d procession greatly to heart; and asked me to say that he was "greatly cut up about it"—a rather curious phrase.... He has received dozens of letters from enraged Protestants, who compare him disadvantageously with his revered mother, now with God, and hint that his ultimate destination may be directed elsewhere.[5]

Faced with the king's concerns and voicing his own, Asquith put pressure on Archbishop Vaughan to cancel the procession. In the event, a compromise was reached whereby the Blessed Sacrament would not be carried outside the walls of the cathedral, though a public procession, bereft of the Blessed Sacrament, went ahead. Since it was unclear whether the wearing of monastic habits in public was legal, religious wore ordinary clerical attire but, as a silent protest, they carried their habits over their arms. It would not be until the passing of the Roman Catholic Relief Act of 1926 that the religious orders would finally be freed from the Penal Laws. There was no major disturbance by anti-Catholic demonstrators during the procession, as had been feared, but this might have been due to the large police presence along the route. The enforced compromise was seen by Catholics as an affront to their faith and freedom; it was rumoured that the government's subsequent defeat in the Newcastle by-election was caused by the loss of the Catholic vote.

[5] Nicholas Schofield and Gerard Skinner, *The English Cardinals* (Oxford: Family Publications, 2007), 186.

Irrespective of his misgivings about the eucharistic procession, King Edward VII still exhibited an openness to Catholicism. Earlier in the same year, he had attended a requiem Mass for the assassinated king of Portugal, accompanied by both Queen Alexandra and the prince of Wales, the first time a British monarch had publicly attended Mass since James II had done so in the seventeenth century.

It was also in 1908 that G. K. Chesterton's *Orthodoxy* was published, a seminal work which would prove instrumental to the conversions of countless people in the years and decades ahead. The same year also saw the publication of Chesterton's finest novel, *The Man Who Was Thursday*, a timeless cautionary tale of the dangers of nihilistic philosophy and of the necessity of Christian faith as the only means of escape from the nihilistic nightmare.

Such was the influence of Chesterton, in league with his great friend Hilaire Belloc, that Fr. Alexander wrote that "Chesterton and Belloc ... have determined the course Catholic literature has taken in the twentieth century."[6] "To me," wrote Ronald Knox, "Chesterton's philosophy ... has been part of the air I breathed.... His paradoxes have become ... the platitudes of my thought."[7] With the emergence of Chesterton into the intellectual and literary fray, the Catholic literary revival entered its second dynamic phase, the first being the period following Newman's conversion. Indeed, it would be no exaggeration to say that Chesterton's role in popularizing Catholicism in the twentieth century was as crucial as Newman's had been in the previous century.

---

[6] Calvert Alexander, S.J., *The Catholic Literary Revival* (Milwaukee: Bruce Publishing, 1935), 242.

[7] Claude Williamson, ed., *Great Catholics* (London: Nicholson and Watson, 1938), 548.

As for the literary revival itself, it rested largely on the shoulders of converts. This was true to such an extent that Hilaire Belloc, as a cradle Catholic, was the exception that proved the rule. Apart from Chesterton, who was seen as a Catholic writer many years before his belated reception into the Church in 1922, and R. H. Benson, whose novels were very popular in the years before World War I, there were many other significant literary converts in the early part of the twentieth century. Maurice Baring, whose novels would prove popular in the years between the two world wars, was received into the Church in 1908; Lord Alfred Douglas, Oscar Wilde's nemesis, became a Catholic in 1911, with his wife and fellow poet Olive Custance being received in 1917; and the historian Christopher Dawson joined the Church in 1914, his influence rivalling that of Belloc with respect to the popularizing of Catholic historical revisionism.

Events in England and Europe took a devastating turn in 1914 with the outbreak of World War I. The old recusant families, now accepted as part of the aristocratic establishment, were at the forefront of the war effort. The Duke of Norfolk organized the reception of Belgian refugees at the outset of the conflict, and many of the most prominent Catholic families were well represented in the military. Major General Sir Francis Howard became inspector general of infantry, and his brother, Sir Henry Howard, was the wartime British envoy to the pope. Lord Stafford's brother, Edward Fitzherbert, commanded HMS *Colossus* in the Grand Fleet, becoming an admiral. Lord Denbigh commanded the Royal Horse Artillery, whereas Lady Denbigh turned the family's stately home into a hospital.

In Belgium, the elderly nun Mary Towneley, who had been English provincial of the Sisters of Notre Dame of Namur since 1886, was at the motherhouse of her order

in Belgium at the time of the German invasion. When
the Germans entered the convent searching for arms, the
old nun held open a bag containing her knitting, asking
the German officer if he wished to search it. The officer
clicked his heels, saluted, bowed, and withdrew.

As the fighting began in earnest, becoming entrenched
and bogged down in a seemingly interminable stalemate,
the English Catholic nobility paid the price in terms of
casualties. David Kerr, the devoutly Catholic nephew of the
Duke of Norfolk, was killed in October 1914. In the following year, the young Lord Petre died from wounds
received in battle, the first of three Petres who would
be killed during the conflict. Other members of the old
Catholic families killed in action included two Welds, two
Weld-Blundells, and their cousin Kenelm Vaughan, as
well as two Stonors and no fewer than four de Traffords.
Colonel Courtenay Throckmorton was killed in 1916,
as were Sir Hugh Clifford's son Hugh and his brother
Brigadier-General Henry Clifford, their cousin Walter
Clifford being killed in the previous year. Lord Clifford's
sister, Lady Denbigh, lost two of her sons, and another
of his sisters, Blanche, lost her eldest son, Thomas, while
her youngest son, Cuthbert, was severely wounded. Alexander de Lisle, another relation of the Cliffords, was also
killed, and Francis Plowden died of wounds in 1918, his
younger brother Godfrey having fallen on active service
the previous year.[8]

The sacrifice of these descendants of the old recusant
families, who had suffered so much during the centuries
of persecution, was not lost on Evelyn Waugh, one of
the generation of postwar literary converts, who wrote

---

[8] Mark Bence-Jones, *The Catholic Families* (London: Constable, 1992),
269–71.

in *Brideshead Revisited* of the futility of their deaths in the light, or shadow, of the postwar wasteland. These sons of recusants "in all the flood of academic and athletic success, of popularity and the promise of great rewards ahead," were the "garlanded victims, devoted to the sacrifice": "They were the aborigines, vermin by right of law, to be shot off at leisure so that things might be safe for the travelling salesman, with his polygonal pince-nez, his fat wet hand-shake, his grinning dentures."[9]

Bede Clifford, who survived the war, wrote in his diary during the Battle of the Somme of the sheer hell in which the combatants found themselves: "On all sides the sickly stench of dead men and beasts assails the nostrils. Everywhere the cries of wounded men pleading in vain to be evacuated."[10] J. R. R. Tolkien, who had been received into the Church following his widowed mother's conversion in 1900, was also at what he called the "animal horror" of the Somme.[11] Had he been one of the victims of this most deadly of battles, during which more than three hundred thousand men were killed, the world would have been bereft of *The Lord of the Rings* and his other works. One wonders indeed, how many great writers were lost during the First World War before their gifts could bless the world.

By the time that the war finally ended, in November 1918, there were few in England who had not suffered bitterly through the death of loved ones. G. K. Chesterton lost his beloved younger brother Cecil at the very end of the war, and Hilaire Belloc lost his eldest son, Louis, who was killed in August 1918 during a Royal Flying Corps

[9] Evelyn Waugh, *Brideshead Revisited* (New York: Alfred A. Knopf, Everyman's Library, 1993), 124–25.

[10] Bence-Jones, *Catholic Families*, 271.

[11] Humphrey Carpenter, *J. R. R. Tolkien: A Biography* (London: George Allen & Unwin, 1977), 91.

bombing raid over enemy lines, only weeks before his twenty-first birthday, his body never being found. (Belloc would also lose his youngest son, Peter, during the Second World War, who would be killed while on active service with the Royal Marines in 1941.)

The spirit of decadence and nihilism that pervaded English culture in the years following World War I was encapsulated by T. S. Eliot in poems such as "The Waste Land" and "The Hollow Men". This spirit was countered by a resurgent and confident Catholicism. The appearance of the poetry of Gerard Manley Hopkins, published for the first time in 1918, almost thirty years after the poet's death, signalled the vitality of the Catholic literary presence, Hopkins being the most influential poet of the following decades, with the exception of the aforementioned T. S. Eliot, who would announce his own conversion to "anglo-catholicism" in 1927. This revitalized literary presence was accompanied by a robust apologetic presence. The Catholic Evidence Guild, founded in 1919, took the teachings of the Catholic Church onto the streets. Its members would set up a platform on street corners and in parks, surmounted by a crucifix, and then one of them would give a talk on some aspect of doctrine, fielding questions and handling hecklers with eloquence and charity. The most celebrated members of the guild were the holy Dominican Fr. Vincent McNabb and a young couple, Frank Sheed and Maisie Ward, who, after their marriage, would found Sheed & Ward publishers.

Chesterton's belated reception into the Church in 1922 heightened the Catholic presence in the culture, as did the popular works of apologetics that he wrote in the years following his conversion, such as *St. Francis of Assisi* (1923), *The Everlasting Man* (1925), and *The Catholic Church and Conversion* (1926).

Another major literary presence, as has been mentioned, was that of Maurice Baring, whose neglect by later generations should not be allowed to eclipse his popularity as a novelist in the 1920s and 1930s. *C*, published in 1924, was highly praised by the French novelist André Maurois, who declared that no book had given him such pleasure since his reading of Tolstoy, Proust, and E. M. Forster.[12] As such a comment would suggest, Baring was as popular in France as in England, with one of his novels, *Daphne Adeane*, going through twenty-three printings in the edition of the Librairie Stock. His novels were also translated into Italian, Dutch, Swedish, Hungarian, Czech, Spanish, and German. *Cat's Cradle*, published in 1925, was considered by Belloc "a great masterpiece ... the best story of a woman's life that I know".[13] Belloc also expressed great admiration for *Robert Peckham*, a historical novel by Baring, set during the penal times, which is reminiscent of R. H. Benson's historical fiction.

Chesterton shared Belloc's high opinion, writing to Baring in 1929 that he had been "much uplifted" by Baring's novel *The Coat without Seam*, stating humbly that "my writing cannot ... be so subtle or delicate as yours."[14] Of all the praise steeped on Baring's work by his literary peers, none was more welcome than that received from the French novelist François Mauriac. Baring was "too moved to speak" when he had heard that Mauriac had said that what he "most admire[d] about Baring's work is the sense he gives you of the penetration of grace".[15]

[12] Paul Horgan, *Maurice Baring Restored* (London: Heinemann, 1970), 49.

[13] Robert Speaight, ed., *Letters from Hilaire Belloc* (London: Hollis & Carter, 1958), 213.

[14] Emma Letley, *Maurice Baring: A Citizen of Europe* (London: Constable, 1991), 217.

[15] Laura Lovat, *Maurice Baring: A Postscript* (London: Hollis & Carter, 1947), 4–5.

Another major literary figure, neglected today but very popular during his own day, was the poet Alfred Noyes, who was received into the Church in 1927, the same year in which Eliot embraced the "catholic" remnant in the Anglican church. More were to follow. Graham Greene and Evelyn Waugh were received into the Church, the former in 1926 and the latter in 1930. Waugh's conversion caused quite a stir, being received with astonishment by the literati and the media. On September 30, the morning after his reception, there was bewilderment in the *Daily Express* that an author notorious for his "almost passionate adherence to the ultra-modern" could have joined the Catholic Church. Two leaders in the *Express* had already discussed the significance of Waugh's conversion before his own article, "Converted to Rome: Why It Has Happened to Me", was published. It was given a full-page spread, boldly headlined. The following day, E. Rosslyn Mitchell, a Protestant Member of Parliament, wrote a reply; the day after, Fr. Francis Woodlock, a Jesuit, wrote an article entitled "Is Britain Turning to Rome?" Three days later an entire page was given over to the ensuing letters.

Was Britain turning to Rome? The number of adult converts during the period indicated that increasing numbers were doing so. Between 1912 and 1927, there were 167,135 converts received into the Church, an annual average of more than 10,000 people.[16] Among the more famous converts was Katherine Asquith, wife of the former Prime Minister, who was received into the Church following her husband's death in 1928. It was, however, the number of literary converts which really caught the eye. Frank Sheed, who was at the very epicentre of this seismic cultural revival, wrote that "the twenties ... saw writers converted to the Faith in England in numbers

[16] Anonymous, *Catholic Emancipation*, 260.

which could not be matched in any previous century." Prior to Newman's conversion in 1845, the only literary converts which spring to mind are John Dryden, who converted to Catholicism in 1685, and the martyred saints Edmund Campion and Robert Southwell, who converted in the sixteenth century. In Newman's wake, a host of writers joined the Church, some of whom are still well-known and others, popular in their own day, are now forgotten. It was, however, in the twenties and thirties that the number of literary converts increased rapidly. Apart from those already mentioned, others included the biographer D.B. Wyndham Lewis, the satirist J.B. Morton, actor-writer Robert Speaight, the artist-writers Eric Gill and David Jones, the poet Roy Campbell, and the novelists Compton Mackenzie, Philip Gibbs, Arnold Lunn, and Sheila Kaye-Smith. Such growth prompted the historian Sheridan Gilley to declare that "the era between the world wars was something of a golden age in the history of Catholicism in England."[17] In fact, the whole period from Newman's conversion in 1845 and Chesterton's death in 1936 was a golden age. The Church, which England's rulers had done their best to kill during a war of attrition conducted relentlessly for three hundred years, had well and truly risen from its presumed grave. It was, therefore, fitting, following Chesterton's death, that Cardinal Pacelli, the future Pope Pius XII, should send a telegram on behalf of Pope Pius XI to Cardinal Hinsley, the Archbishop of Westminster, which was read at the requiem Mass for Chesterton at Westminster Cathedral: "Holy Father deeply grieved death Mr Gilbert Keith Chesterton

[17] V. Alland McClelland and Michael Hodgetts, eds., *From Without the Flaminian Gate: 150 Years of Roman Catholicism in England and Wales 1850–2000* (London: Darton, Longman and Todd, 1999), 23.

devoted son Holy Church gifted Defender of the Catholic Faith. His Holiness offers paternal sympathy people of England assures prayers dear departed, bestows Apostolic Benediction."[18]

There was an ironic twist to the pope's telegram because the English press refused to publish it on the grounds that "the Pope had bestowed on a British subject a title held by the King."[19] That the title of *Fidei Defensor* was originally bestowed upon the king by the pope was, of course, overlooked, Henry VIII being awarded the title by Leo X for the king's theological defence of the seven sacraments, prior to Henry's rebellion against the Church. The irony was delightful, especially in the light of the canonization in the previous year of Thomas More and John Fisher on the four hundredth anniversary of their martyrdom. One can venture to conjecture that Chesterton, a true defender of the faith, was welcomed into paradise by the two newly canonized saints, his reward for a lifetime of service as the towering presence in the Catholic literary revival.

---

[18] Maisie Ward, *Gilbert Keith Chesterton* (London: Sheed & Ward, 1944), 553.
[19] Ferdinand Valentine, O.P., *Father Vincent McNabb* (London: Burns & Oates, 1955), 276.

Chapter Twenty-Seven

Beyond Modernity

In breaking of belief in human good;
In slavedom of mankind to the machine;
In havoc of hideous tyranny withstood,
And terror of atomic doom foreseen;
Deliver us from ourselves.

—Siegfried Sassoon,
from "Litany of the Lost"

If G. K. Chesterton's death in 1936 marked the end of the second phase of the Catholic literary revival (the first phase being that under the paternal patronage of Newman), the third phase began in 1937 with the publication of *The Hobbit* by J. R. R. Tolkien. The works of Tolkien, together with those of his good friend C. S. Lewis, would become some of the most popular ever written. By 2017, *The Hobbit* had become the sixth bestselling work of literature of all time, with over 100 million copies sold. As if this were not enough in itself, the adventures of Bilbo's nephew, Frodo, as told in the later book, *The Lord of the Rings*, have proved even more popular, more than 150 million copies being sold, making it the third bestselling book of all time. Only *Don Quixote* and *A Tale of Two Cities* have proved more successful in terms of sales.

The secret of Tolkien's popularity, apart from his power as a storyteller, is rooted in the perennial truths which animate his work, truths that are themselves rooted in Tolkien's devout Catholic faith. Tolkien stated unequivocally that "*The Lord of the Rings* is, of course, a religious and Catholic work";[1] it is this moral and spiritual dimension that undergirds the narrative, even if many of Tolkien's millions of readers fail to realize it. *The Hobbit* and *The Lord of the Rings* shine forth something beyond the world of mere power which is taken so seriously by those who are its servants. They show that ordinary people are not the absurd creatures that the Dark Lord's servants claim that they are. They are not postmodern nonentities, nothing but meaningless mortals living meaningless existences in a meaningless cosmos. On the contrary, they are what history and tradition, and good theology and philosophy, have always taught that they are. They are those who are called to look beyond themselves to the goodness, truth, and beauty of objective reality and whose lives are a meaningful journey, a quest, an adventure, the purpose of which is to get to the heaven-haven of the reward, as Gerard Manley Hopkins would say. *The Hobbit* and *The Lord of the Rings* look beyond the darkness to the light that transcends it and is beyond it. They reflect the faith and hope of Samwise Gamgee, who proclaims in one of the darkest moments in *The Lord of the Rings* that "above all shadows rides the sun".[2]

It is significant that much of *The Lord of the Rings* was written during the darkness of World War II, the second of the global conflagrations of mass destruction that modernity had unleashed in the twentieth century, the

[1] Humphrey Carpenter, ed., *The Letters of J. R. R. Tolkien* (New York: Houghton Mifflin, 2000), 172.

[2] J. R. R. Tolkien, *The Lord of the Rings* (London: HarperCollins, 2004), 909.

bloodiest so far in human history. Tolkien's friend C. S. Lewis became something of a national celebrity during the war, his booming voice reaching millions of people in several series of radio talks broadcast by the BBC. Like Tolkien, he wrote some of his best work in the war years. *Out of the Silent Planet*, the first part of his space trilogy, had been published in 1938, just before the war; *Perelandra*, the second part, was published in 1943; and the final part, *That Hideous Strength*, was published at the war's end in 1945. Although Lewis would never join the ranks of the twentieth century's many literary converts to the Catholic faith, his own conversion from atheism to Anglican Christianity had been greatly influenced by his friendship with Tolkien and his reading of Chesterton, whom he described as having "more sense than all the moderns put together".[3]

The leader of England's Catholics during the war was Cardinal Hinsley who, like Lewis, became a popular radio broadcaster. Describing the Nazis as "a pagan clique of upstart tyrants", he distributed what became known as "Cardinal Crosses" to thousands of soldiers as a symbol of their fight "for Christian truth and justice".[4] Following his death in March 1943, his requiem was attended by many luminaries, including the leaders of governments in exile General de Gaulle and General Sikorsky, the latter of whom would be killed in a plane crash only four months later. One notable absentee from the requiem Mass was King George VI, who wrote to his mother, Queen Mary, that "no one was more annoyed than I when I was 'advised' not to be represented at Cardinal Hinsley's funeral."[5]

[3] C. S. Lewis, *Surprised by Joy* (London: HarperCollins, 1998), 166.

[4] Nicholas Schofield and Gerard Skinner, *The English Cardinals* (Oxford: Family Publications, 2007), 197.

[5] Ibid., 198.

At the end of 1943, Evelyn Waugh fractured a fibula during parachute training, having previously served with the Royal Marines in West Africa and in a commando unit in the Mediterranean. During his recuperation, he would write *Brideshead Revisited*, arguably the finest novel of the century and certainly a jewel in the crown of the Catholic literary revival. The novel is set in the world of the English aristocracy, both Catholic and Protestant, which Waugh knew well. Among his many blue-blooded friends was Edith Sitwell, daughter of Sir George Sitwell, Fourth Baronet, of Renishaw Hall in Derbyshire, a stately home which Waugh visited frequently. Sitwell, one of the leading poets of the interwar years, shared much in common with Waugh, including the latter's contempt for the civilization of "talking cinemas and tinned food", as he had described it in the article he had written for the *Daily Express* following his conversion.[6] This deep mistrust of the scientism and technolatry which idolized technological "progress" would contribute to Sitwell's own conversion and reception into the Church in 1955, Waugh serving as her godfather. She was especially horrified by the use of destructive technology during the war and had written one of her most famous poems, "Still Falls the Rain". The poem was about the bombing of London during the Blitz, seeing it as being expressive of the destructive and perennial presence of pride in every generation, a continual nailing of Christ to the Cross:

> Still falls the Rain—
> Dark as the world of man, black as our loss—
> Blind as the nineteen hundred and forty nails
> Upon the Cross.

[6] *Daily Express*, October 20, 1930.

Similar imagery was employed by Sitwell to convey the horror of the dropping of the atomic bomb on Hiroshima in 1945. "The Shadow of Cain", the first of her "three poems of the Atomic Age", was, she explained, about "the fission of the world into warring particles, destroying and self-destructive. It is about the gradual migration of mankind ... into the desert of the Cold, towards the final disaster, the first symbol of which fell on Hiroshima."[7]

> We did not heed the Cloud in the Heavens shaped
>   like the hand
> Of Man ...
>   The Primal Matter
> Was broken, the womb from which all life began.
> Then to the murdered Sun a totem pole of dust
>   arose
>   In memory of Man.

The dropping of the bomb on Hiroshima and Nagasaki also shocked Siegfried Sassoon, who had written some of the most disturbing poems of the previous war. In 1945, he wrote "Litany of the Lost", which lamented the "slavedom of mankind to the machine" and the "terror of atomic doom foreseen". Humanity was "chained to the wheel of progress uncontrolled" and in spite of its "marvellous monkey innovations" was "unregenerate still in head and heart". The poem is transformed into a prayer by the haunting refrain at the end of each verse: *Deliver us from ourselves*. Another writer provoked into a creative reaction by the dropping of the bomb was Monsignor Ronald Knox, who wrote *God and the Atom*, published by Sheed &

[7] Edith Sitwell, *Taken Care Of: An Autobiography* (New York: Atheneum, 1965), 153.

Ward in November 1945, the opening chapter of which was headed "Trauma: Hiroshima". Knox and Sassoon, already kindred spirits, became friends, and it was Knox who shepherded Sassoon into the Church, albeit that Sassoon's reception in September 1957 came a month after Knox's death. Although Sassoon was seventy-one when he was received into the Church, he wrote some of his finest poetry, much of it explicitly religious, in the years following his conversion, most notably "Lenten Illuminations".

In 1950, the centenary of the reestablishment of the Catholic hierarchy, the position of the Church seemed stronger and more secure than at any time since the Reformation. According to the historian Sheridan Gilley, the Catholic Church in England a century earlier was "a body quite inconsiderable beside the massed ranks of the Establishment and Nonconformity", whereas a century later it was "probably in terms of practising adherents the largest church in England ... almost a rival Establishment, with a prominence and profile made the more conspicuous by the decline in the forces of popular anti-Catholicism".[8]

The sense of disgust with the destructive forces unleashed by modernity, so evident in the postwar poetry of Sitwell and Sassoon, illustrates a deep disillusionment with the modern world and its cult of "progress". The countless converts to the Church in the previous century were longing for depth in a world of shallows, permanence in a world of accelerated change, and certainty in a world of doubt. Unfortunately, this power of the Church to attract refugees from modernity's culture of death was compromised in the postwar years by the efforts of a new

[8] V. Alland McClelland and Michael Hodgetts, eds., *From Without the Flaminian Gate: 150 Years of Roman Catholicism in England and Wales 1850–2000* (London: Darton, Longman and Todd, 1999), 23.

generation of modernists hell-bent, seemingly, on under-
mining the Church's timeless teaching and desecrating the
beauty and mystery of her liturgy. Perceiving these dangerous trends, Evelyn Waugh wrote in 1964 that "throughout her entire life the Church has been at active war with
enemies from without and traitors from within."[9] To his
great distress, he began to feel that the "traitors" within the
Church were working to deliver the faithful into the hands
of the "enemies" without. Alarmed at developments, he
devoted a great deal of time during the last few years of his
life to opposing the modernist tendency in the Church,
especially with respect to its desecration of the liturgy.

In a postscript to his biography of Waugh, Christopher
Sykes sought to put Waugh's obstinate opposition to "the
reform-movement" into perspective:

> He believed that in its long history the Church had de-
> veloped a liturgy which enabled an ordinary, sensual man
> (as opposed to a saint who is outside generalisation) to ap-
> proach God and be aware of sanctity and the divine. To
> abolish all this for the sake of up-to-dateness seemed to him
> not only silly but dangerous.... [H]e could not bear the
> thought of modernized liturgy. "Untune that string," he
> felt, and loss of faith would follow.[10]

Waugh collapsed and died on Easter Sunday 1966, only
an hour or so after attending a private Latin Mass celebrated by his friend Philip Caraman, S.J. His daughter
wrote to Lady Diane Cooper of the "wonderful miracle"
of grace that attended her father in his final hours: "Don't
be too upset about Papa. I think it was a kind of wonderful

---

[9] *Catholic Herald*, August 7, 1964.
[10] Christopher Sykes, *Evelyn Waugh: A Biography* (London: Collins, 1975),
449–50.

miracle. You know how he longed to die and dying as he did on Easter Sunday, when all the liturgy is about death and resurrection, after a Latin Mass and holy communion would be exactly as he wanted. I am sure he had prayed for death at Mass. I am very, very happy for him."[11]

In his panegyric at the requiem Mass for Waugh at Westminster Cathedral, Fr. Caraman emphasized the place of the Mass at the very heart of Waugh's life and faith:

> The Mass mattered for him most in his world. During the greater part of his lifetime it remained as it had done for centuries, the same and everywhere recognizable, when all else was threatened with change. He was sad when he read of churches in which the old altar was taken down and a table substituted, or of side altars abolished as private Masses were held to be unliturgical or unnecessary. With all who know something of the pattern of history, he was perturbed.[12]

A positive reminder of the "pattern of history" was the canonization in 1970 of the Forty Martyrs of England and Wales who had laid down their lives, many suffering torture and torturously agonizing deaths for the preservation of the very Mass that the "reformers" were trying to abolish. In the following year, *The Times* published the text of an appeal to the Vatican to preserve the Latin Mass, which was signed by a host of well-known Catholics, as well as many non-Catholic dignitaries and celebrities, including Harold Acton, Vladimir Ashkenazy, Lennox Berkeley, Maurice Bowra, Agatha Christie, Kenneth Clark, Nevill Coghill, Cyril Connolly, Colin Davis, Robert Graves, Graham

---

[11] Alcuin Reid, ed., *A Bitter Trial: Evelyn Waugh and John Carmel Cardinal Heenan on the Liturgical Changes* (San Francisco: Ignatius Press, 2011), 98.

[12] Ibid., 101.

Greene, Joseph Grimond, Harman Grisewood, Rupert Hart-Davis, Barbara Hepworth, Auberon Herbert, David Jones, Osbert Lancaster, F. R. Leavis, Cecil Day Lewis, Compton Mackenzie, Yehudi Menuhin, Nancy Mitford, Raymond Mortimer, Malcolm Muggeridge, Iris Murdoch, John Murray, Sean O'Faolain, William Plomer, Kathleen Raine, Willliam Rees-Mogg, Ralph Richardson, Joan Sutherland, Bernard Wall, Patrick Wall, and E. I. Watkin.

Robert Speaight, actor, writer, convert, and biographer of Hilaire Belloc, wrote in his autobiography, published in 1970, of the spirit of modernism and rebellion that was rife in the Church, complaining that "authority is flouted" and "basic doctrines are questioned": "The vernacular Liturgy, popular and pedestrian, intelligible and depressing, has robbed us of much that was numinous in public worship; there is less emphasis on prayer and penitence; and the personal relationship between God and man ... is neglected in favour of a diffused social concern."[13]

Ultimately, Speaight's frustration with the modernists was linked to their evident contempt for tradition: "What exasperates me in the attitude of many progressives is not their desire to go forward or even to change direction, but their indifference to tradition which is the *terra firma* from which they themselves proceed."[14]

Following on the heels of this abandonment of tradition was the all too predictable abandonment of faith. The English seminaries at Lisbon, Upholland, Ushaw, and Wonersh all closed, the inevitable and God-forsaken fruits of theological modernism and sexualized relativism, liturgical abuse and sexual abuse going hand in hand. As in

---

[13] Robert Speaight, *The Property Basket: Recollections of a Divided Life* (London: Collins, 1970), 308–9.

[14] Ibid.

penal times, the lack of bona fide seminaries in England has led to many young men and women looking beyond England's shores to pursue their vocations. In 2020, there were over a hundred priests, seminarians, and religious sisters and brothers from the British Isles in solid, tradition-oriented orders in various parts of the world. There is no vocations crisis in these orders; perhaps, as in days of yore, these English men and women, forced into exile to pursue the priesthood and religious life, will return as missionaries to their native land, filling with evangelical zeal the vacuum caused by relativism.

Such dauntless optimism in the face of adversity was expressed by Sir Alec Guinness, another prominent convert who expressed concern at the iconoclastic spirit that held sway in the 1960s and 1970s. Writing in the 1980s, he lamented the damage that the modernist revolution had done: "Much water has flown under Tiber's bridges, carrying away splendour and mystery from Rome, since the pontificate of Pius XII." He was, however, confident that the Church would survive this latest assault on her integrity as she had survived many other such attacks in the past:

> The Church has proved she is not moribund. "All shall be well," I feel, "and all manner of things shall be well," so long as the God who is worshipped is the God of all ages, past and to come, and not the Idol of Modernity, so venerated by some of our bishops, priests and mini-skirted nuns.[15]

Sir Alec Guinness' positive and largely optimistic appraisal of the prospects for the Church in the 1980s was echoed, no doubt very grudgingly, by A. N. Wilson, writing at the end of the decade. At the time, Wilson had

---

[15] Alec Guinness, *Blessings in Disguise* (London: Hamish Hamilton, 1985), 45.

rejected Christianity and all religions and would soon publish a book entitled *Against Religion: Why We Should Live Without It.* Considering Wilson's anti-Catholic and indeed anti-Christian perspective, his assessment of the position of the Catholic Church in England in the eighties is intriguing and encouraging:

> Nowadays in England, the Roman Catholic Church numbers more regular adherents than any other Christian body; there are more Roman Catholic churchgoers than there are practising members of the Church of England. Though not all Christians accept their doctrines, the Roman Catholic Church is by far the most vigorous of all the denominations. Though pockets of prejudice against it remain, and presumably always will remain, it is now a fully accepted part of the British religious scene. As a result of the Act of Settlement at the close of the seventeenth century which determined that the British monarchy would be Protestant, the Sovereign is still forbidden either to be or to marry a Roman Catholic. But it is now a familiar part of public ritual that the Cardinal Archbishop of Westminster, or some other public dignitary of the Roman Catholic Church, will take part in such events as royal weddings, along with representatives from the Non-conformist churches.... The Roman Catholics have arrived.[16]

Wilson wrote these words at the beginning of his discussion of John Henry Newman in his book *Eminent Victorians*, stating that the present strength of Catholicism made it "almost impossible to imagine that only 140 years ago, the Roman Catholic Church in England barely existed".[17]

---

[16] A. N. Wilson, *Eminent Victorians* (New York: W. W. Norton, 1990), 135.
[17] Ibid.

There is little doubt that the most significant event in the decade was the visit to England in 1982 of Pope John Paul II, the first ever visit by a reigning pope to England's "green and pleasant land". St. John Paul visited Canterbury Cathedral, praying at the spot on which St. Thomas Becket had been martyred in 1170; he celebrated Mass at Wembley Stadium in the presence of eighty thousand people, in Coventry with three hundred thousand people in attendance, and in Manchester with two hundred thousand in attendance, after which he proceeded to Scotland and then to Wales. Another significant event was the pope's meeting with Queen Elizabeth II, the queen having been received by Pope John Paul two years earlier in the Vatican.

Unlike her predecessors, Queen Elizabeth has not been coy about meeting the many popes who have occupied the Chair of Peter during her long and illustrious reign. She had met John XXIII at the Vatican in 1961 and 1965 and would meet the ailing John Paul II once again in 2000; Pope Benedict during his hugely successful visit to England in 2010, during which he beatified John Henry Newman; and Pope Francis in 2014.

In 1987, eighty-five of the English martyrs who had died during the penal years were beatified, belated recognition of the heroic sacrifice these holy men had made for the Church of Christ.

In April 1994, Graham Leonard, formerly the Anglican Bishop of London, was received into the Catholic Church, the most prominent of the numerous members of the Anglican clergy and laity who have converted to Catholicism in response to the Church of England's ordination of women. In what can only be conceived as providential irony, the Catholic Church was the beneficiary of the Anglican church's capitulation to the Spirit of the Age, a recompense perhaps for the suffering of the Church for refusing to capitulate to the Spirit of the Age at the behest of Henry VIII all those centuries ago. Even today, those descendants of the recusant families who suffered during the dark years of persecution gather in London to commemorate and celebrate the holy legacy of their ancestors. These are members of the exclusive "15 Club", the sine qua non of membership of which is a direct link back to the time of Henry VIII. The members meet annually, under the presidency of the Duke of Norfolk, to toast the health of the pope and to remember the sacrifices made by their ancestors.

Today, however, the old Catholic nobility is being joined by a new Catholic nobility, which includes members of the royal family. In 1994, the Duchess of Kent was received into the Church, the first member of the royal family to convert publicly since the passing of the Act of Settlement in 1701. In the same year, Frances Shand Kydd, mother of Princess Diana, was also received into the Church. In 2001, Lord Nicholas Windsor, son of the Duke and Duchess of Kent, was received into the Church, thereby forfeiting his right to succession to the throne under the terms of the Act of Settlement. At his baptism as a child, Lord Nicholas had both the heir to the throne, Prince Charles, and Donald Coggan, the Anglican Bishop of York and later Archbishop of Canterbury, as two of his godparents. In 2006, as required by the Royal Marriages Act of 1772, he needed the consent of the monarch for his marriage to a Catholic, the queen's granting of the necessary permission being further evidence of her cordial attitude to the Church. Since his conversion, Nicholas Windsor has been a tireless and outspoken advocate for the protection of unborn children. In December 2019, Queen Elizabeth's former Anglican chaplain, Gavin Ashenden, was received into the Church, his having served the queen as her personal chaplain from 2008 until 2017. "I had ... begun to realize, with an increasing urgency, that I had a personal responsibility to heal the schism in Christ's body that my spiritual ancestors had created," Ashenden said. "And that could only really be done by returning, in all humility, to the Mother Church, in penitence for the schism and by being received penitentially into full Communion."[18]

More important than the reception of royalty into the Church is the confirmation of the reception of a saint into heaven. Such was the joyous reality confirmed by Pope Francis in October 2019 with the canonization of St. John Henry Newman, a crowning moment in the history of the Church in England. Begging to differ with the words of A. N. Wilson, the Church had not "arrived" but had returned. More than that, as the Mystical Body of Christ, she had risen from the dead.

---

[18] *National Catholic Register*, March 8, 2020.

Chapter Twenty-Eight

The Return of the Queen

I look'd on that Lady,
and out from her eyes
Came the deep glowing blue
of Italy's skies;
And she raised up her head
and she smiled, as a Queen
On the day of her crowning,
so bland and serene.

"A moment," she said,
"and the dead shall revive;
The giants are failing,
the Saints are alive;
I am coming to rescue
my home and my reign,
And Peter and Philip
are close in my train."

—St. John Henry Newman,
from "The Pilgrim Queen"

If England can rightly be considered a Christ-haunted country, it would be equally true to say that she is haunted by the heavenly ghost of Christ's mother, the exiled queen of whom St. John Henry Newman writes. Her ghostly presence is felt in place names like Ladywell or Ladywood, or in the names of flowers, such as marigolds (Mary's gold). This haunting presence of the ghostly queen was evoked by H. M. Gillett in his book *Shrines of Our Lady in England and Wales*:

English folklore is full of analogy to Our Blessed Lady. One has to reflect only upon the beauty of the white masses of "May" flowers in early summer, or the almost forgotten joys of the maypole to realise that.

May was the month for the crowning of England's Heavenly Empress and she it was who was true Queen of the May. Likewise it was she who was Queen of the Harvest, and in harvest-home processions Our Lady played her part, even as she did in the festivals of spring.

Dour-faced Puritans were hard put to it to abolish such innate happiness. In their smashings of beauty, whether in wood or stone or glass, which had once been the glory of so many of our country churches, they had succeeded almost to their liking; but they forgot about the flowers, the harvest and the children's games.

Without knowing why they did so, children continued to choose the prettiest maid among them to be crowned by way of substitute for the true May Queen, the real Fairy Princess of their dreams. All unbeknown to themselves—and who was there to remind them?—they were but carrying on the English tradition of love for Our Lady.

Deep down in English hearts this forgotten loyalty came to express itself in terms of wishful thinking and even hopeful wishing. A day would come, it was said, when Mary would return to her Dowry. Tucked away in the recesses of East Anglian folklore was a legend that one day Englishmen would turn back to Walsingham and then "the Lady" would come back to England.[1]

[1] H. M. Gillett, *Shrines of Our Lady in England and Wales* (London: Samuel Walker, 1957), 286.

This "wishful thinking" or "hopeful wishing" is present in Newman's song of praise to "The Pilgrim Queen".
It evokes England's Catholic past, the mythic Merrie
England that still held the power to move Newman's contemporaries to feelings of nostalgia for a lost pastoral idyll
in which people were united by sure and simple faith. This
idyll had been lost, Newman laments, being replaced with
"a palace of ice":

> And me they bid wander
> in weeds and alone,
> In this green merry land
> which once was my own.

The sense of betrayal, the desolation, the melancholy,
are all reminiscent of the anonymous verse "The Ballad of
Walsingham", which laments the destruction of England's
Marian shrine, once the most prestigious in Christendom, during the tyrannous reign of Henry VIII. Yet
unlike the sorrowful and plaintive passion of the "Ballad",
Newman's "Pilgrim Queen" transcends and transforms
the sorrow with a promise of future glory. Beyond the
Passion is the Resurrection. The Queen will rescue her
people and, aided by the company of heaven, she will be
restored to her rightful throne. The balance, the symmetry, of "The Pilgrim Queen" is the balance and symmetry
of the Rosary. England's destiny, past, present, and future,
is reflected in the Rosary's mysteries. From joy, through
sorrow, to glory. As such, England emerges as a subplot in
a far greater mystery play.

In the years following Newman's death, perhaps on
account of his prayers, people began to turn to Mary and to
return to her ancient shrines. In 1893, on the Feast of Saints
Peter and Paul, the bishops of England and Wales consecrated England to the Mother of God and to St. Peter, in

response to the wishes of Pope Leo XIII, who had recalled that England had long been known as Our Lady's Dowry. Two weeks later, Bishop John Butt, serving as the papal delegate representing the Holy See and Pope Leo XIII, performed a ceremonial crowning of the Mother of God at the restored shrine of Our Lady of Consolation in West Grinstead in Sussex, the first time since the Reformation that such a privilege had been granted to England. In the following year, it was recorded that a child who had been born blind received the gift of sight while on pilgrimage with her mother to the shrine in West Grinstead, a miracle ascribed to the Blessed Virgin's intercession.

In 1897, a pilgrimage was held to the Slipper Chapel in Walsingham, the last intact vestige of the ancient shrine, which had been restored to Catholic ownership after centuries of neglect. The resurrection of the shrine at Walsingham seemed to serve as the fountainhead for the restoration of old Marian shrines and the dedication of new ones. In 1902, the Order of Canons Regular of Premontré established a shrine to Our Lady of England at Storrington in Sussex. It was under her patronage that St. Mary's Priory was built, at which Francis Thompson wrote many of his finest poems and which also inspired Belloc's poem "Courtesy", of which this is the second stanza:

> On Monks I did in Storrington fall,
> They took me straight into their Hall;
> I saw Three Pictures on a wall,
> And Courtesy was in them all.[2]

In 1903, a solemn procession of Our Lady was held to the recently restored mediaeval shrine of Our Lady of Willesden. For the first time since the Reformation,

---

[2] As a related aside, Belloc's local parish church was the shrine of Our Lady of Consolation in West Grinstead, at which he is buried.

a statue of the Virgin was publicly carried through the streets, attended by pilgrims from far and wide carrying banners. In the following year, a group of militant Protestants caused a disturbance and attempted to seize the statue; a year later, an unsuccessful attempt was made to have the procession banned by order of law. In spite of such agitation by the shrinking and shrivelling remnant of England's hardline Protestants, the processions continued, becoming an annual pilgrimage.

Other Marian shrines, old and new, sprang up across the country, most notably at Buckfast Abbey in Devon in 1905, at Hartley in Kent in 1913, and at Prinknash in Gloucestershire in 1929, to name but a representative few. It was, however, in August 1934 that the Queen could well and truly be said to have returned to rescue her home and her reign. It was then that the aging and ailing Cardinal Bourne led the first national pilgrimage to Walsingham, assisted by many bishops and archbishops and accompanied by almost twenty thousand pilgrims. Since then, the "Walsingham Way" or "Holy Mile" between the priory ruins in the village and the Slipper Chapel has been thronged with pilgrims on countless pilgrimages. The Archdiocese of Westminster began its own pilgrimage in 1935, on the four hundredth anniversary of the martyrdom of SS. Thomas More and John Fisher; since then, many dioceses and parishes have followed suit, holding their own pilgrimages to Walsingham annually.

A pilgrimage to Walsingham by the parish priest of Sudbury in Suffolk and some of his parishioners inspired the restoration of the mediaeval shrine of Our Lady of Sudbury on the Feast of the Assumption in 1937. Around four thousand pilgrims attended the ceremonial blessing and resurrection of the shrine, the like of which the small town of Sudbury had not seen since the days of Henry the Tyrant.

In 1938, with world events dark with devildom, portending war, almost twenty thousand young people joined the National Pilgrimage of Catholic Youth to Walsingham, an expedition and exhibition of hope in desperate times. Organized by H. M. Gillett, a young man who had been received into the Church five years earlier, the pilgrimage represented a rejection of, and a positive alternative to, the nihilistic negations of communism and fascism.

With the onset of war, Walsingham became a prayerful haven for refugees from France, Belgium, Holland, Poland, and other countries occupied by the Nazis. Before returning home at the end of the war, a pilgrimage of Italian prisoners of war came to Walsingham to offer prayers of thanksgiving for the end of hostilities. A similar pilgrimage of thanksgiving was made by members of the United States military, especially members of the U.S. Air Force who had been stationed at airbases in Norfolk and Suffolk during the war. These U.S. servicemen showed their gratitude to Our Lady of Walsingham on May 17, 1945, nine days after the war in Europe had ended, by arranging for the first Mass to be said in the priory grounds since the Reformation.

In April 1947, Pope Pius XII accepted a gift of a replica of the statue of Our Lady of Walsingham from a delegation of the British military forces, still stationed in Italy after the war, "in token of gratitude to His Holiness for the countless manifestations of his paternal solicitude towards them and their country".[3] The pope received the gift with a promise to keep it close to his person, describing Walsingham as "England's Loreto" and promising to pray that "the Blessed Mother may win the favour of her Divine

---

[3] Gillett, *Shrines of Our Lady in England and Wales*, 320.

Son for you ... yes, and for the entire English nation, and its gracious Sovereign."[4]

In July 1948, fourteen separate groups of priests and laymen set out from fourteen different parts of England, from Canterbury in the south to Middlesbrough in the north, for a fourteen-day pilgrimage on foot to Walsingham. Each group carried a nine-foot cross of solid oak as an act of penance for a world plunging from World War to Cold War. H. M. Gillett witnessed the culmination of this marathon "way of the cross" as the pilgrims arrived:

> This Pilgrimage of Prayer and Penance, which created a profound impression throughout the realm, was timed to reach the outskirts of Walsingham by midnight on July 15th, to coincide with the arrival of the National Pilgrimage of the Union of Catholic Mothers. At day-break on the 16th, Feast of Our Lady of Mount Carmel, the fourteen crosses were borne in silence to the Slipper Chapel, where Masses were being offered in continuous succession at a large number of altars. Pontifical Mass was sung at an open-air altar and then, after noon, began the solemn procession of these crosses along the Pilgrims' Way, led by His Eminence, Cardinal Griffin ... and a considerable number of prelates, to the site of the old Priory, and the shadow of the one remaining, lonely, arch. This was the occasion when the Cardinal, fulfilling the request made by Our Lady of Fatima, dedicated the Country to the Immaculate Heart of Mary.[5]

In 1949, the Carmelite monastery at Aylsford in Kent was restored, close to the site on which, 702 years earlier, St. Simon Stock is said to have received a vision of

[4] Ibid.
[5] Ibid., 321.

the Virgin. The formal return took place on All Hallows Eve, with a solemn profession of many friars in their habits. Thousands of pilgrims were present, some travelling from oversees to give thanks at this historic restoration of Our Lady's presence at another of the mediaeval shrines dedicated to her. H. M. Gillett evoked the full traditional import of the moment: "To Father Malachy Lynch, whom he installed as first post-Reformation Prior of Aylsford, the Prior General, the Most Reverend Killian Lynch, O. Carm., direct successor of St. Simon Stock in authentic and unbroken line, presented a facsimile of the original Conventual Seal. This was an event without parallel."[6]

In July 1952, another of England's ancient Marian shrines, that at Evesham in Worcestershire, was resurrected. A procession of four thousand pilgrims followed the new statue of Our Lady of Evesham from the new church and shrine to the site of the ancient shrine. In the same year, many thousands attended Fr. Peyton's Rosary Crusade, held at Wembley Stadium, England's national football stadium; in the following year, thirty priests were ordained at the Vocations Exhibition held in London.

During the Marian Year celebrations of 1954, Cardinal Griffin, Archbishop of Westminster, solemnly crowned the statue of Our Lady of Willesden in a momentous event at Wembley Stadium. The coronation was performed by the cardinal in the name of Pope Pius XII and in the presence of the pope's apostolic delegate and many bishops. The stadium, which had a capacity at the time of one hundred thousand people, was thronged with pilgrims. According to H. M. Gillett, ten thousand came from the Essex Diocese of Brentwood alone.[7]

[6] Ibid., 39.
[7] Ibid., 384.

Following the coronation, and after the singing of the *Te Deum*, the apostolic delegate read a letter from Pius XII to the tens of thousands of pilgrims:

> To Our Beloved Son Bernard Cardinal Griffin, Archbishop of Westminster:
>
> With pleasure have We learned that you are solemnly to crown the statue of Our Lady of the Shrine as Willesden, as a culmination of the manifestations of Marian devotion in this year dedicated of Our Blessed Mother.
>
> This touching ceremony, which you propose to perform in the presence of a great multitude of the clergy and faithful, is not only a public demonstration of love and veneration towards the Mother of God, but also an open and appropriate act of reparation for what happened to her hallowed image centuries ago.
>
> We cherish the prayerful hope that the processional return of the newly crowned statue of Our Lady to her ancient shrine at Willesden may be a presage of the return to Mary of her pristine Dowry, your beloved country.[8]

At the conclusion of the ceremony, the newly crowned statue was borne from the stadium shoulder high and taken back to the shrine through thickly lined streets, escorted by 230 seminarians and 2,000 others representing multifarious Catholic organizations. In the same year, also as part of the celebrations for the Marian Year, the statue of Our Lady of Walsingham was solemnly crowned under the shadow of the ruined priory's one remaining arch, the ceremony being performed by Archbishop O'Hara, representing the pope as his apostolic delegate to Great Britain.

As we move towards the conclusion of this two-thousand-year history of True England with a celebration

---

[8] Ibid., 384–85.

of the return of the Queen, it would seem appropriate that the first should be last. Glastonbury, England's first Marian shrine, established within a few decades of the Crucifixion of Our Lord, was finally restored in July 1955. The apostolic delegate, Archbishop O'Hara, who had performed the papal coronation of Our Lady of Walsingham the previous year, blessed the new statue of Our Lady of Glastonbury, which was then formally enshrined in the new church dedicated to St. Mary which had been built to house it.

Many of the pilgrims who attended the crowning of the Queen of Glastonbury made the customary ascent of the Tor, the hill that dominates the surrounding landscape, to pray for the intercession of Blessed Richard Whiting, the last Abbot of Glastonbury, who had been martyred for refusing to surrender the abbey to the king. "How greatly would that holy Martyr have rejoiced to see that day," wrote H. M. Gillett, who added that "one may be sure that it is by his prayers in heaven that this restoration has been brought about."[9]

Today, the shrine of Our Lady of Walsingham attracts 150,000 pilgrims every year during the "pilgrimage season", which spans from Easter until summer's end. Apart from individual pilgrims or groups of pilgrims, there are thirty-five major pilgrimages, organized by dioceses, parishes, Catholic organizations of various types, and by ethnic groups. The Tamil community holds two pilgrimages annually, numbering around 6,000 in May and 15,000 in July. In addition, the Syro-Malabar community, who are Catholics of Indian origin, bring around 5,000 pilgrims on the National Pilgrimage, which is held in July each year. Much has changed ethnically and culturally since the days of Merrie England, but the faith remains.

[9] Ibid., 161.

On March 29, 2020, England was rededicated as the Dowry of Mary in a solemn ceremony held at Our Lady's shrine in Walsingham, a renewal of the entrustment vows of King Richard II in 1381. With the country in COVID lockdown, more than half a million people watched the rededication ceremony online. Much has changed technologically since the days of Merrie England, but the faith remains.

H. M. Gillett saw the return of the Queen as a sign of hope that the England of the future might be as she used to be "in the days when every Englishman was by nature a pilgrim, and heart and soul a child of Mary, in this her Dowry".[10] True England had died, but True England had also risen because, as G. K. Chesterton reminds us, she worships a God who knows the way out of the grave.[11]

[10] Ibid., 123–24.

[11] G. K. Chesterton, *The Everlasting Man* (San Francisco: Ignatius Press, 1993), 250.

EPILOGUE

True and Timeless England Revisited

Here, the intersection of the timeless moment
Is England and nowhere. Never and always.

. . . .

What we call the beginning is often the end
And to make an end is to make a beginning.
The end is where we start from. . . .

A people without history
Is not redeemed from time, for history is a pattern
Of timeless moments. So, while the light fails
On a winter's afternoon, in a secluded chapel
History is now and England.

— T. S. Eliot, from *Four Quartets*

England, like all things, is subject not merely to the truth but to the Truth Himself.

It is this true England, an England "charged with the grandeur of God" and in communion with Christ and His Church, which is celebrated in these pages. It is an England which is as alive as the saints because, like all the saints, and like all of time and all of eternity, it exists in God's omnipresence.

If the reader has experienced a sense of déjà vu in reading the preceding lines, it is because they are the same lines

with which we began, in the Prologue, all those many
thousands of words ago.

What we have witnessed in the preceding pages is the past
lived in God's presence. It is history seen as God's omnipresence in time prefiguring His eternal presence in heaven.
The mystics understand this. The poets understand this.
T. S. Eliot understands this. As he says so eloquently in *Four
Quartets*, "history is a pattern of timeless moments" which
is woven in God's eternal presence. It is God who is the
end of history, as he is its beginning. He is the alpha and
the omega, the beginning and end of each timeless moment.

C. S. Lewis also understands this. In the final glorious
pages of *The Last Battle*, the children and the other characters have all died. And yet they are not dead. Nor is the
place in which they find themselves. On the contrary, they
are more alive than ever, as is the place in which they find
themselves. It's all so real. More real than anything they've
ever experienced. And it's all so familiar—but more so.

> "Those hills," said Lucy, "the nice woody ones and the
> blue ones behind—aren't they very like the Southern bor-
> der of Narnia?"
>
> "Like!" cried Edmund after a moment's silence. "Why,
> they're exactly like. Look, there's Mount Pire with the
> forked head, and there's the path into Archenland and
> everything!"
>
> "And yet they're not like," said Lucy. "They're differ-
> ent. They have more colours on them and they look fur-
> ther away than I remembered and they're more ... more
> ... oh, I don't know...."
>
> "More like the real thing," said the Lord Digory softly.

Lord Digory, with his platonic understanding of forms,
has already guessed what Farsight the Eagle now proclaims: "Narnia is not dead. This is Narnia." As he tells the

children, where they had lived during their mortal lives "was not the real Narnia":

> That had a beginning and an end. It was only a shadow or a copy of the real Narnia which has always been here and always will be here: Just as our own world, England and all, is only a shadow or copy of something in Aslan's real world.... And of course it is different; as different as a real thing is from a shadow or as waking life is from a dream.

Later, as they go "further up and further in" to the reality beyond the shadowlands of mortal time, they find themselves in England; not the England they had known but the real England. They "are now looking at the England within England, the real England.... And in that inner England no good thing is destroyed."

Lewis knows what Plato knows. The good is imperishable. So is the true. And so is the beautiful. That which comes from God cannot die. On the other hand, that which does not come from God has never truly lived. All of the evil with which True England has been afflicted will pass away because it never truly was. Only the truth remains. Imperishable. Holy. Eternal. In heaven.

True England will not perish because it is made of imperishable things, such as truth itself. It exists in eternity liberated from the shadow of transient things, such as evil. C. S. Lewis truly understands this, as did his friend J. R. R. Tolkien, who, in his poem "Mythopoeia", describes evil as the "malicious choice".

In paradise, St. Thomas More is not afflicted by the "malicious choice" of Henry VIII, any more than Christ is afflicted by the malicious choice of Caiaphas. In paradise, True England as a "blessed land" will be taken up into that Blessed Land where "all is as it is, and yet made free".

This is the eternal destiny of that True England of which its history in time is but a mere prefiguring, or what Lewis and Plato would call a mere shadow.

As for England's saints, "we can most truly say that they all lived happily ever after." All their life in this world and all their adventures in England had only been the cover and the title page: now at last they were beginning Chapter One of the Great Story which no one on earth has read, which goes on forever, in which every chapter is better than the one before.[1]

[1] This last paragraph is adapted, of course, from the final paragraph of C.S. Lewis' *The Last Battle*.

INDEX